John Whitford

Trading Life in Western and Central Africa

John Whitford

Trading Life in Western and Central Africa

ISBN/EAN: 9783743383937

Manufactured in Europe, USA, Canada, Australia, Japa

Cover: Foto ©Suzi / pixelio.de

Manufactured and distributed by brebook publishing software (www.brebook.com)

John Whitford

Trading Life in Western and Central Africa

TRADING LIFE

IN

WESTERN AND CENTRAL

AFRICA.

BY

JOHN WHITFORD, F.R.G.S.

LIVERPOOL:
THE "PORCUPINE" OFFICE, CABLE STREET.
1877.

PREFACE.

This Book is not a record of wonderful explorations. It is simply the experience of frequent travel and residence upon the West Coast of Africa, between the years 1853 and 1875.

In the first place, the contents were written in the form of friendly letters, without any literary pretence, and were thus published weekly in the " Porcupine," and then I thought I had done with ·them. But so many readers, in various parts of the world, (some of whom had only seen a letter occasionally,) requested the whole to be re-printed, that I was induced to yield to their desire, and have, therefore, revised the letters, and now respectfully submit them to the public.

Imperfections, and possibly inaccuracies, may be detected, and the difficulty of avoiding these will be increased by my absence from England during the printing of the work.

J. W.

Alfred Street, Liverpool,
December 7th, 1876.

CONTENTS.

CHAPTER I.

Madeira, Teneriffe, the River Gambia, Sierra Leone, and the River Sherboro' . . . 1

CHAPTER II.

Republic of Liberia, Monrovia, Cape Palmas, Cape Coast Castle, Accra, and Quitta . . 44

CHAPTER III.

The Slave Coast, Whydah, Lagos, Ikorodu, Badagry, and Porto Novo 81

CHAPTER IV.

The Niger Delta, Missionaries, Cannibals, River Pirates, and the Yarn of a Castaway at the Benin Branch of the Niger 119

Map of River Niger 120

CHAPTER V.

The River Niger, from the Upper Part of the Delta to its Confluence with the River Binur 158

CHAPTER VI.

The Confluence of the Rivers Niger and Binue.   199

CHAPTER VII.

The Upper Niger, and Return to the Atlantic .   236

CHAPTER VIII.

Bonny, Old Calabar, Fernando Po, and Cameroons   283

CHAPTER IX.

Rivers Gaboon and Congo, and on to St. Paul de

Loanda.—Conclusion   315

CHAPTER I.

---

*"Thus we took leave of our poor father, who, having no money, gave us his
blessing."—Benvenuto Cellini.*

WHEN long voyages were not undertaken so readily as
now, friends accompanied a traveller on board the
ocean steamer by the tender from the Landing-stage to see
him fairly off. These well-wishers and boon companions
concealed the contents of bottles beneath their waistcoats,
thereby trying to hide grief at parting. Stewards rushed
frantically to and fro with rusty corkscrews, the relics of
former voyages. The steampipe howled with fifty hungry
menagerie power. Her Majesty's mails were thrown on
board and bundled into the mail-room. Shore porters earned
rich harvests. Disputes took place amongst warriors as to
precedence for berths, which were settled by reference to the
dates of their commissions in the Army and Navy Lists of the
period. Struggles to wriggle big portmanteaus into tiny
cabins caused great confusion. People were apparently mad;
they fell over luggage in dark passages, and swore heartily.
But now all is calm and serene, and changed, certainly for
the better. Experience in despatching steamers has resulted
in system and order. Very few cronies go even as far as the
Landing Stage to see the wanderer depart. The steampipe,
peaceful as an infant, softly breathes. No rude noises occur.
To the minute, the tender starts from the Landing Stage,

and the ocean floating village, like a well-conducted railway train, gracefully and quietly glides from Great Britain.

The first duty of a full-grown male passenger when the steamer begins to glide is to open an account with the chief steward by filling-up a card ordering something cheering. Then to smoke a pipe, pace the deck, and inwardly observe—Good-bye, Landing Stage; farewell, Rock—and shake hands with the pilot, the last fond link of home. When Holyhead fades into the mist, the loneliest man begins to feel comfortable, forms acquaintances, laughs and tells stories; and when he thinks of the home to which he never may return——but no matter,—it is time to drop sentiment and arrange his cabin for the voyage. British birds of passage are naturally reserved. They fiercely walk the deck, staring hard at unknown fellow-voyagers, each with a wonderful opinion of himself expressed by the walk. But the welcome dinner-bell rings, · the ice breaks, and before the termination of a voyage firm friendships are established. In the African boats four distinct classes are conveyed—viz., naval men, military men, colonial or civil men, and traders. And it is a remarkable circumstance that the three former look upon the latter with amusing contempt. It appears very strange that the mercantile community, which so freely supplies the others with bread, cheese, and bitter-beer, should be so lightly esteemed. Verily, it is not so in other countries.

After six days on uneasy billows it is very pleasant to land at Madeira, one of the loveliest islands upon earth. On first sighting Porto Santo, the Dezertas, and Madeira, the impression is that they are barren rocks rising abruptly from the sea. But after steaming past Porto Santo, rounding the eastern end of Madeira, and approaching Funchal, the beauty of the place bursts upon you suddenly. It is like the bright scene at the end of a pantomime; with this difference, that it is real. Most people are aware that Madeira is a Portuguese island, in latitude 32 degrees north ; situated south of the Straits of Gibraltar, and 450 miles west of Morocco, north-western Africa. Vessels anchor in the roadstead on the south side of the island, abreast the town of Funchal. This town is built comfortably above the sea-level at the base of hills which rise to the height of five and six thousand feet. There are terraces of houses, churches, castles, villas, and villages jotted over the slopes of the hills, mixed up with vineyards, clusters of trees, sugar-cane plantations on a small scale, bananas, and a few delicate palm-trees. Sunshine on the hills and valleys in the clear atmosphere shows intense light, and the shade, and variety of colour, so refreshing to the eye, yield perpetual delight. The roads up the hills are steep, and constructed zig-zag fashion, so that no inconvenience is felt excepting the extra exertion required to ascend. Pleasant parties are formed from nearly every steamer to ride up to the church on the mount on small, sure-footed, strong ponies. The view from that church is photographed on memory as long as life lasts. As you ascend you forget all earthly cares, you inhale the invigorating air, and feel what a delightful thing it is to live. After enjoying the atmosphere several thousand feet above the sea, it is pleasant to descend in a different manner. Small skid sleds, after the manner of sleighs, are provided, something like a Norwegian carriole without wheels ; one or two men steer the conveyance. The motion is exciting, to feel yourself all but flying through the air as swiftly as an arrow, yet this lively mode of transit is not at all dangerous. The zig-zag roads give rest at corners, yielding admiration of the strangely beautiful scenery and the interesting manners and customs of the island Portuguese. Far out on the sea you observe tiny specks—steamers going to and fro : West

African, Cape or South American, Pacific, and other boats, most of which call for coal and refreshment, thus giving time for the weary sea-rovers on board to vary the scenery.

To appreciate Madeira properly, one should leave England in the winter time. By doing so you are almost certain to experience east winds, fog, and peradventure snow on deck in the Channel. And then, in less than a week, you wander through avenues of blooming roses, and enjoy the gentle sea-breeze, beneath the shade of semi-tropical vegetation, not to speak of looking at the sun, and feeling comfortable after chilly England. The mildness of the climate all the year round—in winter the thermometer averages 65° Fahrenheit —causes Madeira to be very suitable for invalids, but the five or six days' run from England prevents many suffering patients venturing afloat. Nervous people are, however, getting bolder as they observe the great increase in the numbers of those who go down to the sea in ships, and— come back alive. This feeling of security will spread amongst delicate folk, and increase the number of English hotels at Funchal from three, as at present, to a dozen before long. Living is most excellent, but the good appetite is better.

Ladies can safely and comfortably travel, if even alone, by any of the numerous steamers going there, for the stewardess of the vessel attends upon them, and the captain, officers, and crew show the honest British sailor's tenderly true care of womankind, or invalids of either sex, and the proprietors of the hotels board every steamer on its arrival, so that passengers for Madeira may rely upon being safely landed and comfortably "hotelled" without any trouble.

I can fancy no life on this planet during the winter time happier than that of a family, with their own servants, occupying a furnished house here, and each day enjoying

open-air exercise, flavoured with agreeable society. There
are many who live so; others occupy lodgings according to
their income, and the hotels are generally full. Very many
martyrs to disease have recovered health and strength, who,
had they not ventured to sea, would long ago have worn
wooden overcoats, and been labelled, and snugly shelved in
his or her own particular family vault. It is, therefore,
surely better to brave a few days at sea in a comfortable
drawing-room steamer—literally a Pullman car on the ocean
—and prolong life, than calmly, and without a struggle,
shuffle off this mortal coil; but invalids should not put off
coming south until it is too late.

Those who land casually are subjected to importunity on
the part of guides, and boys following them to learn the
dragoman business, including broken English, which, as a
rule, they handle just as Englishmen do other languages.
These attendants fight and wrangle, and their shouting—
based upon the fact that all visitors desire to carry away
some souvenir is very amusing—"I say, Englishman, me
show you Reid's hotel, Miles' hotel : you want to buy lace,
me take you to de mount church ; you want to buy feather
flower, me take you to the convent ; you want to buy pretty
flower basket, Madeira chair, Madeira shoes ?" Enduring
this for a few minutes, it is well to select the most athletic
applicant. Big Antonio rules at present ; he stands 6½ feet
high, and he wears a huge nose several sizes too large for even
his stature. As soon as he is appointed body-guard of a
party, the rest get out of the road, for Antonio is powerful.
He clears the track, and keeps off numerous persistent
beggars, takes you to all sorts of shops, and gets commis
sion from the shop-keepers, and commission from you also.
By this sublime system of double entry—not altogether
unknown, neither unpractised, by estimable mercantile

characters in all countries—Antonio has waxed wealthy. He
owns and lets "Quintas" (furnished houses) and even selects
his own collection of voyagers, knowing well, by sage experience, those who pay the best. But, nevertheless, as
Shylock remarks, " An-to-ni-o is a good man," and attends
upon you faithfully. If you have ladies in company, he
quietly suggests a carriage sled without wheels, and in this
conveyance, drawn by two bullocks—which is quite an
institution of Madeira, and holds four people—you are gently
drawn over the smooth pebbly-paved streets peculiar to
Funchal.

Madeira is not yet ruined by tourists. Hotels charge
£12 10s. per month each for board and lodging, including
the run of the house, gardens, croquet ground, and monkey
house. Bullock carriages are moderate as to charge, and the
easy motion beats a tramway car, although I wont say it
does so for speed. Hammocks and cots for invalids are
plentiful and cheap to hire. Two men trot along one at each
end of a pole, and the body of the patient swings between.
The motion is jerky but not unpleasant. Food is abundant ;
lots of fresh fish and vegetables ; no end of live turtle, good
beef, oranges, green figs, limes, bananas, and other fruit.
The residents at hotels get friendly at once with well-
behaved countrymen and countrywomen landing to take a
meal on shore and be off to sea again. These visitors take
on board of the products of the island, easy wicker chairs
and sofas, onions, photographs, white leather shoes, lace-
work, new potatoes, feather flowers, green peas when in
season, and all kinds of strange things which excited ramblers, with money rattling in their pockets, must buy,
although they do not want anything. Everybody speaks
well of Madeira, and, as the boy said about his mother,
" What everybody says must be true."

Traders bound for Africa generally get their flowing locks cut off close to their intellect, preparatory to going it "bald headed" on the hot coast. The barbers have raised the price to casuals from sixpence to one shilling for the operation. They purchase baskets of large refreshing onions, thoroughly enjoyed in Africa, also baskets of potatoes; and they get photographs taken of shorn humanity to send home. They like to linger as long as possible listening to the numerous church bells, all at variance in tone, but somewhat resembling village chimes rung by unmusical amateurs. They love to listen to the military band and watch the youth and beauty of Maderia promenading beneath the trees in the Almeida, and telling the old, old story in Portuguese, which they hope to repeat in dear old England. They bathe in the sea here from the ship's ladder, and at Teneriffe for the last time, as sharks on the African Coast, like marine policemen, patrol and preserve the waters. They chum with hotel residents, and good kind Mrs. Miles frankly tells them, "I hope to see you return, but you must take care of yourselves, for very many stay in Africa for good." They go on board their ship with the happy recollection of kind white faces around the genial table, a last fond imitation of home which they may never witness again. It is really parting from England leaving Madeira, but somebody must go to Africa; and, whether it is to the polar regions or down a horrible volcano, our countrymen are always ready.

It is not often, after leaving th's beautiful island for countries situated further south, that bad weather is experienced, such as gales of wind, sleet, snow, hail, rain, fog, and a general shakiness of climate peculiar to temperate and frigid zones, tropical tornadoes and occasional outbreaks of nature, excepted. The dreaded Bay of Biscay has been screwed through, the latitude of the "roaring forties" left

behind, also " waves rolling mountains high "—a phrase
which sounds lofty and damp, and, although utterly untrue,
it is still considered correct to startle sympathising listeners.
The idea probably originated in the imagination of some
eloquent teacher of the people on a voyage from Southport
to Lytham, as the lively motion of the swift steamer battling against wind and tide caused the reverend gentleman
to reel to and fro and stagger like the individual mentioned
by David, thus enabling him from experience to draw an
impressive, heart-rending, and appalling picture of the
dangers of the sea.

Twenty-four hours' run from Madeira and then Santa Cruz,
the principal town on the Island of Teneriffe, is reached.
Teneriffe is one of the Canary Islands; Palma, Gomera, Ferro,
Grand Canary, and two or three others form the group. The
latitude is about 28 degrees north, a few degrees above the
tropic of Cancer. They are situated closer to the African
coast than the Madeira Isles. Should a case of measles at
Orkney or Putney find its way into the English newspapers
left by a preceding steamer, the healthy health officer, from
his boat alongside, solemnly announces " No pratique," when
instantly a yellow flag is hoisted to the masthead. This
intimates that nobody must come on board from the shore
unless they are going to Africa, also that nobody can land from
the steamer supposed to be infected. You can amuse yourself,
as you do at Funchal, or Malta, or other warm-water seaports,
by watching little shivering naked boys jump into the sea
from boats alongside, following three-penny pieces, or six-
pences, or, if you are generously disposed, shillings, thrown
into the transparent water. You observe them, like sunburnt
frogs, or aquatic street Arabs, diving after the glittering silver.
They grab the coin in diving long before it reaches the level
of the anchor, put it into their mouths, and paddling upwards

to air and sunshine, exhibit the treasure to show you " there is no deception, ladies and gentlemen." It is great fun, and profitable to the boys, but more so to the male and female parents, executors, and guardians, who may be observed hovering around in other boats. These affectionate relatives seize the bullion rescued from the sea in the most summary manner, thus preventing reckless expenditure on the part of youth and inexperience. Other boats also come alongside as close as permitted, loaded with fruit, cigars, tobacco, canaries, poodle-dogs, and a variety of curiosities and comforts. They contain floating shop-keepers, who do a roaring trade with all classes on board the steamship, and take the measly money, and appear to like it. Much more would be expended in the marts of commerce on shore if the authorities were liberal in granting pratique. But the mandates from Madrid, like those of the Medes and Persians, must be obeyed. Hence, Richardson's English hotel, once a comfortable resting-place at Santa Cruz, is now closed. Nobody can depend upon being allowed to land at Teneriffe ; so, rather than spend days in a miserable lazarette, passengers for that island prefer to stop short at Madeira, or else go on to Africa. Thus the influx of visitors is almost nil, excepting by their own wretched, second-hand, shaky craft from Spain. During quarantine, a Government boat, with the national flag of authority flying, hovers about watching to see the law carried out. If anyone on board attempts to swim ashore he is liable to be shot ; so very few try to do so.

As there was only one case of insignificant malady reported in the English newspapers previous to our arrival, we were graciously allowed to land and expend loose sovereigns, rapidly changed into dollars and smaller coin. The ship was anchored half a mile from Lord Nelson's celebrated Mole, discharging cargo into barges, and thus we were enabled to take a jolly run on the island.   Teneriffe is about the most ragged and jagged collection of sharp peaks ever jerked above the surface by volcanoes or earthquakes.   It must have been a great day for the elements to shoot up the Peak of Teneriffe 12,182 feet above the level of the sea.   But it was a good job, and it was well done.   Ben Nevis, Snowdon, and Vesuvius, piled one on top of the other, would not reach the altitude of the Peak.   It can be seen on fine days at a distance of 180 miles, just peeping above the horizon.   Fancy that as you gaze at the Welsh mountains.   When thirty or forty miles away from the island, it stands out fine and sharp against the clear blue sky.   During mid-day, clouds are addicted to floating about and obscuring it, but at sunrise and sunset it generally shows.   In winter and spring snow appears, and then the island looks like a gigantic bridecake.   The snow is collected and " cooked " all the year round at the Santa Cruz domino-playing, coffee-drinking restaurants.   The crater has been quiet for a long time, but it is very easy to trace the desolating belts of black and grey lava extending for miles from the crater down the huge mountain side into the sea, relics of eruptions during bygone ages long before history or languages were invented or written.   The lava appears not so hard as that about Vesuvius.   It is porous, and filters are made from it, called " dripstones."   Muddy water percolates through and comes out clear. They are largely exported, and afford great comfort and luxury, especially in Western Africa. Similar filters are in use all over the land of Egypt to render clear the muddy Nile water.

We wander through the town of Santa Cruz, buying cigars imported direct from the sister colony of Cuba— Havana cigars—also others manufactured on the island.   It is interesting to watch beautiful girls making them.   They select one good leaf of tobacco ; and on their right is placed a heap of broken leaves, which the exquisitely delicate fingers adjust in the centre of the outside leaf. By wriggling into shape and trimming the ends, thus is formed the graceful cigar of commerce.

We go to a wretched native hotel and eat sweet cheese and drink wine, which we do not require ; for which, however, the usual exorbitant price levied upon foreigners is paid. Indigestion and temporary misery ensue. Then to the house belonging to the worthy agent for the African and other steamers. It is a large establishment, iron-barred on the lower story against invasion, similar to strong stores peculiar to insurrection-loving countries. A wide double gate, open during the day, admits visitors into the courtyard, and also carts to take away for shipment bags of cochineal and barrels of wine, stored conveniently for that purpose in the ground floor warehouse rooms. Ascending by an inner staircase to the first floor, a broad verandah comes in view overlooking the courtyard. The first floor consists of business offices, also reception and dwelling rooms. Flowers and plants cultivated all about give pleasure to the eye and create a feeling of comfort. If we happen to be personally known to the agent, we are cordially invited to partake of more refreshment, which is simply unnecessary. We decide to take a drive, so a carriage is ordered. It is like a covered shandry on four wheels, fitted with side curtains, and drawn by uneasy-looking mules. In this conveyance we rattle through the narrow streets ; lattices, disclosing glimpses of bright eyes, are lifted as we rush along. The driver is unhappy unless we visit the Cathedral, where a very polite sexton goes through the well-worn service for tourists. It is not pleasant to be shown the flag taken from Nelson, glass-cased high overhead ; nor agreeable to be informed that a silly young countryman, a long time ago, tried to steal it, and came to grief. It is better to sit quietly in the Cathedral, and think and become cool. But the driver cuts short our devotions. He is anxious to drive us up hill five or six miles to the town of Laguna. We take our seats, and, as we speed through the suburbs of Santa Cruz, admire the pretty country residences of the merchants, and inspect the cultivation of cochineal. Cochineal is a small insect yielding a crimson dye. It attaches itself to the cactus plant, which grows extensively. To encourage its propagation the plant is partially covered with thin white cotton cloth in strips, underneath which the insects breed very fast. At the proper time they are collected, packed in bags, and exported ; but of late years the market value of cochineal has gone down, other and cheaper dyes having been invented.

The road from Santa Cruz is in very good order ; it winds after the manner of a section, or front view, of boyhood's idea of the Tower of Babel. Arriving opposite a house situated about half-way, the mules suddenly stopped. Nobody asked them to stop ; it seems to be a matter of course, and the mules know it. The driver would like a flagon of wine. We feel inclined for beer, but, as it is not to be had, we imbibe the wine of the country, and partake of raw red herrings, hard boiled eggs, and bread. Mountain air creates hunger. This eating-house is not after the manner of a civilised restaurant ; on the contrary, it rather suggests the haunt of brigands. This absurd idea is engendered by the weird-looking, barren, and rugged mountain scenery, and the presence of quaint but natural rocky caverns, occupied as dwellings by dirty-faced tenants of ferocious aspect. You would not be surprised if fishermen and bandits suddenly appeared on the scene, armed with stage-daggers, singing " Behold how brightly breaks the morn," clutch you by the neck after the most approved manner, rifle your pockets, and confiscate your person, assisted by a band of music. The public room of this wayside .inn contains a very suspicious "bed by night and chest of drawers by day ;" there is also a greasy dressing-table, on which is a ricketty-looking glass. Scattered about amongst pomatum pots and hair-pins, are a variety of combs and hair-brushes of suspicious aspect, which evidently have had a hard life of it. Amongst this collection, like a guardian angel, sits a huge lean cat purring ; to our surprise this cat refused to eat herrings or egg, but ate bread contendedly. After the mules, the driver, and tourists were refreshed, the latter were invited to look at the back part of the house. In a sort of kitchen we discovered a girl grinding wheat into coarse but wholesome flour, with ancient grinding-stones made of lava. These are worked in a very primitive manner, by means of a supple, loose stick, the lower end of which is stuck into a hole in the side of the top stone, whilst the other end revolves in a pivot fitted into the beam overhead. These grinding-stones were used by the aborigines of Teneriffe, the Guaches, extinct long ago ; and similar stones are dug up in parts of Ireland. Our driver again urges the obstinate mules by blows, varied with alternate entreaty and strange oaths, to drag the loaded conveyance to Laguna, elevated three thousand feet above the sea. We get there, and find a two or three hundred years' old city of the dead on a small scale. The streets are grass meadows, apparently many of them uninhabited. Houses might be let at the rental of a dollar a century and pay better than they do now, but tenants are scarce. Churches are numerous ; some half-built, others in working order, and several in ruins. In the Cathedral the highly-ornamented, armorial-bearing, illustrated tombstones tell a melancholy tale of the past wealth of Laguna, mixed up with the departed glory of Spain. The climate is bracing and the air is pure and wholesome. It is a very suitable site for a city of hotels to entertain those who love to wander south; but Laguna belongs to Spain, and Spain does not want tourists.

Everything about Teneriffe induces a tendency to do nothing and enjoy it. Camels, muzzled with iron cages and heavily laden, appear to walk slower than in other camel countries. They know exactly were to stop whilst their drivers drink wine and play dominoes. Country rustics, wrapped in ordinary white blankets with the usual black border near the edge, and a string at the neck contracting the blanket into a cloak, lie about on the shady sides of the streets, smoke cigarettes, and go to sleep. Padres, attired in broad-brimmed shovel hats and black cloth coats extending to the heels, talk at corners with chance friends for hours. Nobody is in a hurry. Shop-keepers, during mid-day, take a siesta; their stock-in-trade might be carted away without awakening them. But when the afternoon military band plays in the Plaza, or in the gardens by the Mole, the whole population turns out to listen and be happy. Lovely senoritas appear in brilliant array, attended by the youthful male aristocracy of the island. Young military officers come out strong in attractive uniforms tightened at the waist. These heroes have been occupied during the day drilling rustic boys into soldiers, to be shipped off to fight for Alphouso. They revel during afternoons in the eyes of beauty, and at night enjoy the theatre, the masquerade, cafés, dancing parties, ices, and dominoes. The sea dashes on to where Lord Nelson lost his arm at the Mole; the spot is pointed out to strangers. It is a marvel how boats could disembark an attacking party at such a place in the face of an enemy. It was true bull-dog courage, and ought to have succeeded. Had England appropriated the island, it would now have been the Brighton, Scarborough, Harrogate, Cumberland Hills, Isle of Wight, and general sanatorium for Europe and America.

Once upon a time, a governor of a colony on the coast of Africa—I will not say what colony—visited Teneriffe. The following is his graphic description. It must be read with rich brogue to be properly appreciated.

> " In Teneriffe, for a time brief,
>   I wandered all around,
>   Where shady bowers and lovely flowers
>   Spontaneously abound.
>
> " Where posies rare perfume the air
>   In festoons o'er your head.
>   Brave sheep and cows in pastures browse
>   Without remorse or dread.

The author of the " pome " was an invalid ; he recovered.

The fatigue consequent upon a long day's rambling and jolting excursion in a strange country induces sleep. Passengers for Africa get on board the steamer by instalments, each having amused himself according to his inclination, and presently they quietly creep into bed. Two rollicking young dogs arrive on board after the others have retired. The captain is on the bridge, officers and crew at their posts. The anchor weighed, steam up, so off we go. But the two revellers enter without ceremony into the cabins of other lively-inclined but fast asleep fellow-voyagers, and make them turn out in midnight costume. The moon is shining brightly and the sea smooth, so it really appears a sin to sleep. Madeira wicker chairs are arranged in a circle on deck, fluids produced, songs sung all round, varied by exaggerated recitals of adventures ashore. Meantime, the steamer rushes along towards Africa, leaving behind a track of frosted silver. One by one the congregation slink off to bed ; some are caught in the act, replaced in their chairs, and good-naturedly compelled to sing or listen to another song. At length the chairs are empty, and dreamily we agree with Humboldt that "no place appears more fitted to dissipate melancholy, and restore peace to the perturbed mind, than Madeira or Teneriffe."

On the following morning, the pleasant heave of the vessel announces that she is going ahead before the north-east trade-winds. We feel that sail is set to propel the ship in addition to steam, and, drowsily wondering what sail, gradually awake, and turn out of bed before sunrise with—headache. Others are on deck to look at the sunrise, but, as we lean on something solid to look at the sun, a sense of unhappiness is apparent. We really cannot properly appreciate the burst of bright light over the waters. The honourable member for Sierra Leone moves that copies of "brandy-and-soda" be laid upon the table. They are laid accordingly. It is the very thing to call for under the exceptional circumstances of having the previous day—partaken of say—radishes—on shore. After rolling in the bath in water pumped from the sea, or having had the deck-washing hose, like a fire-engine nozzle playing fierce streams over the person, a sense of liveliness returns. Breakfast is announced and enjoyed, after which all adjourn to the deck.

The sun now shows heat; on touching brass or iron work exposed to its rays, fingers instinctively shrink. So awnings are spread fore and aft, affording shade. The wind, blowing beneath the awning and fanning the face, is delightful. Amusing games are got up, such as "bull," played by throwing round pieces of sheet-lead, or cunningly devised circles of rope called "grummets," on to exact spaces marked on a board, or similar spaces chalked on the clean deck, registering numbers; to spot upon which requires not only sea-legs but a correct judgment of distance. At length noon approaches. The captain and chief-officer appear with sextants

to ascertain the latitude of the ship by observation of the sun.
Sights were taken after breakfast—viz., the altitude of the sun,
and, at the same instant, Greenwich time, noted by the
chronometer, to fix the longitude.   The mirror glasses fixed
on the sextant bring the image of the sun down to the edge
of the horizon.   The sun still rises, when delicate adjusting-
screws on the sextant bring it down to the horizon again.
The lower limb of the sun appears to dip into the sea instead
of rising into sky.   The instant of dip is high noon.   The
sun is at its meridian.   The altitude is noted, eight bells
struck, and the watches changed.   Luncheon-bell rings, and
the smiling captain takes the chair.   If he is a decent fellow,
he mentions the exact position of the ship on the broad
Atlantic.   In many steamships it is customary to issue a public
notice announcing the distance run up to noon, latitude,
longitude, and the number of miles from the next port.

After lunch, idlers smoke pipes and watch porpoises
gambolling and skipping over the waves as lambs do in
green pastures.   Shoals of flying-fish rise from the water,
occasionally skimming the tops of the waves to moisten their
finny wings, and continue the flight until exhausted.   Then
they drop into the water, prey to the swift and brilliant
dolphin chasing them.   During their flight above the water,
if seagulls happen to be about they dine on flying-fish.   A
few trying to fly over a vessel, striking against booms or other
obstructions, fall on the ship's deck, and are rapidly cooked
in the galley.   The dressing-bell arouses many who have
fallen asleep.   After dinner, coffee and talk and various
amusements occupy time until bed is sought.   The next
day the same sort of life is repeated.   After twenty days
spent in a similar manner, the dearest friends commence to
quarrel.   Existence appears to be considered a nuisance.
You want to see land and talk with other human beings.

Some find fault with the food, or the attendance, or anything, in fact, to relieve their unhappy minds. If you are addicted to a churlish disposition—but you must be a pugilist to try it on—you desire nothing better than to have a row with the good-humoured captain and punch his head. Our sea voyage, however, is but short. Four days' steaming and Cape Verde, the western point of the continent of Africa, is passed. Dangerous shoals have to be avoided. A low, uninteresting vestige of land above the sea appears in front. Dreamily snoozing over a dull book, you are startled by a gun fired, the anchor chain rattling, and the screw stopping. You are in the River Gambia, off the British colony of Bathurst.

Bathurst, St. Mary's Isle, is situated on the south side of the River Gambia, and close to its entrance, in latitude 13 degrees north, longitude 17 degrees west. A tidal stream, called Oyster Creek, from the quantity of oysters growing on the branches of trees dipping into it, separates St. Mary's Isle from the continent. The streets of Bathurst are composed of fine sand. It is charming to think of, or look at, " Afric's golden sand," but half-an-hour's locomotion through it dissolves the charm. Walking is hard labour. Shoes rapidly fill with it, progress is slow, and extra exercise creates perspiration too freely. The streets are laid out at right angles. The principal one fronts the river, and has the advantage of enjoying more sea-breeze than those behind it. On the front street are built substantial stores occupied by Europeans, the ground floor used for trade purposes, and above that the residence. It extends towards the sea, and on the healthiest sites are constructed Government-house, the barracks, and hospital. Between it and the water grow wide-spreading india-rubber and silk-cotton trees, affording shady retreats for the populace and itinerant traders. The market is crowded; the multitude of black men and women apparently only half-dressed, and the children not dressed at all, bewilders Europeans on first landing. They wonder where so many negroes, negresses, and picaninnies come from; just as a Krooboy, dropped direct from his native lair into St. John's Market, would be lost in amazement to see so many pretty pale faces. Representatives of many tribes come from long distances, by the river, to barter produce for goods. Trading in the large stores is orderly compared to the Babel of languages shouted and yelled amongst the small dealers. In the back streets there are some good houses occupied by Europeans, rising above clusters of bamboo enclosures, each containing from ten to twenty native houses. The native dwellings are cheaply constructed of uprights fixed in the sand, covered by strips of bamboo, and roofed with palm-leaves. On entering an enclosure, the unwelcome presence of fleas is detected, so it is not good to linger. The tall Mandingoes, Jaloffs, and men of other tribes, having laid aside their walking robes, extend their noble forms on the sand, surrounded by women and children laughing and squalling. At night, they organise festivities; drums are beaten, the elegant tom-tom is heard—dance and revelry continue until long after midnight. And thus they enjoy life.

Youthful Europeans, arriving for the first time, admire groves of the graceful cocoanut palm. Vivid tales of infancy and boyhood suddenly strike memory as to how negroes climb to get at the fruit. They wish to emulate the negro, but they find biting insects on the trunks of the trees; so, therefore, postpone climbing, especially as the cocoanut milk and fruit can be obtained in the market without incurring fatigue. They wander about, fascinated at the strange variety of a race of human beings so different to what they have been accustomed. Tropical fruit and vegetation often read and dreamt of, but now before them, afford intense interest and delight. They eat pine-apples and mangoes, drink cocoanut milk, palm wine, and perhaps imbibe London stout to wash down a few oysters. Such a mixture to digest necessitates borrowing a horse, on which to scamper about the swampy district. The human face divine becomes very red, clothing is saturated with perspiration. Dinner and revelry follow, and then a boat to go on board. Getting swiftly to sea after such ebullition only saves the patient from his first African fever. On subsequent visits to the Gambia, horses are not asked for ; the dim, religious light, during dazzling sunshine outside, afforded in the hospitable mansions of merchants, is preferred to rushing about the country. The value of life is better understood.

Amongst other quaint appeals to the public is an advertising sign—" First-class tailor's shop. . . . . Master, bring your clothes and call for any pattern, and we are ready to do them." The descendants of liberated slaves, who have been educated at the expense of Government, or by the aid of missionaries, gradually amass wealth ; in the first place as clerks or labourers to merchants, subsequently as full-blown traders on their own account. They import books of fashion, get clothes made to resemble the illustrations, and turn out dandies. They imitate the walk of Government officials, and like to talk with a tone of authority. If a young army officer wears an eyeglass, they also mount eyeglasses, and frequently become blind in consequence. If the young army officer gets tipsy over his mess dinner, they get drunk in that circle of society in which they are ordained to move, and consider themselves, as 'they are, lords of the creation. They assist trade wonderfully.

In no part of Western Africa do European residents require better-built and cooler dwellings ; and here they have them.

Every contrivance to admit air and exclude sun is practised. Draught stout, in silver tankards, taken whilst panting on easy-chairs and enjoying the sea-breeze, filtered through venetian blinds, adds to their happiness. Country houses and farms on higher land about Cape St. Mary, fronting the Atlantic, tend to prolong existence in this' horribly dismal swamp—" This old sandbank in Africa they call St. Mary's Isle." The River Gambia, navigable for a considerable distance inland, flows through fertile regions, but it brings down at present only driblets of immense produce which will come at some future time. Ground-nuts, yielding clear oil, produced in enormous quantities, are almost entirely shipped to France. Gum, ivory, hides, bees-wax in cakes, a trifle in gold-dust, and, when cotton is high in price at home, Gambia can produce it to pay. When cotton is not sufficiently remunerative to gather, to gin, and to pack it into bales, it is allowed to waste, and other cheaper cotton-producing countries enjoy the advantage. Everything that tends to make life happy is within the reach of the native peoples without working for it. The women till the soil and cook the yam; a few of the men only work to buy rum and other luxuries. As negroes become educated, they covet things unknown to their fathers; their wants become more numerous and must be supplied. And thus trade with Africa increases year by year.

Some of the merchants, although kind-hearted and hospitable and sensible in every other respect, are yet afflicted with vanity. They are naturally inclined to assume a haughty bearing, from having every little want immediately attended to by the crowd of servants surrounding them. On brief visits to England they do not meet with that attention to which they are accustomed. The fact is, they are lost in the crowd; and, instead of being petty monarchs, find themselves very "small potatoes," and they cannot stand it.   The West-end of London is their haunt.   They bring home a couple of male negroes, who are speedily attired in buttons surrounded by livery.   A furnished house is taken, a carriage hired, and they "go it" for six or twelve months, until ready cash becomes scarce.   They then suddenly remember an appointment with a native king up the Gambia about purchasing—"ah ! yas"— an estate growing rice, coffee, cotton, indigo, "and all that sort of thing, don't you know."   During their brief burst of second-hand grandeur they manage to find happiness in that branch of society which is always ready to dine at other people's expense.   As to their associating with shop-keepers, it is utterly out of the question ; they enlarge to their dinner companions on the exorbitant charges of London tradesmen compared to prices in "the Gambia, sir ; in Africa, sir." They know well how to compare prices, although they foolishly endeavour to ignore all trade and appear as princes. Do they not sell at the Gambia—

> "Onions strung on ropes,
> And cold boiled beef, and telescopes,
> And balls of string, and shrimps, and guns,
> And chops, and tacks, and hats, and buns ? "

It is very pleasant to get away to sea from the River Gambia and enjoy the cool breeze beneath the ship's awning. Three days' run to Sierra Leone.   Now begins a change in the nature of the passengers.   Numbers of negroes and negresses of various tribes crowd the deck and sleep upon packages of goods belonging to them.   They are nearly all traders ; many come from long distances high up the Gambia ; they are going to Sierra Leone, the big city of their imagination.   One of them, a mulatto woman from the French colony of Senegal, interests all on board.   She has a nearly white boy baby.   Her mother is with her, acting as nurse to the boy ; she is a pure negress.

It is Sunday morning and nobody knows it. A missionary informs us that it is our second Sabbath at sea; that on the previous one he was indisposed, or he would have asked permission from the captain to conduct divine service. At half-past ten—after the crew have breakfasted, smoked pipes, inspected the contents of their sea-chests (their invariable weekly custom,) and donned their best attire—the ship's bell rings for church. The ensign is spread over the meat-safe on the poop, and on it a cushion, with Prayer-book and Bible. Copies are distributed on chairs and seats placed handy for all who wish to attend. Beneath the awning, with the strong sun shining on the waters outside, all enjoying the gentle motion of the ship over the ocean, the beautiful Church of England service is read. Diamond tears sparkle and trickle down sunburnt features, as thoughts of loved ones at home naturally fill the mind. It is to be our last day at sea all together. Although we can see nothing but calm water, serene sky, and a hot sun overhead, yet it is known that in the morning we shall separate at Sierra Leone, on the sixteenth day from England, and become as before we met—strangers. Although long-life friendships are cemented amongst many on board, the chances are that we shall see each other no more.

It has often been remarked that only a sheet of brown paper separates Sierra Leone from the habitation of fallen angels; but upon approaching it from the sea, such certainly is not the impression. On the contrary, to the eyes of a new comer, Sierra Leone appears a perfect Paradise, or the realization of dreams about Robinson Crusoe and his island. The land inclines gradually upwards into hills about 1,500 feet above the sea level. The hills are abundantly covered with tropical vegetation. The Cape, on which is fixed a lighthouse, is the object towards which the steamer from

England steers to pick up the pilot. This is a great annoyance to captains of steamers calling at Sierra Leone. They know better than pilots how to take their ships to the anchorage during night or day. They have to take the same ships into many places where no pilots are. But the colonial law of Sierra Leone states that pilots must be taken, or, whether or not, paid for. The pilot is a respectable negro; he comes alongside, from a snug bay behind the Cape, in a boat manned by negroes. The steamer stops, the pilot gets on board. If a ladder is not lowered for him, he growls worse than the First Lord of the Admiralty. He wont take a rope over the side and climb up, not he; the First Lord would be happy to do so. But let the pilot go on the bridge, and immediately we are in the land of enchantment. The Arabian Nights are realised. Fairyland is arrived at. Six miles' steaming from the pilot's den, passing pretty bays, fringed with golden yellow sand interspersed by rocks, delights everybody, young and old—from the small, lean stowaway boy—who was discovered half-starved when three days at sea, but who is now well-clothed, as, thank Providence, always is the case, by contributions from the poorest men on board the ship—to the wealthiest. A gun is fired announcing our arrival, and its report rattles up the mountain sides and echoes back over the bay.

Kind-hearted Artemus Ward amused his congregation with a funny remark about the roses abounding in Africa. But here you must not allude to his joke about the "white rose, the red rose, and the negroes." You are cautioned to be affable, and specially warned not to use the word negro. It is absolutely necessary to control feelings, and on no account speak otherwise than gently to the black fellow British subjects who await your landing at the wharf. If they smite you on one cheek, you are told to turn the other also. It certainly requires all the meekness that you can muster to appear calm. Approaching in a boat from the steamer, yells of entreaty to carry luggage are shrieked. It is difficult to ascend the steps on the wharf without being hustled into the water. Hideous visages, spluttering foam into your face, are your welcome. You may be the senior officer of the African fleet, or the cook's mate, it does not matter which, the reception is the same. A policeman, with his staff wielded as if for instant use, quietly looks on and grins and enjoys the fun. It is well to select the biggest, noisiest, and ugliest nigger—

> " His sigh is a hullaballoo,
> His whisper a horrible yell—
> A horrible, horrible yell !"

But he is useful; he organises a procession of negroes, each carrying some article of luggage. You are escorted by a mob to the customs shed; then, after the luggage is examined, the procession reforms and conveys it to where you are going to stay. Each individual claims separate pay. To gain the goodwill of the porters you pay them what they ask, when instantly they whine for more money, which you give, and then you are hailed as " a good massa." That is satisfactory, and it makes you happy. You are sure to see the well-paid porters daily, and they on each occasion levy further toll, following in your footsteps, pathetically appealing for recognition—" Massa, massa, you 'member them time I carry box for you ?"

The white population seldom exceeds seventy-five in number, so that new comers speedily become well known. There is no hotel at Sierra Leone, but the few Europeans who visit the colony are cheerfully accommodated at private houses. If you are connected with the cloth, missionaries entertain you; if a military or naval man, you have the run of the mess at the barracks; and traders or chance travellers are hospitably received by the merchants. Before you have time to sort luggage and enjoy a bath, a deputation is announced by the chief steward—as the head servant is called—of the home of your adoption. It consists of washerwomen. You receive them as a prime minister would; but, before the deputation can settle on one spokeswoman, a dozen arms are extended, each handing well-worn pieces of paper with writing on. These are "books." "Massa, look at my book." You take the nearest piece of paper and read,—"This is to certify that the bearer is a thief; she stole my good shirts and substituted inferior ones." Others are similar, but many give really good recommendations widely apart from qualities pertaining to a laundress. The chief steward, observing your delicate hesitation amongst ladies, quickly drives the deputation downstairs and into the street. He gets your washing attended to properly, and during your stay in the colony is your guide, philosopher, and friend.

The thoughts and feelings of people landing at Sierra Leone vary according to the nature of what they have come out to do. Many, no doubt, are bursting with zeal to propagate Christianity. They are obliged to land immediately below the Cathedral. Perhaps that intensifies their feeling as they joyously take long strides up the steep road and stand before the ugly building to rest and recover breath whilst reeking with perspiration. Some, on the contrary, feel like nigger minstrels, ready to dance on boards, with the accompaniment of a banjo, and finish in the usual manner with a smash-down of boots. It appears natural that all negroes should sing and dance, that African life should consist of sentimental songs, varied by jokes from the "bones"; but such is not altogether the case here. You jump from practical, hard-thinking mercantile life in England, to what is only a parody of the same sort of thing. You observe, with the difference of colour only, the knit brow and anxious expression of plodding but very petty traders. The whole trade of the colony is far exceeded by many mercantile houses in Liverpool. It is a sham, a miserable pantomime of business.

Sierra Leone is in $8\frac{1}{2}$ degrees north latitude, and 13 degrees west longitude. The principal place is Freetown, behind which are hills sloping from the sea to an altitude of about 2,500 feet. The settlement was first started in 1787, and in 1808 it was turned into a colony. It was used as a home and a refuge for slaves captured on slave vessels along the coast by English men-of-war. The slave vessels were condemned, cut into two parts, or destroyed, and the living freight scattered about the colony. The descendants of those slaves constitute the chief population. Kroomen and their families, from a country two to three hundred miles further south, form another portion of the community; they live entirely apart from the others. There are also natives from various districts between the upper waters of the River Niger and Sierra Leone. The latter dress in the graceful loose garments peculiar to the Mahommedan countries. Kroomen, or, as they are generally called, "Krooboys," attire as close to nature as the dressing laws of the colony allow. When out of the public streets, a good-sized pocket-handkerchief forms their entire suit. They are the Irishmen of Western Africa; the only African race on the West Coast that can be depended upon to work for merchants or on board ships. All vessels going down the coast take either here or from the Kroo coast—the latter is preferable—gangs of them to do the rough work of the ship.

Ships-of-war employ them to save the white crew labouring too much in the sun. Every trader from the Gambia to the Equator annually obtains a supply. The commerce of Western Africa could not be conducted without Kroomen, but residence at Sierra Leone demoralises them. The bulk of the population of the colony prefer to lead an indolent life. Those who can live without working, cheerfully do so. Gangs of strong men hire themselves out only for a day or two, receive their wages, abandon labour, and get drunk until the money is finished. Although the colony grows ginger, pepper, arrowroot, coffee, rice, palm-oil, and other tropical produce, yet cultivation of the land is their last resource. Petty shop-keepers fill the market-place and line the streets. Crowds of insolent vagabond loafers abound everywhere. But for the inducement to purchase gorgeous apparel and truly ardent spirits, very few negroes would work at all.

The mountain slopes afford a variety of climate suitable for European residence; but, strange to say, only one good house is built high above the low region of malaria. I mention this to show how careless Europeans are about breathing pure air. Government-house is pleasantly situated on a hill overlooking Freetown. The barracks are built upon still higher ground, and overlook Government-house; but the merchants and colonial officials prefer to live in the town or outskirts, as near to the level as possible. Almost every house has got its garden, growing the delicious avocada pear, orange, citron, pomegranate, mango, banana, cocoanut, pine-apple, and various other fruits, most of which are unknown in Europe. The surface rock is iron sandstone, beneath which exists granite. Walking along the red-powdered streets during the heat of the day is disagreeable. It it interesting to take, as Hamlet did Yorick's scull, a fragment of the heavy iron rock, and reflect that at some future period of the rolling of this earth, ironstone from Africa can supply the world. Old writers prophesied that when England ran short of timber, her shipbuilding supremacy would cease. Iron was substituted. It has been high in price during late years, and the time will come when competition entailing lower freights will bring the valuable ore from Western Africa to furnaces in England, and it will pay well.

It is a very difficult matter to sleep on shore in the tropics after a sea voyage. In the first place, you miss the sound of the propeller blades striking the sea; next, you hear, instead, a chorus of bull-frogs and crickets. It is difficult to reconcile such entirely different sounds so as to produce sleep. Added to which, you are compelled to listen to the noise of the drum and the tom-tom, and the laughter of the people enjoying midnight parties. Gradually the prevailing noises modulate to that of the steamer, and gentle sleep follows, but only by fits and starts. You are glad when day breaks to justify you in the act of turning out. A cup of tea is ready, and, with fresh milk brought from the high land, it is thoroughly enjoyed. Then a walk of little over a mile westward from the Cathedral to a small sheet of water fed by a rivulet and surrounded by overshadowing bamboo trees. In this pretty romantic pond you splash, and roll, and revel, and love to linger. An attendant negro supplies towels, dries your feet, and throws in religious advice for sixpence a head;—it is good. After the bath you walk about the town before the heat of the sun becomes oppressive.

The business hours are from six until eleven A.M., when most of the stores close for breakfast and repose during mid-day. Breakfast is most enjoyable. Friends assemble

and talk business, or colonial politics, or the latest news from
England.   They partake of good country beefsteaks, Madeira
potatoes and onions, turtles' eggs (rare delicacy), and the
contents of various tins of preserved provisions, mellowed by
Allsopp, or Bass, or claret, followed by a cup of tea when
reclining on easy-chairs in the verandah outside the dining-
room.   All doors and windows are opened to admit the
welcome sea-breeze.   But for the sea-breeze, life in Sierra
Leone would be unendurable; it sets in strong before ten
o'clock in the forenoon and lasts until four o'clock in the
afternoon.   The thermometer ranges from 84 to 90 degrees
in the shade.   When the sun goes westward, and the cares of
the day are over, another bath and change of clothing is
desirable, after or before which some go out riding on
horseback, others walk on the green by the battery.   Black
soldiers are there drilled by white sergeants.   When the
band plays, thousands of people assemble to hear the music.
If the green is not occupied by troops, young men play
cricket; they have acquired the game by education in
England.   The sun sets at about six all the year round, and
darkness soon follows, as there is little or no twilight in the
tropics.   Europeans then hurry home to dinner, which is the
same as breakfast, with the addition of soup.   Friends drop
in after dinner, and sit and spin yarns and smoke.   Cards
frequently are produced, and played until sometimes it is
difficult to distinguish between the knave and king.
Abstemious members of the assembly disappear one by one.
Then to bed.   It is a very weary existence.

The heat so enervates Europeans that they only care for
accumulating money to spend afterwards at home.   They
count the months and days of their painful stay as boys do
at school for holidays in the dim future.   They investigate
the time-tables of steamers, and joyfully state—" Ah! I'll

go home with 'Long John Griffiths'; and wont we be happy?" or they praise any other favourite captain. Many are fond of "Old Digges"—the coast name of the worthy commodore of the oldest line of steamers—Captain Davis. They have no idea whatever of constructing healthy residences on the hillsides. They simply are content with dwellings which others have occupied before them, and which their successors will exist in. They live on the first floor overlooking the usual garden. In this garden, in many cases, exists a pump drawing water from a well. Within a few yards of the well is a cesspool, carefully housed over, but never emptied. It is a horrible abomination; quantities of chloride of lime thrown into it, and strewed about, will not drive away the foul stench emitted. Everything that goes into the cesspool is consumed, or it percolates, perhaps, to the well. You lower a lantern through a hole and observe a mass of reptiles and foul insects gorging on filth and offal, and on each other. Waterworks have been ably constructed by Mr. Jenkins, the present colonial engineer, and pipes laid in the streets. A good public fountain is erected opposite to the Postoffice, and others are in course of preparation. But unless house-holders are compelled to pay for and use the good water, they stick to the wells, or else get water in jars, carried on the heads of young girls long distances from springs. Heavy rains run down the streets in torrents, and abundance of water is wasted. If the colony could afford to fill up the cesspools, and construct drainage below the surface, the place would have a chance of becoming healthy. As it is, after heavy rains the sun shines fiercely, and fog—foul malaria—spreads over the low lands, breeding fever and death. Is it any wonder that Sierra Leone is "the white man's grave?"

The Cathedral is a very unprepossessing looking edifice.

The expenditure on it is variously stated at from £100,000 to £150,000. In England a better building could be constructed for £3,000. It is asserted that certain parties, who had a hand in the contract, found (after getting cash in advance) that it was more convenient to break their engagements than to fulfil them ; so they gracefully left the colony, and the Cathedral had to build itself or grow. It is of stone and is slated ; the walls are very thick, and the ground floor is paved with stone flags. When any breeze prevails outside, it blows pleasantly through. It is certainly the coolest place in the whole colony ; but, with the exception of the services on Sundays, and occasionally during the week, the doors are closed. It is melancholy to note on the walls tablets, in both marble and brass, to the memory of departed countrymen. Illustrious natives also urge a claim to posterity ; one inscription states that the defunct was a member of the committee appointed to welcome Prince Alfred on his visit to Sierra Leone. Some one, whose ideas were evidently practical, once proposed to clear away the ugly pews and utilise the cool building during week-days as a promenade. But the Bishop—and very properly—refused his sanction. The better educated negroes use the Cathedral to doze in during Sunday services. The mob flock in crowds to the numerous Dissenting places of worship, where stirring hymns, fitted to the most lively tunes, enable them to join in the singing, thus happily combining a Christy Minstrel sensation with the exercise of a religious duty.

I spent a very pleasant evening at the country house of a wealthy native who was once a slave. He has amassed wealth, and his sons and daughters have been educated in England. To my surprise, the young people were practising on the piano and singing Moody and Sankey's hymns. On the following morning, when visiting the trading store of mine host, I found it full of people listening with strange delight to one of the sons singing "Hold de Fort." These hymns will doubtless be very shortly heard in every conventicle in Sierra Leone. Such melodies go straight to the hearts of the congregation. Singing seems to form the chief attraction of Christianity in Africa. Negroes will go to sleep under a sermon that has no excitement, only longing for its conclusion that they may "go ahead mit de moosic." As they daily eat hot peppers for the nourishment of their bodies, it is not strange that they should require sermons which abound with terrific allusions to the Old Serpent tormenting lost spirits in the lake of fire and brimstone, contrasted with glowing descriptions of celestial bliss in the inheritance of the saints of light. Unless highly-flavoured spiritual food is administered, Sierra Leone Christians wag their woolly heads and remark of their pastor—"He be no nuse" (of no use). They have certainly not much cause of complaint against their shepherds on this point.

On Sundays every place of worship is densely crowded. It is marvellous to observe the inordinate love of dress which is implanted in the negro nature. They will cheerfully expend their last coin to appear in brilliant array. The latest fashions from England are not only copied but exaggerated. The ladies adorn themselves with silk dresses, and they flourish parasols of the brightest hues; and all the gentlemen who can afford to do so wear black broadcloth suits, brilliant neckties, two-story hats, patent leather boots creaking wonderfully, and they carry umbrellas to preserve their complexion. As they troop home from forenoon service, under the dazzling sunshine, the varied colours of their clothing form a kaleidoscopic addition to the beautiful tropical scenery which charms the eye in every direction.

Families who have ample means have adopted English

habits, manners and religion, and they are invariably
hospitable and kind. I dined with one of this class after
Sunday mid-day service. We enjoyed a plump turkey, which
was well cooked, likewise several highly-seasoned dishes, one
appropriately called "palaver sauce," in which the flavour of
palm-oil was not unpleasantly apparent. Claret and
champagne disappeared rapidly after the turkey and yam.
There were two lovely daughters, fashionably attired ; both
engaged to be married to black missionaries. The reverend
lovers were themselves present, and talked in the goody-
goody strain, each striving to win the smile of beauty. The
girls were not quite at their ease, their Balmoral high-heeled
boots causing them much discomfort; their light silk
dresses, too, in places acquired a deeper hue somewhat
foreign to the natural colour. It was broiling hot, which
accounted for their uneasiness. Under ordinary circumstances, loose and more appropriate dresses and easy slippers
would have been worn, instead of imitating the unsuitable
fashions of Europe.

After dinner the parents slept and snored. I was odd
man out, so I told the young couples (each individual of
whom was at that moment occupying the extremity of two
sofas, after the manner of courtship before strangers) that I
would go "into the garden, Maud," and smoke. No objections
whatever being raised to this suggestion, I strolled forth and
found a wicker sofa beneath the shade of a palm-tree, and
there, lulled by the inward satisfaction of having played "gooseberry," I slept the sleep of champagne and turkey until sunset,
when I was awoke by a beauty inviting me to tea. The
missionaries, I found, had already gone forth to conduct the
service and arrange with the choir what hymns were to be
sung. I was asked to accompany the ladies to a revival
meeting. As I wanted a change, I went with them, and

found myself comfortably seated, flanked on each side by folds
of silk. The meeting was lively. Sir Charles Coldstream, in
"Used Up," would have discovered a new sensation here. The
eloquence of the black preacher was something to remember.
Loud shouts of "Hallelujah!" "Amen!" and "Glory!"
during the sermon were enough to keep the sleepiest sinner
wide awake. And the hymns, both before and after the
sermon, fairly "knocked" the congregation. The following
verse is imprinted upon my memory for life, and the peculiar
style of music with which it was sung :—

> " Eve ate de apple,
> Gave one to fadder Adam ;
> And so came mis-e-ry
> Up-on dis world.
>
> Chorus, repeated twice :—
> Oh sor-row, oh sor-row,
> Tri-bu-la-tion,
> Until Sal-va-tion day."

After the benediction, sinners were invited to remain ;
repentant sinners were entreated to come up to the penitent
form, in front of the communion rail, and "seek peace." If
my two young lady friends had not kept on their gorgeous
attire, I have no doubt that they would have gone up to
the penitent form and wept. Those who did go up and kneel
cried a good deal. The feelings paramount at the time with
me were rather those of thirst than of devotion ; so that,
observing how fairly fatigued the girls were, I quietly suggested that they also really must feel "thirsty." They took
the hint, and we took our departure from the tabernacle.

Law is a favourite study of many ambitious young negroes
after they have finished their education at the mission or
government schools. Even when they gain a livelihood as
clerks in stores, they keep concealed books relating to law.
When the eye of the master wanders abroad, these books are

furtively produced and read and re-read.   Hence the negro
lawyer is anything but a scarce article ; but very few of them
are noted for integrity or honour, in fact they are exceedingly
captious and pettifogging.   If a white man should happen to
forget himself and call a negro a " nigger," the negro goes to
his lawyer, a summons is at once issued, and the poor white
is fined five pounds for the abusive language.   Should a white
man push an unfortunate nigger on one side, it is pronounced
a case of assault, and it is a grand thing for the lawyers. The
white man may have to pay fifty pounds, peradventure more.
A friend of mine, once being annoyed by a negro importuning
him for money, said, in a tragical tone, " Away, you vegetable
marrow !" and this abominable language so horrified the
witnesses that they hurried off the insulted negro to obtain a
summons.   A deputation of policemen (of the Dogberry genus)
waited upon my friend, and, with ominous nods, cautioned
him against using such expressions in future.

Englishmen, on first landing, are generally full of that
indefinite national and natural desire to fraternise with
coloured people—to show kindness and sympathy to the black
race, having been educated to know no distinction between
white men and negroes.   If they are sensible, they will not
hesitate, as they generally do, to freely associate with the
well-educated coloured families ; and I promise them they
will thereby find continual amusement, provided that they
keep aloof from domestic feuds, which unfortunately exist
here as well as in small communities elsewhere. But the half-
educated young male negroes, who spend all their money in
fine clothes and jewellery, are most offensive and insolent.
It is well to avoid them.   It is also well to avoid disputes
with the mass of the people.   Each man or woman in the
colony is a British subject, and fully entitled to all the
privileges of British subjects, the same as in England.

Strangers, however, soon perceive that the law is exercised entirely in favour of the black man, and that black juries simply ignore all idea of justice. Englishmen, therefore, become disgusted. They are continually hailed in the streets as "white hounds" and "white niggers." If they die (and that is too often the case) as the hearse—a handcart drawn by hired black men—is conveying the corpse to the cemetery, the mourners hear, as they walk behind, remarks similar to this :—" Dere goes another white beggar to his grave; I wish dey would all go to ——, and leave the colony to ourselves."

One morning, as the five o'clock gun was fired from the fort, the house steward came into my room and stated that a gentleman wished to see me. " What does he want?" I said, only half awake. " Not time for tea yet; begone !" "He want look you partiklar, saa." But the fellow was already in the room, flourishing a white handkerchief perfumed with eau de Cologne, and blowing the burgomaster's solo in "Genevieve de Brabant " on his nose, which thoroughly awoke me, although the report of the big gun had failed to do so. I sat up in bed and said, " What the ——" No, that won't do. " My good Christian brother, what—do—you—want?" Handing me his card, upon which was printed the illustrious names James Babington Macaulay Bismarck, he replied, " I am de gentleman managing a ball to-night of coloured ladies and gentlemen, saa. I thought that I would find you disengaged, saa. De tickets are two shillings each, saa," "All right," I said, " I'll take a ticket. Hand me my purse. No, wait; I'll get up; it is no use trying to sleep after your charming solo. Bless you, here is the money ; ta-ta."

When night came, I persuaded a white resident to go with me. The ball took place in a couple of tolerably-sized rooms on the first floor of what was (for the colony) a large house. Wide folding doors between the rooms were thrown open.

The staircase was lighted by grease-dropping candles. Candles fixed into chandeliers hung from the centre of the ceilings illuminated the rooms also. The springing of the floor, acting upon the beams overhead, caused these candles also to shed their drops. My visitor of the morning, the early bird, was factotum; he took tickets, played a fiddle, and, stamping time with his boots, acted as a master of the ceremonies generally. The ladies were decked out in full ball costume, and most of the gentlemen wore evening dress. At first the dancing was extremely proper and stiff, but gradually the dancers warmed to their work. A refreshment stall, situated outside the dancing rooms in the cool verandah, lighted by lanterns, had a rare time of it. The really delicious home-made ginger-beer was in great demand, also lemonade, price twopence per bottle, taken neat at first, but subsequently strengthened by the addition of rum, gin, or whisky, supplied at very moderate prices. Each gentleman gallantly and regularly after every dance took his partner to the verandah, if not for refection, at any rate for a rest, the chairs having been removed from the dancing rooms for that purpose. Trees laden with strange fruit overhung the verandah; the cool air was inhaled with delight, and the repose was welcome. Between the dances, songs and popular sacred hymns were sung with a chorus by the whole company. I never witnessed such a mixture of religion added to what Byron calls "Fiddling, feasting, dancing, drinking, masquing." In the middle of the tenth dance my partner, who seemed distressed about her understandings, whispered softly, " Come into the verandah, saa, and tand before me, only a little bit, saa; I want to take my tockings off, de room it be hot too much." She actually, and with perfect innocence, peeled off her stockings, placed them carefully in the bosom of her dress, pocketed her shoes, and then danced in her bare feet so vigorously, and with such extra velocity, that I had fairly to give in and exclaim with Macbeth, " Hold, enough !" It was great fun.

A portion of the banks of the river Sherboro' belongs to the colony of Sierra Leone. This river empties itself into the sea by two mouths, the Sherboro' and the Shebar. Both of them are navigable; the former for vessels drawing nineteen feet, and the latter for vessels drawing fourteen feet. Without the revenue collected from Sherboro' the colonial coffers would not have wherewithal to pay expenses. The Governor of Sierra Leone delegates his authority to an administrator called the Commandant, who, with a few coloured policemen, and a collector of customs, assisted by a black staff, levy and collect tribute. No protection whatever is afforded to the merchants, although they are compelled to pay heavy duties on the principal articles imported, and also, strange to say, a very heavy tax upon all produce exported ; the unwise policy of the latter materially limits the trade, and prohibits the legitimate development of the enormous resources of the surrounding country. It is supposed that the Sherboro' takes its rise in the same range of hills as the Niger and Senegal. Natives report that it runs out of a greater river. If that is true, the greater river must be the Niger; but I receive this tale with doubt, as it remains to be proved. One hundred miles is the farthest that any white man has ascended it. Wherever it, and the numerous navigable branches that run into it, flow, the districts teem with valuable products. Near the sea the nature of the country is swampy, but the land gradually rises sufficiently to give water-power for running saw-mills at a few miles from the coast, and the further inland the more elevated it becomes. It is abundantly covered with excellent hard timber, of which the American missionaries know the value ; for, in addition to their schools and services, they have constructed, and work, an American made saw-mill.

Alluding to the missionaries here. The Church of England have the usual schools and church house, but the Americans have hit upon the proper plan of educating youth and adults in useful mechanical pursuits. The greatest credit is due to Mr. D. W. Burton, the head of the American Mission, who has spent twenty years of his life in doing that good work. Mr. Burton is now about to found a colony of the freed negroes from the United States, who will work after the manner of the Basle mission, paying its own expenses.

I visited Sherboro' with a friend who had a trading factory there. He was anxious to look after thirty thousand pounds owing to him by black traders who had migrated from Sierra Leone, and also by the native chiefs about. During ten days' stay we had interviews with many of his debtors, some of whom were full of promises to pay, but meantime they wanted more credit. Others were rudely insolent. One man was especially overbearing and arrogant ; he owed nearly six thousand pounds. This nigger was a beggar before being trusted ; he now owns sailing craft, has built a large house in the centre of a beautiful park, where he lives like a nobleman and laughs his creditors to scorn. I forbear at present enlarging on the evil of merchants giving niggers extensive credit, as I shall have to allude to that subject further on.

The Sherboro' tribes are peacefully disposed towards white men ; but, as usual, on other parts of the coast, they, and tribes of the interior, are frequently at war with each other, and then trade suffers. Before 1870 a company of black soldiers under English officers was stationed here, but it was then withdrawn. It would be satisfactory to the

merchants to have soldiers in the vicinity for the protection
of commerce, and also a court to decide law cases, for at
present trials take place at Sierra Leone, and many of them
are vexatious suits, entailing trouble, expense, and time wasted
in travelling to and fro. The merchants speak highly of
the late acting governor, Dr. Rowe, as a man who thoroughly
understood the best means to keep the tribes in order and
also to grant facilities for the extension of trade.

There are five European factories on the Sherboro', besides
smaller native trading posts. The Europeans have established their business places far apart on both sides of the
river. I think that this is a mistake ; for, if they were
clustered together, they would form a town of considerable
size, and be well able to protect themselves against savage
attack and plunder, but, unfortunately, they are jealous of
each other. We resided at Mocolo factory. The site was
selected at a deep part of the river, where, on its hard sandy
bank, canoes from the far interior could conveniently land
produce and receive goods in return. When first started, a
dozen years ago, a small house was sufficient; year by year, as
the barter business prospered, other buildings were added.
On the beach is a large brick and slated store, two stories
high ; on its right is the powder magazine, and on the left are
strongly-constructed stores to hold palm-kernels, palm-oil in
casks, and salt in bulk. On the land behind the beach,
twenty-five feet above the river, is an enclosure measuring
two hundred yards square, containing the agent's dwelling-
house, gracefully shaded by trees. The sheds and stores are
all built well apart from each other, so that when one takes
fire it can be destroyed to save the rest. The cost of the
buildings was six thousand pounds. The agent employs
three or four white clerks, and from one hundred to a
hundred and fifty black mechanics and labourers, who reside

outside. In the enclosure only the agent, one clerk, and the domestic servants live, besides a watchman, who keeps a huge fire burning all night inside the gate.

Everything that the negro heart can fancy is sent out to barter. Powder to devastate tribes is a favourite medium of exchange, but when the stock is large climatic influence renders it damp, and then it has to be dried in the sun. One day several men were detailed to this duty. Taking the kegs from the magazine up to the enclosure, they opened them, spread the powder out upon sheets of brown paper laid on the burnt-up grass, and, as it dried, they repacked it into new kegs, leaving the broken ones lying about. Some of the damp powder stuck to pieces of the wood, and some of it was scattered amongst the grass. That night, about nine o'clock, the watchman, smoking a short pipe, was rooting amongst the broken kegs to find enough small timber to light his midnight bonfire. A spark from his pipe dropped on to a cake of powder, which instantly exploded, and then a running fire took place of all the powder left amongst the grass. A brilliant glare flashed for a few moments, then dense smoke followed. All the white men were enjoying coffee and pipes in the verandah after dinner. We instantly rushed across the garden to where the explosion took place, and found the poor Krooboy watchman in terrible agony. He darted towards the well, intending to jump into it, calling out, " Oh, I done die, I done die." His cloth was burnt into the flesh, and even the wool of his head destroyed. We covered him with oil and cotton. An alarm was raised. The labourers from their outside village flocked to the gate. The women suggested rolling the poor man in plantain-leaves. We could do no better, so they took him; but he died a few hours afterwards.

We travelled by a little French steamer called " L'Afri-

caine." Leaving Sierra Leone at noon one day, we anchored
for the night to the leeward of the Banana Islands; started again
at daybreak, and at' ten o'clock that forenoon made fast to the
wharf of Bonthe, about 120 miles from Sierra Leone. At
night all slept upon the little deck, and it was a strange
medley group of Europeans and Africans. The captain
spoke half-a-dozen words of English, and we possessed about
the same proficiency with French. But speedily it appeared
that we were Masons; apart from that, he was a hearty good
fellow, but with it, he was perfection. He acted not only as
captain, but chief mate and cook. The pilot who steered
and the rest of the crew were negroes. Frenchmen are proverbial for getting up dainty messes. We all assisted at the
cooking, as there was nothing else to do. Walking was out
of the question, as the little vessel was crowded. We were
afraid that some of the children playing upon the sea-sick
forms of their mothers would fall overboard, as the rail was
only about one foot high, so the liveliest of the plump,
bright-eyed little woolly heads had to be tethered like sheep.
The skipper instructed us in the art of making Mayonnaise
sauce. We caught fish enough to feed everybody on board,
and going to and fro, enjoying the balmy open air sleep at
night, entirely free from mosquitoes, was very pleasant.

CHAPTER II.

A SHORT residence in and about Sierra Leone is quite sufficient to gratify the curiosity of any traveller. We had had enough of the colony, and therefore prepared for our departure and paid our washing-bills. It is one of the articles of a sailor's creed to do so. Having made up our minds to travel further southwards, we anxiously looked seawards through a "spying-glass," as dear old Robinson Crusoe called it, to descry on the horizon a tiny streak of smoke, the expected steamer. As it became due we gazed intently. A gun fired from the top of a hill (where a look-out house, with a flagstaff has been erected) announced the approach of one from the north, long before we on the level could possibly see it. It is the boat from England, and it at length duly arrives and delivers mails and cargo. It is not, however, until the following day that we go on board, and we are not sorry when our boat puts off from the wharf. It was difficult to make our way through the crowd of other boats to the gangway of the steamer. Luckily, we happened to have selected a crew of able-bodied negroes, who, by freely using very wicked-looking boathooks, worked through all obstacles to the vessel's side in the most determined manner, as if they wanted to get rid of us quietly and seek for another job. At the top of the gangway are two of the colonial "police" vainly struggling to establish some kind of order. They roll their eyes about, foam at the mouth, and wield their truncheons lustily ; but

the negro skull is as hard as a grindstone.   There are about
thirty coloured folks going on with us southwards, and each
of these has at least ten friends to see him or her off, so that
the crush may be imagined, but the yelling cannot—it is
simply indescribable.   At length the steam-whistle shrieks,
drowning all other noise, and it distinctly warns visitors to
hurry into the boats for shore.

There were several young English naval officers on board,
on their way to join the African fleet at Lagos.   Their
behaviour was more lively than would have been compatible
with the discipline of a man-of-war, but here they were only
passengers, and had spent a jolly day on the land.   There
happened to be, as usual on all steamers leaving Sierra
Leone, bunches of bananas hanging underneath the awning.
The gentle youths referred to amused themselves with
pulling the fruit off the bunches and pelting the boatmen
alongside with it.   This riles the boatmen, and, accompanied
with really only good-natured chaff, works them up to such
a fearful rage that, in retaliation, they take to throwing back
empty bottles (doubtless stolen from the ship.)   Now
bottles, hurled under circumstances of mad aggravation, do
not make accurate flights.   Nobody is ever certain, when he
shies a bottle, under the influence of temporary insanity,
where it will go to, so that innocent people generally take
the place of the target aimed at.   Thus the waistcoat
of our quietest missionary, who was on deck at the time
trying to read, became a bull's-eye for one of these stray
projectiles ; his hat fell off, and his book flew away out of
his hand, but the meek man merely said " Dear me," and
then moved his chair quietly out of the line of battle.

A number of well-dressed, aspiring young negroes,
flourishing fancy walking-canes, are in the saloon drinking
champagne and talking very loudly.   I do not believe that

it is physically possible for negro lips to execute a whisper;
like the mouth of a foghorn, they seem constructed only to
bellow. The steward respectfully intimates to these gentlemen that the ship is about to proceed on her voyage, and he
requests them to go into the boats waiting for them. But
the steward's advice is disregarded. "Ethiopia still stretches
forth her hands "—for more champagne. Europe adores the
sparkling fluid, and why not Africa? But meantime the
steamer is off. The boats, with the men in them holding on
to the ship's ladder, are dragged through the water, as
the talented champagne-drinkers jump into them, till at
length the speed of the steamer being too much for the
strength of the boatmen, they are obliged to let go, and so
drift away. One of these (literary) howling swells, however,
is left on board, who yells out, "Captain, 'top de steamer,
saa! 'top de steamer, I tell you! Why you not tell gentleman
you go! Why you no ring bell, saa! D—n you, you white
rascal, I make you pay! I make "—— But the owner of
the voice suddenly disappears; in the fulness of his wrath he
had backed on to the ladder, and, in some unaccountable
manner, gave a lurch and fell overboard flop into the sea.
A shining hat dancing on the waves, a woolly head emerging
from the billows snorting sea-water, and a boat containing
his festive friends, who laughingly apply a boathook and
pick up the dripping clothes containing his living carcase
shrieking with vengeance, were our last reminiscence of the ·
colony.

It takes a few hours to settle down after leaving Sierra
Leone. The stewards are busily engaged in turning steerage
passengers out of the saloon to the other end of the ship,
their proper place according to their tickets. Men can be
driven if necessary, but women will seldom go further
forward than the main hatchway; here they place their

luggage, sleeping mats, and pillows, and cooking and other utensils, and squat·down, with their "fixings" located like settlers in the backwoods of America, for the week or fortnight, or whatever the time may be, until they arrive at their destination. In the ladies' cabin we have four black women and ten children. The husbands óf these women are clergymen of the Church of England proceeding to Lagos to be distributed by Bishop Crowther throughout his diocese. One of them is placed in the cabin with two of the naval officers. In the middle of the night, however, the white men leave their berths and take up their beds and walk—to sleep on deck, preferring the open air to the insufferable exhalation from the negro epidermis. Gentle reader, when you or any other praiseworthy philanthropist, come out here to fraternise with your black brethren, if ever you find yourself in the same state-room with any of them, you will do precisely as our naval friends did. Monkeys and skunks yield a well-known offensive odour, so do the drains of Naples and Constantinople ; but our coloured brethren, asleep in their native tropics, beat them all. Shortly after the naval men had proceeded on deck, an amusing incident occurred. The ship's engines were stopped and the lead hove, as it is customary, for we were in the vicinity of St. Ann's Shoals, and it was necessary to take soundings. As soon as silence reigned (and it is silence when the screw stops on ·board a steamer at sea), the four women and their offspring in the ladies' cabin set up such screaming and crying and yelling that they awoke the passengers and stewards, who speedily rushed out of their state-rooms in sleeping attire to see what was up. The cries when reduced to language simply meant, " Wat de matta ? Wat de matta ? Oh, my fadder and my lord, wat de matta ? Oh !" As soon as the husbands of these ladies ascertained the cause of the stoppage, they had no difficulty in pacifying their spouses by simply stating, " Ship she feel for watter."

Twenty-eight hours after leaving Sierra Leone the steamer anchored off Monrovia. A very tiny oil lamp, fixed in a lighthouse on Cape Mesurado, showed us the land, and enabled the steamer to anchor and wait for daylight. Cape Mesurado is a small, well-wooded hill jutting out into the sea. The lighthouse is erected on the top, and below it, fronting the water, is a pleasant-looking spot, cleared of trees and bush, and converted into a farm, on which a good house has been erected. This is the country residence of the President of the Republic of Liberia. Monrovia, the capital of the republic, situated on rising land, well adorned with trees, inside the promotory, is a fac-simile of a small town in the Southern States of America. The names " White House " (a very ordinary-looking edifice built of *red* brick) and " Senate House " (a ramshackle wooden structure erected on a stone foundation) tend to mislead strangers as to the importance of the republic. We landed at the beach in one of the ship's boats, and everybody got unpleasantly wet by the waves breaking over the boat as it touched the sand. Although sheltered by Cape Mesurado from the full swing of the Atlantic rollers, it is not safe to land here in boats. But when the tide suits, so that, without going near the beach at all, you can cross the bar of a river into smooth lagoon water skirting the lower part of the town, a ship's boat may be, used without danger. It happened, however, to be low water when we arrived, so that we were compelled to land at the beach in the vicinity of a village populated by the aboriginal natives, who are called Kroo-people. The simple costume of these Kroo-people (not far removed from the primeval fig-leaf) contrasted strikingly with the perfectly American turn-out of the Postmaster-General, who, with his attendants, waited to receive the mails. The President wanted to read his letters before breakfast, so the seals of the Liverpool mail-bags had to be broken, and a swift runner was forthwith despatched to the house fronting the Atlantic.

It was too early to see many people moving in the town as we strolled through the grass-covered streets, which we had nearly all to ourselves. There was a small shanty store apparently open for trade—tobacco, cigars, lollypops, pickles, and ginger-beer being exhibited in the window; we accordingly entered, and, seeing nobody about, knocked sharply on the counter. On the other side a woman half rose up from a bed and exclaimed "Oh my!" Our modesty caused us to turn away our faces, and we apologised, remarking that we had seen cigars in the window, and had just stepped in to buy some. The woman replied, "Well, I guess you can have some." Then she called out in a drawling tone, "Hezekiah! Hezekiah!" To which name a black boy came forward, rubbing his eyes to awake himself. He had literally got "nodings on." The lady resumed, saying, "Hezekiah, them cigars is two cents apiece, and them thar is three cents apiece. Gentlemen, will you help yourselves, and never mind me?" We did so; and, having purchased a box of matches, gallantly deferred lighting our cigars until we were outside the bedroom store. We are under the impression that Hezekiah returned at once to his bed, and that the lady also fell asleep again.

We wandered about until it became apparent that the inhabitants were getting up. Basins of water, soap, and towels, began to appear outside the houses. Costermongers, retailing fresh fish from house to house, commenced to shout. Clerks and labourers hurried down hill to the trading stores and wharves fronting the lagoon. Women stood at house doors relating incidents of family biography, and well-dressed people congregated to discuss the news brought by the mail, and to drink a morning nip of something refreshing ; just as they do in early settlements of civilized beings all over the globe.

We were already upon intimate terms of friendship with the Postmaster-General, and he kindly introduced us to the Secretary of State for War, as well as to the general commanding the troops. It was at first a somewhat stiff and ceremonious proceeding; but "standing drinks" at one of the tin-pot places called "ho-tels" speedily placed us upon a more comfortable footing with those high officials. Every one we conversed with—in other words, every respectable man that we met—for Liberians are very pleasant and affable people so long as you stroke the wool the right way—seemed bent upon giving us the whole history of their colony ; its starting from America about 1822, their internal dissensions and wars with the aborigines; every important event, in fact, was related voluminously, and, of course, highly exaggerated, both to the detriment of their enemies and the glorification of themselves, the narrators nearly always summing up with an imitation of the old American expression, "We air a go-ahead people, sir ; that's what's the matter with us." Everything about Liberia, its laws and government, is a puerile copy of the United States of America. But Liberia is as yet only in its infancy as a nation ; in all probability, it will ultimately become a great country. The peculiar "high-falutin" talk of interested residents should, therefore, be taken with reserve. The real drawback to its advancement is that the majority of the colonists, who were originally sent from America to till the soil, and grow coffee, sugar, indigo, gum, indiarubber, and castor-oil, and to collect palm-oil and palm-kernels—are far too lazy to work. The tract of fertile country capable of being farmed is unlimited in extent. Those who do pay attention to growing produce iuvariably succeed. But far too many have acquired the American habits of ease and luxury, although peculiar only in America to the wealthy classes of society; yet a life of ease is imitated in parody by coloured folks, so that these people prefer to keep petty stores and associate in towns and villages rather than lead the life of farmers. The habits, customs, and love of religious excitement amongst Liberians are very similar to those practised by descendants of slaves at Sierra Leone. America has established the Republic of Liberia more successfully than England has managed with Sierra Leone, and therefore Liberia carries the palm, and will flourish, and some day may absorb the adjacent colony of Sierra Leone.

We invited some of our republican acquaintances to a spread at the hotel, intending to have a festive meeting and thoroughly enjoy ourselves; but, in the midst of our festival, the gun from the steamer, announcing her immediate departure, caused us to call for our reckoning, and hurry off in a boat, kindly placed at our service by one of our guests. The steamer's anchor was hove short as we ascended the ladder; the donkey-engine hoisted it up whilst the screw turned ahead. A bath and a change of clothing made us happy and comfortable, and, beneath the awning, we gazed at Cape Mesurado until it faded into sky; then we conversed and played cards, and, at last, welcome sleep followed, not unaccompanied in my case with dreams; for, in a vision, I thought that Liberia was the greatest and proudest government on earth, that I was ambassador to it from somewhere, and associated with similar respectable parties from Great Britain, the United States of America, Germany, Russia, France, and all creation, more or less. I believed myself to be a benefactor of mankind. I had something to do with constructing a railway (not without much difficulty, however)

from Monrovia or Cape Palmas (not clear which) to the head
waters of the River Niger.   Goods trains, laden with produce,
arrived from the interior alongside wharves, where steamers
were waiting to receive their cargo.   Quaint smiling negresses,
like those depicted upon the crockery ware of the African
steamships, with the motto "Spero meliora," submitted fruits
and tusks of ivory for my acceptance, and they stated in good
English, alluding to the trifle of a railway, "Oh, thank you
very much, you have really opened up Africa."   Strange to
say, I was in indescribable agony to get fish-plates fixed upon
the rails to complete the line, when the firing of the steamer's
gun awoke me, and my imaginary railway vanished into
thin air.   We had arrived at Grand Cess (bad cess to it !)
The steamer wanted Kroomen ; this is one of their villages,
and we make a morning call.

A belt of light yellow sandy sea-beach, with flat country
above it abundantly wooded, stretches north and south as
far as the eye can reach.   It is fringed by the white surf
caused by the long Atlantic waves.   These waves, when the
air is calm, give the idea of rolling prairie country.   They
are then smooth, but undulating, and ever moving onwards,
till, on coming in contact with the shore, they curl their
monstrous heads, and, breaking into foam, hiss upwards and
expend their force. ˙Reefs of rocks extend here and there
at some distance from the land, upon which the sea, dashing
with all its force, makes a tumultous, angry foam.   These
are the breakers so much dreaded by mariners, and
constitute one of the perils of the sea.   Black spots of rock
peep out from the seething waters, and woe to the boat or
ship that strikes on to them.   It means dire disaster,
destruction, and death.   A collection of thatched huts,
peeping out from amongst the trees, is the village of Grand
Cess, Kroo Country.

The report of the ship's gun arouses the inhabitants, and hundreds of dark forms rush at once over the bright beach to launch their canoes into the surf and through it. These canoes go bobbing up and down, dancing on the blue water. They are very light, are carved out of one piece of wood, gracefully formed like a cigar tapering at both ends, and are propelled by one or two men, squatted upon their heels in the bottom of the canoe. If only one man occupies the canoe, he uses his paddle first upon one side and then upon the other; but, if there are two men, each takes his own side, and their well-developed muscular action swiftly urges the graceful skiff towards the steamship. It is a glorious sight to watch the race of at least two hundred canoes. The paddlers yell with ecstasy as they approach, and familiarly hail well-known faces on board. Captains of African steamers have each their favourite head Krooman. The numerous wives of a head Krooman, knowing this, seem to look upon their husband as the real commander of the ship. Their names are peculiar. " Nimbly," " Tom Bestman," " Shilling," " Bottle of Beer," " Prince of Wales," " Salt Herring," " Gladstone," " Flying Jib," " Bismarck," and hundreds of other equally fantastic names, conferred according to the fancy of their employers, stick to them through life, and their heroic deeds are sung and recited to crowds of evening parties in Kroo Country, The head Krooman, as he approaches, absolutely grins with delight, and, addressing the captain, shouts, " Aha, long John, you lib ! " This word " lib," means, I hope, my dear and worthy commander, that you are in the enjoyment of perfect health ; in fact, that you live and move and have your being " proper." The good-humoured captain smiles at the knowing familiarity, and orders his welcome head Krooman to engage so many good, strong men, not " bush boys " (as men who have never worked on board vessels are termed), but experienced hands, to do the hard work of the ship down the coast and back again to Grand Coss.

Whilst the captain is thus engaged, hundreds of natives climb over the ship's side in the ordinary full-dress costume of the country, consisting of a necklace, in addition to which as Mark Twain says, " they wear a smile." The necessary number selected, the steam-winch runs the anchor up, and off we go full speed ahead. The Kroomen who are not wanted (a few have been employing their time on board trading cocoa-nuts, fresh fish, or live birds for biscuits) actually jump overboard to swim to their canoes. The sight of ten, twenty, fifty, nay, sometimes even two or three hundred men springing from the ship's gunwale and splashing into the sea, whilst the steamer is going at the rate of eleven miles an hour through the water, is so startling that you have to rub your eyes, whilst laughing heartily, to look again and realise it. Jumping into the sea and swimming a mile, or perhaps two miles, to your canoe, would be rather a novelty to those who are accustomed to land at a wharf and jump into a cab. If one of the canoes gets swamped, the paddlers and passengers jump into the sea and swim about, whilst one of the party rolls the canoe to and fro with a peculiar jerk, thereby ejecting the water; the swimmers then carefully balance their agile bodies, jump in again, and away they go. All along the Kroo coast, extending from Cape Mesurado to Cape Palmas, it is a common thing to meet with canoes ten or twelve miles out at sea fishing.

Kroomen are a hard-working race, but they are very timid and much given to superstition; unfortunately, they are also naturally born thieves. They come on board the ship as Job entered this world—naked; but there the resemblance to that good man ends. They leave the ship laden with everything that they can lay their hands upon. In addition to their wages, they are paid in kegs of powder, guns, demijohns of rum, cases of gin, and Manchester goods; they have also strong wooden boxes, containing miscellaneous plunder and perquisites freely donated to them by all who admire pluck on the sea. On the whole, they are merry men; and, before residence at Sierra Leone degenerates them, they are comparatively inoffensive. Head Kroomen, who organise the gangs of labourers, are responsible to the mothers of the boys for their proper treatment whilst away from "we country," as they fondly call their home, as well as for their safe return; and, failing that, a satisfactory account must be rendered as to how they died. This is one of those beautiful and affecting "touches of nature which makes the whole world akin." Kroomen prefer to run in the steamers down the coast and back, the voyages being short. Those employed in factories on shore, or on board palm-oil vessels in the bights of Benin and Biafra, only engage themselves for one year, and they calculate the time by the number of moons; one notch for every full moon is carefully cut upon a piece of wood, forming the private diary of each individual. When thirteen moons have thus been worked out, they joyously return by steamer to "we country." There is no disputing their almanac, nor is there any desire on the part of right-minded employers to do so, for no decent white man will break faith with his Kroomen. The experiment has frequently been tried of employing them as firemen on board African steamers; but, strange to say, they cannot stand the heat of the stoke-hole on the coast as well as white men. And then, again, the cold boisterous weather of our northern seas does not agree with them; it fairly frightens them out of their senses. They are as easily alarmed as little children, and cannot understand the short wintry days and long dismal nights peculiar to our latitude, nor the absence of their darling sunshine. They miss also their boiled rice, with which they gorge themselves, and which, with the addition of a salt-herring, their great luxury, makes them perfectly happy and contented.

Three hours' steaming from Grand Cess and the anchor is dropped off Cape Palmas, at about three miles distance from the land. It requires the utmost care to select anchorage-ground, so as to avoid the sunken rocks, or rather rocks which are not visible. We see before us, high and dry upon the beach, at a distance of one mile north of the Cape, the splendid steamship "Yoruba." She anchored in what was considered a safe position; but, on swinging round by the action of tide, current, or wind, she touched upon a rock below the surface. The touch was sufficient to knock a hole in her stern compartment—a rock will rip up an iron ship's side just like tearing your finger through a newspaper—the compartment speedily filled. The officer in charge weighed anchor again sharply, put on full steam, and ran her on to the beach and she was wrecked.

For the first time during the voyage our surf-boat is lowered, the mails from England are placed in it, six Kroo-boys ply the oars, and the third-officer takes the tiller. We gladly avail ourselves of the opportunity of going ashore. Though only a third-officer here, he has commanded a sailing vessel before now, and is working his way upwards to command a steamer; he keeps his weather-eye open for breakers, which he avoids, and for the current, which he carefully estimates, and steers accordingly. We run for a small beach situated between rocks on the north side of Cape Palmas, and for the last hundred yards of our journey the oars simply direct the boat's head; for we are riding upon the crest of a wave, and it rapidly carries us along, with a feeling of delight, until the

crunching of the boat upon the beach causes our teeth to
close suddenly.   Tourists should not talk during these exciting
moments, lest the tongue be caught unpleasantly between
the teeth, producing a worse shock than galvanism.   Before
we can collect our senses and jump out on to the shore, now
dry before us,—the wave that landed us having receded
gracefully, though with a hissing noise, drawing with it sand
and pebbles—lo ! another raises its crest and overwhelms the
boat and its contents like an avalanche.   We get out on to
the backs of Kroomen, who carry us to dry land.   They
shake themselves as ducks do after a thunderstorm, and are
soon all right ; but we feel uncommonly damp.   It is not,
however, an unpleasant sensation ; it is like using a bathing-
machine without the trouble of disarranging your necktie and
paying the customary sixpence.   Well-dressed Liberians,
chewing tobacco, smile and express sympathy with our mis-
fortune.   They introduce themselves, and converse freely ;
of course, the talk turns on the fertility of the country and
the superiority of American negroes settled in Liberia over
the aboriginal Kroo-people, and the history of the republic
attains to about its thirtieth or fiftieth edition.   We are
literally crammed with the subject.

The ship's officer takes the mail to the general post office,
and subsequently informs us that we have got three hours'time
to wander about that portion of the republic.   We proceed
to the lighthouse at the extremity of the Cape, and, mounting
to the top, admire the view inland.   It is certainly a glorious
country.   Calm lagoons, fringed with luxuriant vegetation
springing from a rich soil, everywhere show undeveloped
wealth, only requiring labour and cultivation to yield
valuable produce.   A road, running inland from the Cape, is
studded with pleasant-looking houses and gardens and
schools and churches.   Occasional patches are cleared of

trees; these are cultivated farms, bounded in the distance by the natural bush and forests of untouched indiarubber trees. Seawards, the Atlantic beats upon stray rocks, and upon the Cape are clusters of graceful palm-trees waving pleasantly in the breeze; hence the appropriate name, Cape Palmas.

The American mission-house, built alongside the light-house, attracts our attention, more especially from its general appearance of comfort and the existence of artistically arranged plants and flowers. Although total strangers, we are kindly invited to enter, and the presence of a white lady is at once revealed by the antimacassars and pretty orna-ments that adorn the drawing-room. We are most hospitally received, and feast upon the best of the fruits of the country. Baby is asleep. The fond mamma shows us the wonderful treasure. The little white darling reposes in the centre of a wide bed, surrounded by gauze curtains to keep out the mosquitoes. We approach carefully upon tip-toe, and gaze at its little heaving bosom. Such a memento of home and love we never expected to witness in dark Africa, and it fairly affects the stoutest heart. The clergyman at the head of the mission introduces us to some very sad-looking, woebegone American missionaries, who have come out to spread the gospel of glad tidings in benighted Africa. They give vent to their sorrows, and evoke our sympathy. But see! One of them is inflating his chest, as if about to speak. Is our brother going to start a hymn? Sankey inhales atmosphere considerably when he does so. No; but he commences by observing, "In the year eighteen hundred and twenty-two the foundation of this prosperous repub——" No; pardon me; not if we know it, my friend. We have got that remarkable history by heart, and have it tattooed upon our memories. Forbear. Prythee seal thy

lips, and breathe not a syllable more about your remarkable
republic.   Let us go and inspect the hospital, or the schools,
or anything, even the liquoring-up stores.   Spare us that fifty-
first edition !

America—the United States, I mean—gets up hospitals
wherever the stars and stripes float, with unbounded gener-
osity, simply for the benefit of suffering humanity, without
reference to nationality or religion.   The noble example is
followed out here ; for, beneath the lone star of the Liberian
flag, there is an hospital ready to receive anybody in need of
medical attendance.   We inspect it.   The rooms are lofty
and well ventilated.   Our particular attention is called to a
woman with a singular complaint ; she sleeps for a fortnight
straight off, without waking once.   We observe the happy
woman in one of these slumbers, in a state of coma.   We
have not time, however, to wait until the awakening; but the
doctor informs us that, when her eyes open, she rapidly
devours large quantities of food, and then goes to sleep
again.   This disease is very common amongst Africans, and
it invariably terminates in the long sleep that knows no
waking.

Our garments, instead of being damp by the rude salt
sea-wave which saturated us on landing, have become dried
by the sun, but perspiration has created a counter-feeling of
unpleasant irritation.   We are invited to take a bath in a
cavernous enclosure, formed by the natural rock fronting the
sea, and gratefully accept the invitation.   Sharks are not
admitted into our aquarium.   They would be glad to come
and dine off a human joint; but, as they cannot climb, they
are deprived of that luxury, and we are not sorry.   The
waves, breaking from the sea and running up the cliffs, throw
a continuous supply of fresh sea-water into the cavern.   In
England, from fifteen to twenty minutes in the water is

considered ample, but here half-an-hour is not sufficient.
"We are out of our depth," as the saying is amongst people
learning to swim, but there is no danger; so we combine
the pleasures of smoking with bathing, light our pipes, and
float lingeringly about until the third-officer suddenly
appears, standing on our garments and towels, with a mail-
bag slung over his shoulder. He very curtly observes,
"You fellows had better dry yourselves and come along to
the boat." We "go along" and arrive on board, and Cape
Palmas will always be associated in our minds with the
happy recollection of having seen at the American mission a
living white baby.

To a child studying geography, a Yorkshire ham will be
a good illustration of, and represent with tolerable correctness,
the form of the continent of Africa. Such quaint comparisons
become distinct to comical minds inspecting maps. Italy, for
instance, resembles a Wellington boot, the toe of which apparently ought to have kicked Sicily over to Tunis and
Carthage ages ago; Greenland looks like the snout of a
polar bear; North and South America resembles a modern-
dressed lady going head to wind, or a wasp thin in the waist.
Europe, Asia, and Oceanica, viewed from the moon, will appear
the shakiest portion of the world, and so the appearance of
Africa suggests a ham, and the shank represents the Cape of
Good Hope. On the Atlantic side you observe the slope
above the knuckle to where the fat begins to be prominent,
and where the customary joint causes a redundancy of overhanging flesh to bulge to the left; these form the Bights of
Biafra and Benin. Continuing the simile of the ham, that
part where the fat takes an upward curve is Cape Palmas;
and this brings us into latitude 4° 24′ north, longitude 7° 46′
west of the meridian of Greenwich. "Sultry is it?" "Yes,
it is—hot." We feel it is so, and a ramble on the shore

makes the fact apparent to our external senses also; for we note that our faces have put on the hue of the red comb of a "man" turkey, as male birds are called here by the natives. But another bath and change of raiment, followed by repose beneath the awning on deck, creates a feeling of comfort and peace which passeth the understanding of all who, not having experienced the enervating feeling caused by walking in the tropics, cannot appreciate it.

From Cape Palmas the steamer steers eastward along what is called the Ivory Coast. Opposite the villages, which here and there peep out of groves of cocoanut-trees and eternal bush, sailing-vessels are observed at anchor, engaged in trade with the natives. These vessels all seem to hail from Bristol. In the next map of Africa this region ought to be re-christened—say, the Bristol Coast; at any rate, ivory has now become so scarce that this part of the coast hardly deserves to bear the name any longer. Steamers on their way home generally pick up odd shipments of palm-oil and palm-kernels from these vessels to fill up cargo space, but we are outward bound, and therefore push straight ahead for Cape Three Points. Two nights' elapse, and on the following morning the ship is close to the land abreast of the the trading depôt of Dixcove, which we can see through our opera-glasses distinctly, as well as the mouth of the now celebrated river Prah, and other trading places. We steam close past the fortress of Elmina, and shortly afterwards anchor off Cape Coast Castle.

It is a calm, lovely morning, and we all go ashore in one of the splendid surf-boats which were left behind by Sir Garnet Wolseley. These boats each accommodate twelve passengers, who are placed in the fore part, to prevent their getting drenched on landing through the surf. A dozen Fantees man each boat; they use paddles instead of oars,

which they can't, or won't, understand.　A thirteenth Fantee
steers with a paddle longer in the handle than the others,
and after each dip he flourishes it as high in the air as it will
go, in a semicircle, and with much gusto sings the solo of a
song, taken up by the rest in chorus, in regular and correct
time, as their flexible and utterly unclothed bodies bend over
the sides.　This is a sample :—

Solo—" Massa he be berry good man."
Chorus—" By-a'nd-by he come again, he come again, he come again—Ish!"
Solo—" Whitee man he gotte plenty money."
Chorus—" By-and-by he come again, he come again, he come again—Ish!"
Solo—" Whitee man he gotte plenty rum."
Chorus—" By-and-by he come again, he come again, he come again—Ish!"
Solo—" Massa he gotte biggy roddy nose."
Chorus—" By-and-by he come again, he come again, he come again—Ish!"

The Fantee steering is elected to his position from the fact
of his being naturally comical, and able to improvise in song
any striking peculiarity of his passengers, and thereby obtaining money in addition to the usual fare, accorded freely or
otherwise as the music is appreciated.　The natural and
apparently refreshing ejaculation " Ish !" is uttered after
each stroke of the paddle.　When heard at a distance from
the deck of a steamer, the alternate rising and falling of the
boat on the waves gives the performance quite a concerto
effect.　The song bursts forth and is heard on board during
the few moments that the boat is on top of a wave ; then, as
it descends and disappears from view into a marine valley,
the song is hushed ; presently, it swells forth again like a
grand anthem chanted by a choir of Greek priests.　It is
wonderfully pleasing.　Upon approaching the rocks which
extend in front of Cape Coast Castle, the paddlers cease
singing, and wait to select a wave larger than the ordinary
run ; every seventh wave is generally considered to run up

higher on the beach than the others. The steersman has to calculate his time, and also the force of the sea; for, at the exact moment, he gives the word in his own language to paddle ahead as fast as possible. The men put forth their full strength, and " on the top of a billow we 'ride "—-Oh, so smooth and jolly ! until crunch goes the boat on to a sandy beach inside the rocks at the foot of the Castle, and, before one can wonder at the mass of foam, the Fantees have lifted you out and carried you up beyond the reach of the following wave. This is the only way that anyone can get ashore. It must truly have been a difficult matter with such inadequate appliances to have landed the British army on its way to Coomassie.

I thoroughly sympathise with my fellow-countrymen who had to perform that arduous march from Cape Coast Castle inland. As a rule, when white men take a trip of only a few miles in tropical Africa, a *posse* of niggers is indispensable. It is absolutely necessary that one nigger should carry the soda-water, another something to put into the soda-water, if required, and it generally is required ; a third carries a gun, sometimes more for show than for use, and some hard biscuits, which are very nourishing. How would our gallant soldiers have progressed, encumbered by three retainers for each man ?

Had I been the Commander-in-chief of the Coomassie campaign I should have felt inclined to " sit down " for a couple of years, waiting until the railway was finished and the river Prah bridged over, but Sir Garnet Wolseley took heed to the health of his white soldiers, and did not detain them at Cape Coast Castle ; they were rapidly moved forward across the Prah and into Coomassie. The expedition was short, sharp, and decisive ; and turned out a success. Sir John Glover, whose march from the Volta to take Coomassie in the rear with a fickle, undisciplined, and constantly dwindling army of unmanageable natives was, in a strategical point of view, a no less meritorious achievement than Sir Garnet Wolseley's victorious campaign. He had greater obstacles to overcome; he was a regular scare to the Ashantees, and a strong moral support to Sir Garnet; and it was only the smart success of the latter, backed by the flower of the British army, that took away his (Sir John Glover's) opportunity. Had there occurred a hitch in Wolseley's progress, Glover would inevitably have materially assisted him, and have been better rewarded than he has been. It is to be regretted that the same promptness was adopted in leaving Coomassie as was put forth in the march upon it. The Ashantees were not sufficiently punished; the effect on them was too startling and brief to make a permanent impression. Sir John Glover should have been instructed to remain in possession of Coomassie and reorganise the government, and Coffee Calcalli should not have been deposed; for he was the only man to be relied upon for keeping the other tribes in order, and so preserving peace. This is the opinion of those best acquainted with affairs on the coast here.

Everybody of late years has been made aware that Ashantee is an inland country, situated on what is called the Gold Coast of Africa, or the Guinea Coast; also, that the race of people called Fantees occupy a territory fringing the sea-board, and possess the towns where trade is carried on, which used to be protected in what we already call old times by forts built two to three hundred years ago by the Dutch, French, Portuguese, and English settlers. These forts were built for the accommodation of troops to protect the traders of the period, who used to amass enormous fortunes. In those days the black men knew nothing of the habits,

customs, guns, powder, rum, and other exponents of the
advanced civilisation of the white man, so whites were looked
upon as devils, or fetish-men, who could conjure up in
advance of that dark age anything required for their comfort
or defence, and they were dreaded accordingly. White men
also were not without their dread of black men—fostered
during tender years by nursery tales—but only for the reason
that they knew nothing about them. Hence the necessity
for these forts. But as black men learned from white men to
drink grog, the discovery was soon made that the spirit had
the same lively effect upon both. They then began to open
their eyes to the simple truth that "all two," as Krooboys
remark, were human beings, and that without fear of supernatural results, nay even to mutual advantage, black men
could bring produce to white men, and receive in return
everything necessary to render their life much jollier than
hitherto. This was all very well then, and the forts might
have been shut up or knocked down from the moment that
such confidence was established, as far as Fantees were concerned. But, as the coast people get the principal produce
from tribes inland, virtually they act only as brokers. Now,
the Ashantees are an inland race, who are desirous to save
brokers' commission and trade with the sea-coast direct, and
this is the real point at issue. They have all along insisted
on, sought for, and fought for, have tried by fair means and
foul—and are sure to go on trying still—to accomplish this
object, which they claim as their right. And, as they are
comparatively warlike and enterprising, whilst the coast
tribes are, on the contrary, feeble and degenerate, they must
eventually succeed, in spite of the Fantee brokers, and even
British protection. What have we to gain by bolstering up
these Fantees? Suppose that the braver Ashantees overcome
them, and get to trade directly with the sea-board, what does

it matter to us? We want their produce, and in return for it we hand over British manufactured goods. Why not let free-trade principles prevail, and abolish this mischievous protectorate?

Let merchants occupy the forts as stores and shops, and defend themselves if need be; they can easily do so. It is downright cruelty to send out white men as governors, soldiers, officers and sergeants to drill the native troops, and secretaries, and other officials, to the Gold Coast to waste time and money, and, more likely than not, lose their lives. One of these colonial officials, when seeing some friends off in the mail steamer for home, remarked, " A fella had better be waterman on a London cabstand than be governor of Cape Coast Castle, don't you know." We *do* know, and feel sorry, for most of them are of no use whatever. There has been no improvement made at Cape Coast Castle since its first establishment, and generations of Government servants are to blame. The dangerous landing is exactly as it was when Adam was a boy. It would be a simple matter to extend the existing rocks in front of the Castle by adding masses of concrete, and so make a good wharf for passengers and goods, but nobody thinks of anything of the sort. British men-of-war, cruising about to protect trade, can easily reduce refractory sea-board villages with judicious doses of shot, shell, and rockets. Never mind the interior people *at present;* let them come down and fraternise with or overcome the indolent wretches in possession of the direct trading places. The latter are hopelessly degenerate; they have succeeded in imitating all the vices of the white man to perfection, but have not learned one of his virtues.

Sir Garnet Wolseley left behind him the excellent surf-boats already referred to, which were sold, when the " cruel war was over," to merchants up and down the coast, who find them very useful in discharging or loading vessels. These craft have entirely superseded the old lumbering canoes, and even the more modern canoe-shaped boats. As they were made for the transport of the English army, no doubt the best talent and naval architectural skill would be employed in their construction; they answer admirably. In addition, Wolseley left also a number of wooden houses, which were sent out in pieces from England and put together here for the purpose of being able to secure, under lock and key, our war *matériel*. When the campaign was finished, it was apparent that it would be of no use to pull the houses down, and therefore there they still remain, and will do so until they tumble to pieces. They are occupied as dwellings by the natives. Vast numbers of similiar houses in the Crimea, which had been occupied as dwellings as well as stores, were left standing after that "crueller war was over." Such temporary erections, with their concomitants, are evidence to the traveller that war has taken place, but more they cannot tell; the treasure spent, the noble hearts that have ceased to beat, are things of the past. For further information, newspapers and books must be consulted, and, after a short time, history.

In other respects we found Cape Coast Castle just as uninteresting as ever. The heat obliged us to resort to some place of shelter from the glare of the sun. In Africa the homes of Europeans are always open to the stranger; affording shade, rest, and refreshment, all the sweeter for the hearty welcome. The Castle is first visited. It contains the only object of reverential interest for English people in this truly torrid zone—the grave of " L. E. L.," the celebrated poetess, and wife of Governor Maclean. A Latin inscription on a marble slab, inserted in the Castle wall, points out where she reposes. It is very

affecting to recall her prophetic lines in the " Impro-
visatrice "—

> " And on a tablet hung above
> Was graved one tribute of sad words."

And then again—

> " I ever had from earliest youth
> A feeling what my fate would be."

It was a sin to take that gifted Englishwoman to Cape Coast
Castle to die.

We are kindly invited by the officers on duty in the
garrison to visit the billiard-room, situated on the second
story, up strange flights of tiresome stone steps; having
panted up which, however, the benefit of the delicious sea-
breeze is all the more appreciated. The billiard-room and
officers' quarters overlook the useless old cannons in the
Castle pointing seawards. Soda-water and brandy are
offered to quench our thirst, or bitter beer in honest sized
bottles opened and emptied into jolly tankards. The operation is anxiously watched, and the attendants eyed by us
rather impatiently, as they, with scrupulous care, but, to
our thirsty ideas, slowly (Oh ! *so* slowly), loosen the tangled
wires which detain the corks. But when at length the
foaming fluid *does* touch our parched lips, why, then—
" Richard is himself again." We are not long in becoming
quite at home, and begin to play billiards. Visitors fresh
from Europe generally astonish the spectators with a brilliant dash of good play, chiefly by several successive spot-
shots. But, after a couple of games or so, the steady play
of a resident is almost sure to bring about the discomfiture
of the new-comer, for the simple reason that the resident is
better accustomed to the heat of the climate, and keeps
himself cooler.

Leaving the Castle by the shore front, we wander eastward through that portion of the town containing the worst

of the filthy native residences and their equally unwholesome surroundings. Chubby naked children, and pigs so
lean that you would hardly give them credit for being able
to walk at all, emerge promiscuously from mud huts,
attended by barking dogs, to welcome the unaccustomed
ramblers. Men and women, aroused by the noise, appear
standing in door-ways, or lolling at their lazy lengths upon
greasy sofas placed in shady but shaky verandahs, and so
they welcome the strangers, but with kindly words. We
notice pleasant-looking houses situated upon small neighbouring hills peeping out from groves of trees; these are the
residences of the wealthy natives or of Europeans. The
best of them is occupied by the Governor. It was purchased from the descendants of Thomas Hutton, an English
merchant, who expended £30,000 upon its construction. It
is the most perfect residence on the West Coast. We
retrace our steps back to the Castle, and, passing the shore
entrance, proceed outside the walls uphill to the high-level
entrance, then down again and up another hill, on the top of
which is perched the Wesleyan mission, and it is really the
most salubrious situation in this unhealthy place. As usual
at all missions in Africa, we are regaled with excellent fruit,
and enjoy pleasant conversation.

The time allowed on shore is restricted according to the
fiat of the captain of the steamer; it may be ten, twelve, or
twenty-four hours, according to the amount of cargo to be
delivered at any particular place, or according to his time-
table for the voyage, which will sometimes be extended and
anticipated by dull trade at previous ports, or be curtailed
by the necessity of pushing ahead. The captains of African
mail steamers much prefer this shoving ahead, as, if they
happen to be in advance of their time-table, they can easily
reduce speed, and so economise coal. We on shore, therefore,

have to regulate our time away from the ship accordingly. We inspect the market, situated above the shore at the west end of the Castle. It is crowded with people, buying and selling everything that both buyers and sellers are acquainted with as capable of making life happy. We look at a street above the market fronting the sea and containing some good houses. But what we admire most particularly is an excavation in the rock, intended for the basement of a store, with a dwelling above. The rock is being blasted in the usual manner, by drilling holes into it, filling the holes with gunpowder, and then applying a slow match. When a fuse is fired, the cry is "Stand from under!" Everybody in the vicinity skedaddles immediately. The explosion takes place, and pieces of rock fly in every direction. When the smoke clears away, the black labourers (priding themselves on the idea of having frightened a white man by anything resembling the report of a gun), with good-natured satisfaction, place a ladder to enable us to descend and inspect the excavation. An old Californian gold-digger belonging to our party, after descending with some difficulty, suddenly exclaims, "Why, this rock is granite, and it is streaked with quartz, and that quartz contains gold." He is cut short by a resident reminding him that this is the Gold Coast of Africa, and it is no new thing to wash the earth on the surface and so obtain gold in small quantities. Crushing machines would be required to pulverise the quartz rock and extract the gold to any extent, but nobody seems inclined to attempt the operation. Perhaps when California, Australia, and New Zealand are worked out, the gold mines of Africa may be developed. Sir John Glover, on his march from the Volta to Coomassie, saw where gold was regularly obtained.

With our present large colonial empire, constantly increasing by emigration or annexation, the question, "What

must we do with the savage?" is a very important one. I
have had considerable experience of the tribes on the coast
out here, and think it may be interesting if I attempt to
show how civilisation first strikes the barbarian mind, how it
influences and commends itself to his untutored ideas, and
what is his process of reasoning on what he hears and sees
the white man do; in a word, what kind of raw material
does he make for civilisation to operate upon. Let me, then,
take up my parable by taking a two-bladed knife; a simple
article, but thoroughly useful. One blade is large, the other
small; both are constructed so as to shut up into a handle.
An African savage sees this wonderful weapon, and the
movement is explained to him. He has hitherto carried only
a rude dagger-knife in a sheath slung around his neck by a
fancy leathern thong; and this implement is used either to
cut up meat or to stick into an enemy, as occasion requires.
It is a native-made, cumbersome, and blunt weapon, and has
only got one blade, the point of which continually works its
way through the sheath and unpleasantly scratches the
person of the noble wearer. Now, the savage is not long in
seeing the superiority of the white man's weapon, and his
natural instinct of appropriation tells him that he must have
that Sheffield knife with two blades; but the trader owning
the knife requires, of course, something in return. The
savage scratches his wool to consider, then rushes off into his
luxuriant country, collects cotton-pods, cleans the cotton of
its seeds, and produces the beautiful pillowy article of trade
which all people appreciate; or he goes and kills a wild
beast and prepares its skin, or perhaps gathers a few coffee-
berries, or obtains, by washing the soil, specks of gold-dust,
which he bottles up in a bird's quill, and, with one or other
of these articles, he satisfies the trader and becomes possessor
of the coveted knife. He hugs it and sleeps with it at night

as little girls do with their dolls. Then a difficulty arises; the knife requires a pocket. White men wear pockets, and our savage must do the same; so he abandons his fig-leaf, and organises a pocket, 'in which the Sheffield intrument finds a home. As he oils the springs, he is lost in admiration at the ingenuity of the invention, and says to himself, "Oh, I must most decidedly learn white man fashion." There is no mistake about the fact that the Sheffield blade has proved a valuable missionary. So he obtains employment as a domestic servant, or becomes student to a cooper or carpenter, or hires himself to a tailor. If endowed with intellect above his asserted consanguineous friend, the monkey, he is eager to find out all about the white man's "God palaver man;" by this he means the missionary; and then the savage begins to reflect in earnest. Please to consider him reflecting after having had a big feed, and resting to digest it, lulled by the customary croaking of his native bull-frogs, the hum and buzz of numerous insects and birds, from mosquitoes to flying-fox bats, all gradually mellowed into the greater noise, the ceaseless crash of the Atlantic wave upon the beach. After meditating for some time thus in his barbarian fashion, he will decide (and wisely) to be converted to Christianity; it is the best thing he can do; so, presently, he appears "sitting and clothed in his right mind," partaking of Christian meat and drink, and by the next mail will be reported at Exeter Hall as "one more brand saved from the burning." Thus the missionary does good, if only as a preacher of civilisation, and the trader profits likewise, as both together create wants amongst the heathen which trade has to supply. That is really the main thing; at least, from a secular and commercial point of view.

Although Cape Coast Castle was bathed in sunshine on the morning of our arrival, yet towards dusk the rainy season exhibited its peculiarity. A strong wind, setting directly upon the shore, caused the waves to increase in force. They dashed on to the rocks and created dangerous-looking foam, which extended to some distance from the land. Most of the passengers loafing on shore managed to induce canoemen to paddle us off in a surf-boat just at sunset, and we were soon comfortably settled on board the ship. The steamer had disembarked the passengers, mails, and cargo for Cape Coast Castle, and had received mails and fresh passengers for ports further leeward, but some of the young naval-officers who were proceeding to Lagos to report themselves on board the flag-ship, expected to be at anchor there, were dining at the Castle. The Governor's surf-boat was ordered to bring them off to the steamer after dinner. The run to the next port of call (Accra) only occupying six hours, it was useless to start until late in the evening, so as to time our arrival off there at about daybreak. We fired guns to announce through the dark night to the roysterers at the Castle that we were waiting for them. We waited and waited and gazed at the white phosphorescent breakers fringing the Castle, and we listened intently, trying to discover, above the dull roar of the breakers, the sound of human voices, for if they were coming there would be singing, " Unequal bursts the hum of songs between the roaring winds!" But they did not come, nor did the songs burst. Had they started from the shore, of which through the black night we could only distinguish a silvery, luminous glare caused by the surf, and got swamped and drowned? We were in doubt, and naturally felt very anxious. Rain fell in torrents, the wind increased in force, and the white foam fringing the Castle and shore appeared to become larger. Our captain waited as long as he could do so in justice to keeping up his time-table, and then he sorrowfully ordered the anchor up, and away we proceeded on the voyage. All on board, and you might say even the ship herself, felt melancholy at the absence of the jolly young midshipmen and junior lieutenants, who perpetually sung songs, punched the stewards' ribs, chaffed the skipper, and kept everybody in roars of laughter. Obtaining the consent of the captain, we survivors formed ourselves into a vigilance committee, entered the empty cabins of the gallant naval men, collected their gold watches, rings, stray shirt-studs, and other articles of value left knocking about, sailor-like, including envelopes, addressed in delicate handwriting, containing letters, which we carefully placed beside the jewellery. We then looked for their portmanteaus to stow away the stray articles. The portmanteaus were all open—sailor-like again—so we packed, corded, and sealed up the separate lots to deliver to the first man-of-war we should happen to fall in with on the voyage, excepting toothbrushes and a few singlets, shirts, handkerchiefs, and socks, which we packed up to send from Accra along the shore, by one of the customary native runners, back to Cape Coast Castle. It was a very solemn proceeding, and, as usual at funerals, christenings, and weddings, much brandy and soda-water disappeared amongst the sad vigilance committee on the strength of collecting what we thought were the remains of our departed brothers. But it turned out that the lively young fellows were all right. A runner from Cape Coast Castle brought a letter stating that the Fantee canoemen refused thirty golden sovereigns offered to bring them off to the mail steamer. "Water be too sass; you all go die one time," the Fanteemen observed; and right they were, for the sea was saucy, and the liquid cemetery was handy.

At Accra, polite retainers appertaining to native gold-smiths came on board and offered zodiac rings, watch-chains, and curious-looking representations of butterflies and beetles done in native gold. Many people purchase these articles, but they are not cared for in England; the work is too clumsy, and, however much visitors to Accra may appreciate them, sweethearts and wives at home do not care about them. A suspicion lurks that the metal is too much mixed up with brass to yield more profit to the jewellers, who are really too polite for Africa to sell genuine guinea gold. Often the bright Accra gold turns out to be simply brass gilded.

The ship is anchored abreast James Fort (English), at a distance of a mile from reefs of rocks jutting out several hundred yards from the front of the fort. The sea to leeward of the rocks is studded with fishing canoes. These canoes have more beam than the Kroo canoes, and are safer looking. Two miles eastward a large building stands over the sea; this is Christianborg Fort (Danish.) We embark in surf-boats similar to those in use at Cape Coast Castle, paddled in the same manner, and, landing at the foot of James Fort, toil up an inclined road to the town. There are a few good houses occupied by merchants, but the native dwellings are surrounded by disagreeable garbage, which long-legged, lean pigs and turkey-buzzards eagerly devour, and thereby act as scavengers to the place. From the town we observe hills about fifteen miles inland, and the country between is suitable for farms and plantations. It looks like a healthy district, and, for the Gold Coast, is healthier than Cape Coast Castle, for horses and white women invariably soon die there, but here they live for a longer time. Natives bury their dead inside their houses, underneath the ground, and the earth is pounded down hard over the bodies, and then polished smooth as asphalte. Accra women, when young, are very beautiful; they are addicted to wearing artificial but graceful humps over the lower part of the spine, which, when walking, imparts to the wearers a coquettish, jaunty wriggle.　Many of them migrate to ports windward and leeward, and they love to associate and hold sweet converse with people of other lands.　Accra also supplies excellent coopers to the whole coast; they are chiefly employed to buildup "shooks" sent out from England, and form them into casks to fill up with palm-oil.　The coopers are generally well-behaved and earn good wages.　It is good to instruct Africans in skilled labour; they are apt to learn, and speedily take rank above Kroomen, canoemen, and the generally worthless domestic servants.

Whilst discharging cargo, the rainy season again gave us a specimen of bad weather on a small scale.　It was uncomfortable.　The deck, even beneath the awning, was wet; the water bulged the well-worn awning into holes, forming shower-baths for people disposed to enjoy sousing.　Sitting in the saloon below was found to be so intolerably warm, caused by damp heat creating perceptible fog, that butter, or, as some of the stewards facetiously called it, "Kelly," turned to a liquid, and had to be served out by the aid of a spoon instead of being cut with a knife.　We, therefore, deserted the saloon and dwelt upon the deck, watching canoes alongside receiving Manchester bale goods, cases of Hollands gin, casks of New England rum, tins of biscuits and cases of pickles, and other welcome things for the benefit of people on shore.　It is necessary for each consignment that the man entitled to receive the same produces a bill of lading signed in England for goods received on board.　The officer in charge of the fore or after hold, or wherever the particular cargo is stowed when this document is presented to him, delivers the articles enumerated, and gets the recipient to sign on the back of it, showing delivery from the vessel.　The contract is then completed.　This sort of work is going on, when suddenly we hear a shout.　The chief-officer has allowed an unsigned bill of lading to be blown out of his hand, and it gracefully flutters in the air until it reposes on the water. It is gone; he has got no receipt for stuff delivered, and may be called upon to account for its value upon his arrival in England. In fact, the value of all missing cargo is liable to be deducted from the wages due to captains and mates, and the knowledge of this makes them careful. Our chief-officer calls out to the nearest Krooboy, "Jump overboard and catch that paper." The Krooboy alluded to springs into the water, swims to the paper, catches it and places it in his mouth, and tries to return to the steamer. But the steamer is at anchor, the wind blows strong, the waves are rough, and the swimmer has to battle against fierce opposition. Kroomen are naturally good swimmers, but in this case the man is drowning; he sinks beneath the waves once, twice. The surf-boat is fortunately floating alongside; men jump into it and shove off, and they drag by the wool of the head the unfortunate inanimate bill of lading diver. Everybody suddenly hunts up and reads "directions for recovering the apparently drowned." The fellow-country Kroomen do the best thing, assisted by everybody. The body is placed in blankets on the top of the skylight and rolled to and fro, the breast and stomach rubbed with rough towels to restore animation, the mouth opened . and fresh air from kind Kroo lips blown into his lungs. The man breathes, he opens his mouth and emits the bill of lading, which only wants drying. He has been faithful to his trust—too much so. After that I will never hear a Krooboy maligned.

Our English fowls have waxed very thin during their residence in the hen-coops; cocks, disgusted with the hot climate, have given up crowing and utter a hoarse cackle instead. Geese have been reduced in the census, and survivors can hardly get up a scream. Sheep in their pens pant fearfully; they watch the butcher with a vacant stare as he cuts up into joints their late companions, and they cannot even utter "ba-a." The last home-fed pig escapes from its domicile and wanders about the deck as much a gentlemen as if it were in dear old Ireland. It is a very knowing pig, the last of its race, with all the experience fresh in its memory of all its bacony chums whose joints have already been discussed. It looks into the faces of intercolonial deck passengers, and, grunting expressively, turns away. Anybody personally known to the animal—fireman, sailor, captain, or passenger—it instantly recognises, cocks its ears, looks out of its cheeky eyes and expects a scratch, which is cheerfully accorded. It rubs one of its hams against your own particular calf, wanting to be scratched again; you repel it; it grunts disapprobation mingled with sorrow, and turns sadly away. But that last pig is bound to die; we long for its chops, and from its delicate ears to its tough trotters it goes the way of all pork.

We leave Accra, and shortly afterwards observe a black rock peeping above the water. It is on the meridian of Greenwich. The longitude up to the black rock has been west; at the rock it is 0, and afterwards east longitude. We steam round Cape St. Paul, pass Jella Coffee, and anchor off Quitta. This is the St. John's Market of the West Coast of Africa. Canoes come off to the steamer laden with "man" turkeys and "women" turkeys; live fowls in half-dozens, tied by the legs, but they are very thin fowls; ducks fastened in a similar manner (the ducks are far better than the fowls here), eschalots in baskets, yams in profusion, thin, long-haired sheep, and long-legged, big-eared, hungry-looking pigs. Our hen-coops, sheep-pens, and pig-houses are speedily filled, and it is most amusing to watch the new-comers. Animal or canine etiquette prevails all over creation. The English survivors are scented all over. No doubt some language is common to everything that lives or moves or breathes ; for, soon after coming on board, they wistfully eyed the butcher, who administers judicious refreshment before executing them.

The commandant · of the fort comes on board in his surf-boat to look at fresh faces. We welcome him. He knows somebody that we know, or we are mutually acquainted with some particular lamp-post. He kindly invites us to go on shore and breakfast at the fort. We gladly go and land near to the German mission. The missionaries received us in the most hospitable manner, showed us the schools for boys and girls. Amongst the girls we noticed a wonderful albino with light red wool, bright-coloured eyes, and an almost white skin, but still negro features. One of the missionaries took us to the small cemetery and showed us Captain Croft's grave. A granite slab sent out from England covers it. We were all old friends of Croft, and we felt very sad. He had worked his way up from junior officer to be commodore of the African Steamship Company's fleet, a position enabling him to amass wealth to retire upon. And he was on his fifty-first voyage from the coast ; but, as his steamer laid alongside the hulk at Bonny, fever broke out. Charles Livingstone, consul of Fernando Po, brother to the great African traveller, was a passenger on board, and he proved to be the first victim. He was a very quiet man, and regulated his living by strict abstinence from wine, beer, and brandy ; and yet he went the way of all African travellers. Charles Livingstone died and was buried at sea. The day afterwards Captain Croft breathed his last just as the steamer approached this place. Two big men of the sea—you will always find that the big men of the sea exhibit true love—brought the body of their beloved commander on shore, and the German missionaries accorded the long resting-place for it. On that cape of St. Paul, fringed on each side by the Atlantic—a fitting grave for a sailor—lies one of the bravest sons of Ireland who ever trod a ship's deck.

CHAPTER III.

AT Cape St. Paul the Bight of Benin commences, extending eastward to the Bight of Biafra. The land is
very low, and is only distinguished, when at a distance of
eight or ten miles at sea, by dots of trees on the horizon, in
some cases presenting the appearance of a fleet of ships. As
our steamer has to call at Little Popo, Grand Popo, and
Porto Seguro, to discharge cargo into trading vessels waiting
at those places for it, we are obliged to hug the shore. This
affords us the opportunity of observing through our glasses
many objects of interest on the land. From a little to the
east of the River Volta—the mouth of which debouches into
the sea west of Cape St. Paul—to the River Benin the shore
line of country is separated from the mainland by lakes of
brackish water, called lagoons, which are fed by streams of
fresh water from the interior, and also by occasional openings
from the sea. Lagos is the principal opening. This extensive
district of coast is very monotonous, having a long yellow sandy
beach, above which villages peep out of clumps of trees, and
it is very difficult to distinguish one place from another, all
being so very much alike. On the borders of these lakes, or
lagoons, studded with innumerable islands, exist the strangest
and most delightful looking variety of the tropical vegetable
kingdom. The lagoons afford inland navigation, with smooth
water, for nearly the whole distance, but during the dry
season, in particular places, the communication is interrupted

by the water becoming shoal, and in other parts opposition to transit is offered by hostile tribes. But where we are, upon the open sea, the navigation is as free as the air we breathe.

This part of the coast was the great rendezvous of the now extinct export slave trade, and it still bears the name "Slave Coast." We call at the places before mentioned to deliver cargo, and then we anchor off Whydah for the same purpose. Whydah is the landing-place on the eternally surf-beaten beach for the celebrated kingdom of Dahomey. It is not a port, as it is usually styled in the English newspapers—it is simply an open roadstead ; and to land in a canoe or surf-boat usually entails a drenching of the person, but most certainly of luggage. The town of Whydah is situated about two miles inland, and it was a great place during the days of slavery. Portuguese and Spanish slave-dealers held high revel and lived merry but short lives ; but now it is of very little account. Legitimate trade is not developed as it will be in future years. The annihilation of the slave trade is too recent in slow Africa for the native slave-catchers to collect their thoughts and make their domestic slaves collect produce to barter for goods and luxuries, which were formerly obtained entirely by the sale of slaves.

We timed our departure from Whydah during the night so as to arrive off Lagos about daybreak. The morning was very fine, and our glasses were utilised as we approached and counted two, three, four men-of-war, one mail steamer, ten or a dozen sailing-vessels, and from thirty to forty cargo-cutters, anchored between two and four miles outside Lagos bar,—just as vessels for Liverpool, if it were not a good port, would have to anchor outside the Bell Buoy. As we draw nearer we perceive a little steamer coming out of the lagoon and crossing the bar ; she has to deliver mails to the homeward-

bound steamer, and then visit us to get the English mails.
We anchor, and the cargo-cutters flock alongside like chickens
around the maternal hen. The little tender comes alongside
for a few minutes, and unluckily I send my portmanteau on
shore by one of the passengers, with whom I am invited to
stay. I am not in a hurry to go ashore, so with the captain,
in the ship's gig, we visit the homeward mail boat, anchored
about a mile off, and enjoy agreeable conversation, mixed
with parting glasses. We get into our gig as the steamer
goes ahead, and actually wish that we were going to dear old
England also.

Returning to our ship, we observe a crowd collected aft,
and great excitement is apparent; the boat is swiftly urged
to the ladder, we rush on deck, and find that a shark has
been captured. A piece of tempting.looking pork, about
eight pounds in weight, was bewitchingly fixed on a chain-
hook attached to a stout rope made fast on deck. The
shark could not withstand the enticing bait; it turned over on
its back—the mouth being situated underneath the head,
similar to that of the sturgeon—as is the nature of the
monster, and it made a successful grab at the pork and got
hooked properly. It takes not a few willing-minded men to
haul a moderately-sized shark out of the water and on board
ship, but everybody delightedly. lends a hand. It is the
ship-carpenter's ancient privilege, duty, and pleasure to stand
by with his sharpest axe, and, with a well-aimed blow, chop
off the tail the moment it is landed on the deck. If this is
not cleverly done, the shark, with wriggling its body and
throwing its tail to and fro, smashes binnacles to atoms,
breaks skylights or human legs, if they happen to be in its
way. But the carpenter has the honour of his craft to
maintain, and with one blow the tail is severed and the
shark made quiet. It glares with its unearthly green

demon-looking eyes, opens and shuts its enormous mouth, and exhibits several rows of fearfully-wicked, sharp-pointed teeth in each jaw. Seamen show no mercy to a captured shark; they naturally torment it, and in its own element it returns the compliment. It is very strange how tenacious these monsters are of life; for, whilst part of the fish is being cooked in the galley—a little of it goes a long way—a piece of wood put into its mouth is bitten into two parts, an iron bar applied in a similar manner is crunched and its teeth smashed. Under these circumstances it is not advisable to insert your shoe into its mouth, unless the foot is previously withdrawn.

The cargo-cutters have taken away the goods destined for Lagos. The steamer in which I came from Sierra Leone is preparing to leave for Benin, so I must go and take pot-luck on board some of the vessels at anchor until the tender comes out again from Lagos. Meantime a strong wind sets in from seaward, heavy rain falls, and all communication across the foaming bar is stopped. Fortunately, a man-of-war's boat is alongside waiting for some officers who came on board to get the welcome latest newspapers from home, and to purchase Madeira potatoes and stores for their mess. They kindly invited me to go on board their ship, and I gladly accepted the invitation. Between heavy rain and seas tipping over the sides, all in the boat get wet through; but once on board the man-of-war, the hearty British welcome accorded, and dry clothing cheerfully supplied, speedily transform the civilian to a sort of commodore, not down on the " Navy List," and the sparkling wit and cheerful conversation around the jolly mess-table, make the time pass away pleasantly. For two days it rained in torrents, and the wind blew so hard that navigation over the dangerous bar was impossible; so the little steamer stayed quietly at home in the lagoon, and the

people on shore looked through their telescopes at the vessels
anchored in the roads perpetually rolling to and fro, and
perhaps they wished to change places with us.   At any rate,
without offence to my gallant entertainers, I did ; for a
rolling ship spoils rollicking fun, and however well used to
the sea people may become, yet on board a vessel at anchor
swaying to and fro, when glasses have to be held in the
hand and balanced like a swinging barometer, when soup
goes outside your bosom instead of affording nourishment,
and when cooked legs of mutton and roasted turkeys are
tossed about in the cabin, it tries the sweetest temper.   The
second day on board the man-of-war happened to be Sunday.
I had lost all run of time, it passed so very swiftly, and
every hour and day yielded delight ; but they have a habit
of keeping nautical almanacks on all vessels.   The rainy
season prevented divine service being read on deck, so the
captain descended to the forecastle and there read it.
Several sailors were lying in their hammocks down with
fever ; they produced prayer-books from beneath their
lonely pillows and joined in the responses, learned during
infancy from· their English mothers, who would cheerfully
sacrifice their lives, did they but know, to nurse their brave
but now helpless boys.   The discipline, order, and clean-
liness on board English men-of-war is proverbial, but the
respectful feeling throughout all ranks, amounting to
affection and care for each other's welfare, is most beautiful
and touching to witness.

On the third day the weather moderated, and the little
steamer came out from Lagos to attend upon the men-of-
war. I returned in her, and before encountering the angry
seas foaming over the bar her hatches were battened down
and everything loose about the deck made fast to something
that would not wash away. The billows smashed over her

with great force, making her shiver and quiver, but she rose gallantly to her work and paddled along. In five minutes after crossing the bar we were in smooth water, when she steamed quietly up the sheltered lagoon, four miles from the sea, and made fast to a wharf at Lagos.

The only navigable breach into the system of lagoons before mentioned occurs here. Vessels drawing only twelve and thirteen feet can safely cross the bar and discharge and load cargoes in still water alongside wharves. The River Ogun, flowing from the north from above Abbeokuta, brings down produce in canoes from the Yoruba country, and east and west, along the lagoons, canoes also convey produce previously carried from the far interior upon the heads of natives, along narrow paths winding through bush and forest. Roads are unknown. Lagos undoubtedly rejoices in the best situation for trade in the Bight of Benin, and the merchants are alive to its importance; for, notwithstanding the natural difficulties caused by winds, tides, the rainy season, the rough bar, and the ocean steamers being obliged to anchor for safety far out at sea, they have organised efficient cargo-cutters, sent out on the decks of steamers from England for the purpose, and also small steamers, to work the traffic.

Lagos used to be the greatest slave shipping port on this coast. I first visited it in 1853, and foolishly crossed the bar from the sea in the ocean steamer's gig. As I then approached the town I saw eight or ten strange-looking objects stuck upon stakes over the lagoon, with turkey-buzzards hovering about. Curious to investigate, I steered the boat towards the spot, and, to my horror, found myself amongst a crowd of dead negroes, skewered like sheep in a butcher's shop, with carrion birds pecking off pieces of flesh. The effluvia was powerful, and the oars were plied with extra strength, which made the gig lively as it fairly jumped away

from the barbarous fetish destruction of life.   I came out
from England in the first mail steamer to Lagos, and in those
days everything was very primitive.   The huts of the town
extended to the water's edge, and it was a filthy, disgusting,
savage place, and unsafe to wander about the streets.   In
1861 the British Government pensioned off the King Docimo
with £2,000 yearly, and turned Lagos into a colony.   The
governor immediately cleared the filthy beach of the
wretched native tenements, and for a considerable distance
back from the lagoon border destroyed them and formed a
wide promenade; but he very considerately and wisely allowed
the existing graceful cocoanut trees and several groups of
shady trees to stand.   He also pulled down hundreds of huts
situated behind the promenade, and constructed wide streets
for the sea-breeze to blow through.   The consequence now is
that, on the promenade fronting the lagoon, merchants have
erected brick stores, with comfortable and luxurious dwellings
above, fronting the glorious life-sustaining sea-breeze.
Wharves are also made running into the lagoon, with water
deep enough to berth vessels alongside, and between the
wharves there is plenty of space for canoes coming from long
distances, north, east, and west, to discharge produce and
receive upon the spot goods in return.   Markets have been
regulated, Houssa Zouave-dressed soldiers and a police force
organised, a race-course established, churches, schools, court-
houses, custom-house, Government-house, and barracks built ;
and lastly, a cemetery (which drives a brisk trade) has been
walled in outside the town, but rather too near to the houses.
It is not a pleasant place, for you can tell in which direction
it lies, long before seeing it.

The steamer in which I am going up the Niger has just
returned from that river, but, as she requires a fortnight to
fit out, the governor kindly permits me to accompany any

lagoon trip undertaken by his colonial steamer, so as to fill up the time pleasantly. Meanwhile I amuse myself by walking about the markets and streets, looking at the strange variety of people. Everything is interesting, from the turkey-buzzard floating high aloft in the air, hovering calmly in space and intently gazing for something earthly to pounce down upon and eat, to the land-crab below busily engaged digging a hole in the ground and carrying in its natural panniers tunnel loads to the surface and emptying the earth excavated like a skilful navvy. Nature finds some mischief still for idle folk to do ; so I desire to catch a land-crab, and wickedly taking a box of vesuvians, ignite one, and shove the box by means of a stick into the hole after it, and wait patiently for its bolting out, so as to confiscate the interesting specimen for my collection. Smoke comes up out of the hole, and that is all, for the wily crab has got another entrance to his abode which I wotted not of, out of which it runs and escapes, and I am not at all happy after being sold by a crab. Evidently, elephant-hunting is not my forte.

The town of Lagos is situated upon a lagoon island, which is sometimes called Eko, but oftener Lagos. The soil is of a sandy nature on the surface, covering clay, of which good bricks are made. The island is very little elevated above the sea level, and abounds in swamps. Where houses are not built, rank vegetation flourishes. The wily crocodile and voracious shark exist in the lagoon, and both seem to thrive, but they keep away from the busy haunts of men generally. Sharks, however, often swim into shallow water amongst a crowd of bathers, and occasionally confiscate a stray body for private use. The population of the town is estimated at about 50,000, and it is very much mixed. In addition to the original natives, many people from countries bordering on the River Niger, eager to trade, have settled here. Traders from Sierra Leone, old liberated slaves, or their descendants, have also come to ameliorate their position in life, and they conduct themselves better than they do at Sierra Leone ; for, if they exhibit insolence here, they are liable to be properly punished. Various denominations of Christian missions have planted their Ebenezer in Lagos, and the followers of Mahomet have also established their right to benefit by the religious inclination of the different races. Christian and Mahometan schools abound. In the former Holy Writ is not only taught in English, but translated into the native languages ; and in the latter, the tenets of Mahomet are inculcated in the Arabic language, extracts from the Koran being inscribed upon smooth wooden tablets, which the children readily commit to memory. So the Bible and the Koran have each fair play to assist in educating the rising generation ; and in all the schools the essential three R's are taught in addition to the duties of daily life.

The oriental style of dress and graceful manner of salutation, peculiar amongst Mahometans, is fascinating. The right hand is placed first upon the forehead, then upon the region containing the heart, the body at the same time is courteously bent towards the stranger, and the arms opened out for welcome. It is truly and naturally a most expressive indication of warm hospitality without the aid of language. There are several followers of Mahomet wearing green turbans, to which they are entitled from having performed the pilgrimage to Mecca, crossing and recrossing the continent of Africa from Lagos to Egypt, over the Nile and across the Red Sea to Jiddah, the port for Mecca, and then inland in Arabia the blest, to the birthplace of the prophet. But to comprehend their devotion to their creed, exhibited by this long journey, you must look upon the

map or upon a terrestrial globe, and calmly note the distance
and think what a great amount of hard walking and
suffering that religious rite has taken to entitle the Hadji to wear
the green turban.   Some of the poorer followers of the prophet
sit upon comfortable chairs at street corners, with a small
table placed before them, shaded from the heat of the sun,
and read the Koran.   Good Samaritans collect around to
harken to words of wisdom and donate cowrie-shells, the
current small money of the country.   And thus the Hadji gain
a livelihood somewhat after the manner of blind men in
England, who attract similiar attention by rubbing their
fingers over raised letters and reading the blind-man's Bible.
Mussulmans from Northern Africa, pilgrims from Morocco
and Algeria, earn green turbans more easily than their
Lagos brethren ; for, instead of undertaking the long and
perilous land journey across Africa, at certain seasons
during each year, they flock in crowds—males only—as deck
passengers on board steamers bound up the Mediterranean
to Alexandria, there to break the journey and visit Grand
Cairo, or they go direct through the Suez Canal and down
the Red Sea.   But, even with such modern swiftness of
transit, they suffer much from indifferent food, which they
bring on board the steamer with them.   These pilgrims will
not accept of Christian food.   They suffer also from sea-
sickness, and lie about the deck in heaps, many of them
perfectly helpless, and numbers of them die in consequence.

The trading stores, or factories, as they are called, belong
to English, French, or German firms ; each occupies several
acres of land, enclosed by a high wall, with only one gate,
where a policeman keeps watch day and night.   A factory
forms, in American phraseology, an entire block, square or
oblong, with streets on every side, presenting only the
appearance of high blank walls, excepting the dwelling

building, which rises from groves of acacia-trees, rose-trees, and palms, high enough for the inmates to enjoy the sea-breeze. Inside the walls on three sides are buildings fronting inwards. These are blacksmiths' shops, coopers' and carpenters' places of work, stores for produce, cook-houses, and other buildings, affording shade from the heat of the sun or shelter from the heavy rains to the numerous servants employed. In the front stands the trading store, and on the first, and perhaps the second floor above it, are the living rooms. Inside the store natives stand before a long counter and receive payment in cowries, guns, cloth, or anything from a fish-hook to a cask of rum, for palm-oil, palm-kernals, cotton, or other produce delivered. In the open space formed by the courtyard, beneath the shade of graceful trees, the natives who have come long distances in canoes lie about, and talk, go to sleep, or higgle about trade. They are in no hurry about anything, and often require to be driven outside before the gate is closed at sunset. Meantime, whilst they are resting under the trees, the cotton which they brought is undergoing the process of ginning, to clear it of the seed before it is packed into bales. The palm-oil which they brought in country jars is boiled in huge coppers, and in that state run into casks. Palm-kernels are either packed in bags or left in bulk. Thus these articles of produce furnish continual cargo for homeward-bound steamers. Trading commences with daylight, at about six, and lasts briskly until ten or eleven o'clock, when the heat compels Europeans to shut up shop and go upstairs to breakfast and rest. The stores are closed for the night and locked at about five o'clock, and then riding or walking exercise is practised until dinner-time; after which, tea, talk, billiards, and bed, constitute happiness, and so on just the same all the year round all over this coast.

Cowries form the current coin amongst the market-people here, and also all over Central Africa. They are small sea-shells obtained from Zanzibar, and also from India, and they increase in value as a medium of exchange the further they are conveyed inland. Here one bag containing 20,000 cowries is worth 12s. 6d. only; thus an idea may be formed of the cheapness of living, when in the numerous markets and amongst petty traders everything to make life enjoyable can be purchased for a few cowries. Of course, luxuries, such as rum and gin, pickles and gunpowder, have to be paid for, either in produce, or else with harder and more easily counted coin than cowries. The likeness of the Queen done in silver is, therefore, gradually taking the place of cowries as missionaries and traders educate the heathen.

The women of Lagos are very industrious; they perform most of the hard work pertaining not only to domestic life, but to tilling the soil and buying and selling in the markets. Everything that can be so conveyed is carried upon the head. A little girl, almost an infant, commences the practice by putting an empty bottle upon her head, and thus she learns how to balance; next follow articles of food for retail about the streets, the names of which she shouts in a shrill voice; in time she becomes a market-woman, gets up calabashes or baskets filled with oranges, limes, peppers, kolah-nuts, or anything trifling that the mass of the people require. After this she is not long before she can exhibit her own baby. It is supported by an extra cloth fastened round her body by means of a simple turn made in front, which can be loosened in an instant. Many of the mothers are remarkably young. The little round woolly head of the child and its bright wondering eyes peeping over the back of the mother are extremely interesting to look upon. On seeing the strange sight of a white face, if the face is not one that children will be alarmed at, and infants are not bad judges of character, the little things crow with astonishment. The mother, if notice be taken, appears proud, and lets go the cloth binding the infant and brings it to the front, a perfect babe without a rag on ; and they. look pretty these specimens of innocent humanity done in ebony. They are dandled by their mothers with the same fondness, and chirruped to with the same maternal language, that the noblest ladies of our land delight in with their infants in full dress. All babes, black and white, appear to act alike, and chuckle with fair primitive Garden of Eden fun when pleased.

The principal exports from Lagos are palm-oil and palm· kernels. The variety of the species producing the tree from which the palm-oil of commerce is extracted is thick in the trunk; the leaves start from a few feet above the earth, and as it grows the first set of leaves wither and others appear higher up, withering in their turn as the tree grows higher and older. When it attains to the age for bearing fruit, the graceful leaves spread in every direction, and at the juncture where the foliage branches off is a huge bunch of magnificent bright red and yellow plums, looking like the customary exaggerated gilded emblem peculiar to hotels called "The Grapes." Each bunch of palm-oil producing grapes, or plums, contains from 800 to 1,000 individual plums, and weighs in many cases upwards of half-a-hundred weight. No cultivation is absolutely needed, but where it can be encouraged to develop, especially upon higher land than the ordinary swamp ; where the undergrowth and surrounding high jungle can be cleared away, so as to allow free access of sunshine and air, the oil produced is much finer in quality, and ensures a higher price at home. For a long distance from the sea the palm-oil tree flourishes, and the fruit drops when ripe and goes to waste. It is only in the immediate vicinity of villages that a few bunches are collected and leisurely boiled in water to extract the oil. As it floats on the surface it is skimmed and poured into native earthenware jars or into casks, as the case may be, for conveyance to the nearest port of commerce.

The plum contains a nut, with a covering harder than that of the husk of the well-known almond, which, when broken, discloses a kernel of the same shape as the almond, but much more plump, larger, thicker in the skin, and more oily in its nature. This is the palm-kernel of commerce. Until very recently the nuts were thrown aside as worthless, and they form in some places useful mounds of rising land. The mud floors of houses and yards, and roads leading to wharves, are paved with them, and they set almost as hard as cement. The export from the West Coast amounts to about 50,000 tons annually, but, from the quantity of palm-oil shipped, it is well known that ten times the quantity of kernels should be got ; this shows that the trade is in its infancy. The high rates of freight to England preclude merchants shipping nuts entire, but this difficulty is overcome by boys and girls and old men and women being set to work by the quaint but tedious process of cracking each between stones. The long-neglected simple kernel thus obtained now takes rank in the market of the civilised world as a most important article of commerce. It yields beautiful clear white oil, which is not only used to make the finest kinds of soap, but also for many other purposes ; and, even after the oil is expressed, the residue is formed into meal to feed cattle.

The palm-oil region of this coast has hitherto only been sampled. It is impossible to calculate the extent of the enormous tracts of dense jungle never trodden by man where the valuable produce, amongst other unknown good things, ripens and falls to mother earth, and is never seen.

It is a very difficult matter for the governor of a new colony like this to please everybody. In fact, his every act is canvassed freely for and against him by the three heads of the people—chiefs or petty kings, missionaries, and merchants ; all clamouring loudly for their respective interests. These parties have to be appeased by the governor, so as to give satisfaction to each, or else rows and petty wars are the rule instead of the exception ; and therein lies the necessity for a governor combining common sense with firm administration of the law. At the best of times he wears his honours uneasily. In old-established colonies governors can manage affairs with more comfort, and need not expend the whole of their income, but upon this coast they part with more money than they can afford, principally in entertaining chiefs, missionaries, and merchants, simply with the object of promoting good-will and good government. Suppose a dinner at Government-house, Lagos; time, 7-30 P.M. Oil-lamps are lighted in the reception-rooms, and also in the verandahs. The major-domo of the governor arranges the guests in proper order ; native chief and merchant with a missionary between ; the latter generally acts as interpreter. If there are not missionaries enough, a clever coloured Government official, able to understand and interpret native languages, takes the place of the missionary. At the expense of the governor, a really good banquet is spread, and the guests of entirely different views of life are happily entertained. Each visitor has got some grievance to declare, but during the entertainment, as a well-behaved man, he only opens his mouth to partake of good food and drink, or to talk pleasantly. Meantime the band of the Houssa soldiers plays lively appetite and drinkytite provoking music in the "Arabian Nights" lighted gardens outside. A babel of talk goes on as various native dialects are translated into English. When the dining part is over, the governor gives the word of command, and, all standing up, do due honour to the grand loyal toast, "The Queen." Shortly after which business commences, and it is arranged and recorded by secretaries upon the spot. The chiefs know that the governor represents the majesty of England, and that he can order men-of-war or troops to punish their people if the good laws are broken, and they accordingly keep their tribes in order. If they are right-minded chiefs, they foster trade and respect the colonial laws; but if they are obstinate wretches—sometimes ill-advised to such conduct—they have to be forced into obedience.

The ex-King Docimo, having abdicated in favour of Great Britain, receives a handsome pension. In front of his mud-built palace a very good triumphal arch has been erected. One of the governors subsequent to the cession—Captain, now Sir John, Glover—instructed his colonial engineer to construct it, and it yields great pride to Docimo and the chiefs. It is a very amusing sight to look at the big men of the town or visiting chiefs approaching the arch to the Court of Docimo. A dozen gaily-clothed attendants march in front of the important man, and a dozen behind. They are adorned with little tinkling bells, which give out a jingling sound, reminding one of similar simple music common amongst companies of packed mules and muleteers in Mexico, or of tramway cars, or sleigh bells. The turn-out is also attended by professional musicians. Their principal musical instrument consists of a sort of half-bagpipe, half-drum—a cylinder eighteen inches long and five inches in diameter, covered at the ends with skin stretched tightly. It is placed underneath the left arm, whilst the performer, with the right hand, strikes it with a curved drum-stick, at the same time squeezing the sides to modulate the sound. These drummers keep good time and dance wildly to it, as well as the spectators; for, the greater the noise and dancing, of so much more consequence is the procession. The great man in the centre wears a small turban upon his head, his face is covered by a veil, a long rich silk velvet robe conceals his person, and the train moves along very fast, swaggering like undecided sailors just landed for a spree on shore. Immediately behind the chief trots a tall attendant holding a gig umbrella of brilliant hues over his master's head; which individual must be well up in civil engineering, for, if the cant of the umbrella allows the sun to shine on the chief, he gets reprimanded by being suddenly knocked down. A crowd of boys and girls and lean barking dogs accompany the party as far as the triumphal arch, where they meet a similar procession coming out. Both processions stop, the chiefs kneel to each other, snap fingers, shake hands, exchange salutations, and pass on.

A naval man and myself happen just then to be inspecting that part of the town, and, becoming much interested in the manners and customs, inquire if we can see the ex-king. The reply is favourable, so we wait until the chief comes out. We then pass under the arch and through a couple of courtyards surrounded by apartments, and are shown into a state courtyard, where chairs are offered. We wait for twenty minutes, when Docimo appears from a side door, attired in a clean loose white robe, which leaves his right arm and breast at liberty, the flowing portion of the robe being gracefully thrown over his left shoulder. Red silk-velvet slippers encase his large feet, and gold, silver, and brass rings profusely adorn his thumbs, fingers, and wrists. He is a good-natured, easy-going man. He kindly welcomed us through his interpreter, and seated himself upon a rich cushion placed upon the centre of a hard mud throne. The scantily-attired lords-in-waiting fell upon their faces on the ground in front of the throne, did obeisance, and rose again. A bottle of champagne was produced, which Docimo cleverly opened, and three tumblers were filled. Whilst we drank his jolly good health the attendants fell once more upon their faces at full length, with their noses rubbing mother-earth, cracked* their fingers, and, half rising, clapped hands. Meantime the glasses became empty. Docimo had evidently been under the hands of the court-barber, for a straight broad line of paint or thick blood (fetish) ornamented his forehead from the nose upwards to the wool. Upon laughing, which he did at some observation translated by the interpreter, his mouth expanded like a tunnel fringed with ivory. He requested us to remember him to Queen Victoria, and to tell everybody about his hard case. He said that the governor did not allow him "too much" money, but that still he was better off without the cares of state ; for, when he was king, his chiefs "tiefed" the lion's share of his revenue, which was derived in the usual barbarous manner by levying tribute unfairly, more being demanded from one trader than another.

Retiring from the presence of the monarch to the outside of the arch, we heard the noise of drums and shouts of joy issuing from a courtyard ; entering it, we saw, beneath trees, affording pleasant cool shade, an admiring crowd of excited people, laughing and clapping hands, and encouraging an old man and an old woman who were doing a grotesque dance to the musical time kept truthfully by two kettle-drums. Innocent frivolities peculiar to youth this ancient couple depicted in pantomime, to the intense delight of their audience. They threw their arms about wildly, twisted their bodies, and stepped out with spasmodic jerks ; but yet every action kept time with the strokes of the drums and the clapping of

hands, and also with the appropriate ejaculations naturally
jerked by pure fun out of the spectators. It really looked
somewhat after the manner of our deepest tragical stage-
murderers, who, to slow, shaky, fitful music, look for their
victim everywhere but where the footlights show the innocent about to be slain comfortably reposing upon a sofa.
When well tired out the old people sought repose on mats,
and youngsters brought them calabashes of palm-wine, just
as English children do at Christmas festivities, when grand-
papa has sung the song of his boyhood. Other sets of
dancers then started, and the fun was kept up fast and
furious.

One morning at daybreak a little steamer, commanded
by a naval officer, started up the lagoon for Ikorudu, eighteen
miles in a north-easterly direction, and I gladly accept an
invitation and go with her. The lagoon is so calm that it
appears a pity to cut waves upon it. The sun rising, rapidly,
changes the dense foliage surrounding the waters from sombre
shade to brilliancy. We are interested in observing fishermen
in canoes gathering shrimps from traps set upon innumerable
stakes sticking above the water. The absence of stakes indicates where deeper water exists, so we avoid the stakes. We
steam past the mouth of the river Ogun, which flows from the
north of Abbeokuta, and shortly afterwards anchor and get
ashore to the market-place in a tiny boat, tender to the tiny
steamer, and walk three miles through the bush to Ikorudu.
The path led through swamps, across creeks in which we saw
great numbers of leeches, and on to well-timbered land rising
from fifty to eighty feet above the lagoon level. Here we
find ironstone on the surface, similar to that at Sierra Leone.
The oppression which prevails, on account of being fairly shut
in by the dense low jungle, high trees overhead, and rank
perfume from the vegetation—like that felt in a close, stuffy

ohemist's shop on a hot day when the physic-bottle stoppers are not air-tight—produces a giddy feeling, only to be overcome by smoking pipes of tobacco; from this the blue smoke, curling upwards, forms a new and pleasing feature ·in the lonely landscape.   Large butterflies of varied colours abound, monkeys and grey parrots chatter in the trees, humming-birds perch on strange flowers, but you admire the pretty little birds too much to try to capture them.   Huge trees have fallen across the path impossible to climb over, so the path winds either round the root or where the top lies; this makes the walk appear to be double the distance.   We stop to rest frequently; meantime our attendants come up, and refreshments, which they have in charge, are had and enjoyed.

Ikorudu is surrounded by an irregularly-constructed mud wall, with a ditch outside, but both ditch and wall are overgrown with thick vegetation; however, it affords good cover to repel the ordinary native invaders.   The gates, or entrances, are simply mud thatched houses.   Everybody is obliged to stoop low at the front door, and pass into the town by the back door.   It is a very filthy, unwholesome place ; there is no regularity whatever in the buildings ; they appear to have been thrown together.   The Ikorudus are evidently preparing for war against their permanent foes, the Egbas, for at the blacksmiths' shops men are busily employed hammering iron into bullets.   They firmly believe that leaden bullets are of no use whatever, because they flatten when striking against a hard substance, which iron bullets will not do.   The blacksmiths are also making spear-heads and dagger-knife blades, and the primitive manner in which they blow the charcoal fires to make the iron red-hot is amusing.   Double bladders are fixed with pipes leading to the fire, the blower squats upon the ground and works sticks

attached to the top of the bladders, and he makes the
sparks fly.

In addition to suitable European goods and the variety of
food to make life enjoyable, the market-people drive a good
trade by the sale of dried shrimps, dried fish, and also dried
mice and rats, skewered on sticks, ready to be eaten or
warmed up previously; the latter look anything but tempting.
Tiny heaps of English salt placed on green leaves command a
ready sale; the purchasers lick the salt from the leaf, and
appear to enjoy it. The shopkeepers and market-women look
as easy and contented as traders do in the bazaars at
Stamboul and Cairo. Everywhere a perpetual buzz of
conversation and salutation goes on, and pleasant greetings of
" Oko," " Kaboh," " Akaboh." Infants, clinging to the
market-women, scream at the appearance of white men, and
hide heads beneath mamma's long breasts. Toddlers roar
with affright and flee inside the nearest house. The eight
and ten year olds dodge from corner to corner, taking short
cuts, and occasionally harmlessly crowd around you, just as
adults at home do to see Dr. Kenealy or the Khedive. The
children are decked with bead necklaces and iron anklets, and
fancy patterns are shaved on their round woolly heads like
ornamental parterres.

Our business was with a chief, to invite him to return with
us to see the Governor on some political palaver. We found
the venerable man asleep, but he soon appeared from his
dark chamber. Africans invariably prefer to shut out the
light from their sleeping-places. Taking five cowries from a
bag, he sent a boy to the market, who speedily returned with
a twisted leaf containing snuff. The chief licked the leaf,
placing the snuff in a roll comfortably inside his mouth, so as
not to impede conversation. He then ordered his portmanteau—a green Hollands gin case—to be filled with gala

clothing and placed upon a retainer's head. The return
walk through the bush was very fatiguing and tiresome; but,
once on board the steamer, going ahead created a pleasant
breeze. We enjoyed a good lounge on deck beneath the
little awning, and the old chief proved himself to be "a
pleasant-spoken man and a good judge of liquor." On
approaching Lagos, with the fond recollection of his good old
slave-dealing time, when he made money out of the Portuguese slave-dealers, and they made much more out of him, he
pointed out a shallow bay where, he stated, with tears in his
eyes—you may call them crocodile tears, but they were
honest—that he had seen in that bay as many as sixteen
hundred slaves being washed at one time previous to shipment.

Some years ago I happened to be here, when actual warfare was going on between the Egbas and the people residing
at a small village situated one mile north of Lagos, on the
mainland of Africa, called by the very pretty name of Abutta
Metta. I crossed the lagoon in a canoe to Abutta Metta,
and, inquiring my way through the Zouave-dressed West
Indian soldiers, was ushered to the residence of Lieutenant
S——y, the only white man in command of that outpost.
This young Englishman had a company of negro warriors
under his command, but unfortunately he had nobody wearing
a white skin to talk to but himself, and he repeated aloud
over and over again the Commandments and the Lord's
Prayer, so that he should not forget his mother-tongue. He
was obliged, unless addressing the better educated class of
West Indians, to speak Nigger-English to his army. He had
nobody to open his mind to and converse with familiarly, so
that he felt very melancholy and terribly lonely. I was
disinclined to intrude more than a brief visit to the place, and,
if a fight were on hand, would exercise my legs, as Falstaff

did, in running away upon instinct, but he welcomed me so
warmly that I gladly abode with him for a few days.   His
wooden shanty was raised over the swamp to keep him alive.
The eternal chorus of bull-frogs was only varied by the
occasional call of the sentries.   It is a most extraordinary
thing to note the calm courage and downright determined
pluck shown by our countrymen in this terribly lonely and
dangerous retirement from the world.   We talked about the
theatres and what was going on at home, and we actually
acted "Macbeth," and, after being floored by Macduff,
dropped upon the stage—the floor of his little room—and
died after our own idea, and rose again.   He was most
enthusiastic in collecting insects and butterflies, and
classified them neatly in boxes strewn with camphor to
frighten away the terribly-destructive ants.   Thus the
lonely lieutenant amused himself when not engaged arranging
his troops for fighting.   He was ready for any emergency,
and had his men posted to shoot the wily savages when they
came on.   Once, in the hunt after butterflies, we wandered
into the preserves of the enemy too far to be pleasant.   We
had armed men with us, and, taking a canoe along the
lagoon, landed at a butterfly-looking place, and wandered like
little boys with gauze nets fitted to sticks to capture
the butterflies, dragon-flies, humming-birds, or beetles.
Whilst thus engaged, a peculiarly offensive odour became
apparent, issuing from a dense part of the bush.   We knew
what it was, and, only looking at it with feelings of sorrow,
speedily withdrew.   It was a horrible sight.   Headless bodies
of black men were being devoured by carrion birds and overrun by millions of ants.   We could only account for it that
the Egbas had fallen upon a smaller party of their foes, and
killed them in the most shocking manner.

A small man-of-war was ordered for a week's lagoon cruise

to Badagry and Porto Novo, to act as a moral force in protecting British traders exercising their calling in those districts, and more especially to exhibit to the King of Porto Novo the power possessed by the Governor of Lagos to compel him, if necessary, to allow free trade along the lagoon, and also from the interior through his territory, without "let or hindrance." I was asked to join in the cruise, which I accordingly did with pleasure. The Governor sent with us an intelligent Mahometan interpreter, to talk as instructed by the captain of the man-of-war to the King of Porto Novo.

We steamed westward from Lagos at daybreak on a very fine morning, and, entering a narrow channel, which in some parts widened, passed romantic islands and banks covered with mangrove-trees with roots rising from the water's edge, and dense jungle with tall trees behind. We occasionally caught glimpses of crocodile. Three or four, and frequently more, of these unwieldy and dangerous brutes were seen asleep upon the banks or peeping out of grass. As soon as crocodile hear the steamer approach, they adopt the same rising and falling motion peculiar to lizards, resting upon their fore-legs and elevating and lowering the body whilst gazing intently at the puffing steamer. If it were only a quiet canoe they would not disappear so quickly, but now they make for their proper fighting element, enter with a great splash, and are hidden from view. It is useless to shoot at them from the deck of a vessel, as regularly-organised trips must be got up for the purpose of capturing them ; but very few people take the trouble to do so. The steamer has to keep in the centre of the channel to avoid sticking in the mud-banks on either side. Thus the course requires to be altered continually according to the curves of the lagoon. Comfortably seated beneath the awning, between the guns, which strike mortal terror to the natives, it is most enchant-

ing to look at everything that the real living panorama
exhibits. In the trees monkeys chatter and bend the
branches as they jump from one tree to another. Birds of
beautiful plumage abound, and the sight of a variety of
pretty flowers, strange to European eyes, is thoroughly enjoyed. Lagoon water agitated by the steamer, as it rolls in
waves aft, is the colour of dull brass, caused by being charged
with mud and unwholesome vegetable deposit.

It is interesting to notice, through glasses, canoes
bound for Lagos deeply laden with palm-oil in jars, kernels
in bulk covered with mats, bullocks, goats, sheep, corn, and
various other produce from the interior. In addition to
cargo they are crowded with passengers, chiefly women
traders, who seem to be comfortably reposing on the top of
the cargo. These canoes are made from very large trees
literally scooped out, like a long, cucumber-shaped water-
melon with the longitudinal top cut off and emptied of
fruit, leaving the firm ends intact. They are shoved along
in shallow water close inshore by the aid of long poles made
from the stems of palm-leaves, and in deep water, when
taking short cuts across lagoon bends, they are propelled by
paddles, but with a fair wind square sails are spread. The
sails are made of strong cotton cloth, woven in the interior,
coloured blue or white or striped ; sometimes they spread
butterfly sails, after the manner of Queen Elizabeth's invention of studding sails, and they then go along rapidly.
Lagoon navigation is so well sheltered that rough waves
seldom exist, and when a tornado comes on the canoes can be
tied up safely to sheltering trees.

We anchored towards sunset abreast the town of Badagry,
and the welcome dinner was soon announced. The table was
spread beneath the awning, and was lighted by swinging
lamps, but insects annoyed us terribly. One of the officers

produced a wooden tablet used in Mahometan schools with Arabic inscribed upon it. After dinner the Mahometan interpreter, to our great delight, read and translated the subject of the tablet. It was the account of Pharaoh· and his army being drowned in the Red Sea. We soon get tired of talking after dinner; the air feels heavy, and we can hardly keep our eyes open. The white sailors, excepting those on watch, have long ago crept quietly into their hammocks. If the vessel were at sea, in pure air, they would be dancing and singing. We gradually seek repose on mats on deck, with mosquito-curtains tucked round the edges of the mat, and the top corners made fast with string to stanchfons, rigging, and booms. I sleep alongside a gun, and cool my head delightfully against the iron. It is a great luxury to lie in personal contact with as much iron as you can ;·it creates a pleasant coolness in this tropical night, and gradually sleep follows. The changing of the midnight watch arouses me, and, creeping from underneath the mosquito-curtain half asleep, I observe the solitary swinging lamp under the after awning shedding forth a dim religious light. It shows a collection of squarely-formed mosquito-curtains covering the sleepers, which present a ghastly appearance, and at once suggest the idea of a cemetery of raised white tombstones. You are apt to shudder and wonder what particular graveyard you are reposing in, and you try to recollect how you died and what friends were about you at the time ; but a chorus of snoring, good honest British snoring, far and near, restores confidence. All hands turn out at day-break, and the cemetery changes into a man-of-war again.

Badagry is the first town of any importance after leaving Lagos on our trip, although we have passed many villages where petty markets are held, and. produce is received in exchange for goods. It is thirty-five miles distant from Lagos in a straight line as the parrot flies, but the winding lagoon makes the actual voyage longer. It is situated on the north side of the lagoon, which, opposite to the town, is half-a-mile wide. I resided for a few days at a trading store built of palm-leaf stems, and one floor made of the same material, bound together by strips of palm and roofed by palm-thatch, exactly like living in a wicker picnic basket of suitable dimensions, raised on stout bamboo props, so as to be above the society of big snakes, leopards, and crocodile. There are open spaces in lieu of windows, and the tenement is infested by large rats, which continually run unpleasantly over the face, and by fox-bats flying in and out at pleasure, so that it is very difficult to sleep. The perpetual squeal of each in the same key, tends to keep you awake, but the fox-bats possess voices about six-rat power, added to which the eternal roar of the sea in the distance gives occasion to the same unquiet style of dreams that front bedrooms in the Strand induce.

All over the town, beneath small bamboo-thatched sheds called devil-houses, exactly like temporary pig-sties, open at the front, are stuck up clay figures to represent an evil spirit. Cowrie-shells are inserted by the artist to represent eyes, feathers on the head show the abundance of hair, and leopards' teeth ornamenting the wide mouth denote fierceness. The sacred fetish-ground is a thick plantation enclosed by high bamboo stakes, the entrance to which is concealed by a screen of bamboo network threads. Before the English took possession, human sacrifices were common upon stated occasions in this place; now bullocks are substituted as the victims. Inside the enclosure are three houses; one for cooking, with pots and calabashes pertaining to the last feast lying about convenient for the next; one for repose; and the other containing an enclosed altar stud-

ded with feathers, knives, arrows, spear-heads, red earthenware pots, pans, and bamboo shields like hard wooden
cylinders cut in two parts, two and a-half feet long by fifteen
inches wide, with handy loops for the thumb and finger
inside. The whole of this horrible place is strewn with
human skulls, picked clean by the ants, each skull showing
the fierce cuts which caused death. The annual fetish lasts
for three weeks, during which time drums and other rude
noisy instruments are perpetually played night and day to
frighten the evil spirit away. Trees in town and country are
hung with calabashes, birds' feathers, and jars—all fetish.
Leathern cases are worn round the neck, containing articles
of the same nature. A jar of palm-oil landed from a canoe,
with three cowrie-shells placed upon the top, is sufficient
protection for it ; nobody will have the audacity to steal it.
A man getting into debt and unable to pay, mortgages himself, and works for his creditor until the account is squared.
Should he pay the debt due to nature in the meantime, his
remains are placed in the bush, and whoever removes the
body becomes liable for the amount still owing. On the
death of anyone whose friends can afford the expense, drums
are beaten and guns fired until powder runs short; the body
is then buried in the house, not far from the surface, and the
earth is rammed down tight and polished over smooth in the
same manner as on the Gold Coast. These people do not
worship a good Supreme Being, which they say is too kind to
do any harm, so they worship the devil instead. But it is
difficult to imagine why at certain periods they try to drive
their best friend away.

An intelligent native, pressed for his reasons for fetish,
said, "White man no hab fetish, and no sabby what them
ting be." Pointing to a hat upon the table, he continued—
"Suppose that be fetish, my grandfather he have fetish, my

father tell me to keep fetish, and I tell my pickaninnies the same; what be good for my grandfather and father be good for me and for my picken; all the same white man have hat." This lucid and eminently conservative homily took place at the civil commandant's house; and, as an interesting trial was about to take place, we remained to listen and look on. A woman belonging to a neighbouring village, accused of witchcraft, had fled for protection to the British flag. Four burly chiefs sat upon a bamboo sofa, and the floor was occupied by their retainers and witnesses. All the evidence was translated through interpreters into Nigger-English. It was asserted that the witch had a child dead in her house, that its elder brother remarked to neighbours, " Plenty beef live for our house." A vicious old woman, with violent speech and savage action, much more like a witch than the accused, said that the prisoner had "two eye in her head when she went out, and left two eye in the house also." This statement caused a thrill of horror to pass over three of the chiefs and their partisans. To the fourth chief, who appeared to be a compassionate, stout old man, the poor prisoner crawled upon her hands and knees, and at his feet made obeisance to each sentence he uttered, kissing the ground, and occasionally rising to clutch his hand with agonising gratitude. It was distinctly proved that all the prisoner's goats and other property had been siezed. The civil commandant, through the interpreter, decided, and he had to speak the usual jargon to reach the intellect of the interpreter :—" This woman has come here for British protection, and she shall have it. All you say be old woman talk; she be no witch. Witch no live for Badagry since them time English flag fly. What picken (child) say no one sabby. Now this woman wish to come live for Badagry. She shall come and live here, and all you men and all you big chiefs, you send

everything that belongs to her to Badagry one time. Suppose
you keep one goat, I fine you two bags of cowries. Now all
go, palaver set " (trial over).

Crossing the lagoon, half-a-mile wide, and walking over a
strip of land about one mile across to the sea to inhale the
delicious Atlantic breeze and recline upon the shelving sandy
beach, sheltered from the sun by a thick-skinned umbrella, it
is deeply interesting to look at the remains of old canoes,
stems, ribs, and frames of old whale-boats, which carried in
their time tens of thousands of slaves to vessels waiting for
the living cargoes in the offing. Here also are long sheds,
once called " barracoons," going fast to ruin, in which the
slaves were housed whilst waiting for shipment. High look-
out wooden boxes, formerly used to signalise slave vessels and
announce the coast clear, or give notice of the approach of
British cruisers, are fast tumbling to pieces. It is very
melancholy to look at such diabolical places, and it is better
to be alone and think. You feel proud of your country for
having with strong national will stamped out the infamous
slave traffic.. Thus pondering on that solitary beach, with
the Atlantic rollers fringing the bright sand as far as the eye
can reach with a line of white foam, the moaning of the wild
waves sounds like a perpetual death-wail.

Whilst the man-of-war was at anchor off Badagry, the
captain despatched the Mahometan interpreter by a canoe to
Porto Novo to announce his coming to see the king. In three
days the interpreter returned and delivered the words of the
king. " King he say, what you want, Sheetah? Me no glad
to look you. Why you go tell Governor ting about Porto
Novo? Suppose I cut your head off?" " Well, I say,"
Shetah continues, " suppose you cut my head off, man-of-
war he no find Sheetah, he say, ah, King Porto Novo kill him!
You be big man, king, but Governor of Lagos be bigger. He

send man-of-war blow you up one time. Big gun talk loud. Then I tell king he must do what Governor say (political business). King he say all right, but tell man-of-war no come here. No want him. Big gun he talk too much. He frighten all my people, and they go run for bush. Tell captain I glad he well, but I no want to look him."

Tom Tickel, an Englishman permanently settled at Badagry, living country fashion in a large dwelling-house pleasantly situated amongst trees, in the centre of a compound surrounded by offices and houses for retainers, lives like a sensible man. He has flocks of plump turkeys, fowls, ducks; herds of cattle, goats, and sheep, and a few horses. All the animals are regularly housed each night, to prevent, as far as possible, their falling a prey to snakes and wild beasts. He grows everything that the country produces for use or comfort, even to watercress; and after the manner of his generous hospitality in entertaining all visitors, he gave the naval officers—as many as could be spared from the ship— several resident traders, and myself a good country dinner, wound up by an excellent musical entertainment. The captain asked our worthy host to accompany him to Porto Novo, and also act as interpreter, and he cheerfully agreed to do so.

After visiting the chief man of the town, and receiving his return visit, attended by several headmen, steam was ordered, and the vessel proceeded westward sixteen miles to Porto Novo. We passed several green floating islands covered with long grass; they swarm with myriads of small snakes and creeping things. Floods detach these islands from the lagoon sides; they obstruct navigation somewhat, but gradually become broken up and finally float out to sea. We anchor off Porto Novo; immediately above it the lagoon opens out from half-a-mile to two or three miles in width, and the land

on the north side, behind Porto Novo, rises to from eighty to
one hundred feet above the level, which, showing cultivation
on its slopes and pleasant groves of trees, gives the district a
livelier appearance than the terribly flat, closed-in, dispiriting
country that we have come through.   The gig is manned and
looks, what it is, "a thing of beauty" on the water, with the
union-jack and pennant flying.   The captain, in full-dress
uniform, takes the place of honour, and the two interpreters
and I take our seats.   The coxswain steers, the six oars keep
time, and the boat skims the smooth water gracefully.   But
it is a matter of difficulty to find solid ground, for an extensive floating island obstructs the landing.   It presents the
singular appearance of a tract of green country rising and
falling, caused by similar action on the part of the water
underneath.   Canoes close to the bank look as if they were
docked far inland.   The oars are now of no use, so the gig is
poled through the island until mud is reached.   We are
carried on to dry land on the backs of Kroomen.   It was
comical to look at the captain's sword dangling on a Krooboy's legs, and his spotless white ducks clasped by strong
Kroo hands; the pair resembled a sort of nondescript giant
with brilliant uniform over bare black legs.   Sheetah wore a
flowing white cotton tober extensively adorned with red silk,
and on his head a red fez, with thick blue tassel, falling over
the white turban surrounding the fez.   Turkish trousers and
sandals completed his costume.   He was gorgeous, and he
knew it.

As soon as we landed a crowd of natives collected and
accompanied us to the palace entrance, situated about five
hundred yards from the green island.   A wide house gate,
thirty feet high, roofed with corrugated iron, leads to the
palace grounds.   The house gate is built of sun-dried bricks
and rejoices in two stories, but there are no windows in the

lower story; no doubt it was so constructed for defence. Opposite to the gate outside is a row of mud images of the Porto Novo fancy devil, each housed over as at Badagry; but here they have more consideration for the evil spirit, for a small brass pan is placed before each image, containing water, the rapid evaporation of which induces the natives to believe firmly that the devil drinks it when nobody is looking, and likes it; so they take a religious pleasure in replenishing the brass pans when they become empty. Appropriately placed next to the devil-houses is a shed devoted to the sacrifice of human beings. Beheading is the favourite plan, and blocks of hard wood, similar to those exhibited in the Tower of London, stand in a row. Each block is hollowed to allow perfect rest to the chin and breast, either to render the execution more rapid, or to make the victim as easy as possible under the painful circumstances, or both. We are fairly nauseated with the horrible details, and, gladly leaving the slaughter-house, pass through the palace gate-house. We are ushered through several square courtyards, surrounded by houses fronting inwards, and at each junction we are detained for several minutes. At length chairs are placed for us on the raised platform surrounding what proved to be the audience courtyard. It is well shaded from the sun, but the air is shut out too much, and it is not pleasant. Presently the King sent word that he was not up, also that he was "too much vex," and would not see anybody. The captain, having come a long way to see him, determined to wait patiently. Probably the King wished to consult his headmen, for parties looking like cabinet ministers turned up, to whom courtiers fell flat upon the earth, rubbed their noses in the snuffy dust and sneezed, kissed the ground, and snapped their fingers as the headmen passed into the King's private apartments. After

being detained about an hour the King sent word " Captain
call next week." Captain replied that he would leave for
Lagos that afternoon, and quietly suggested that the King
need not take long to dress. In five minutes the King came
strutting out with an insolent swagger. He wore a wreath
of—— no, there was nothing rosy about him; he wore a
white cap upon his head, a green silk-velvet loose robe
gracefully thrown around his person, leaving his arms and
neck free, disclosing a valuable necklace. His slippers were
made of bright coloured silk-velvet, and he violently smoked
a long reed-stemmed pipe, and jerked from his mouth long
blasts of smoke, which showed, like an index, the state of his
mind. He shook hands all around as a forced duty, and,
with the voice of a buffalo, asked Tickel and Sheetah what
we wanted. First, the captain hoped that his Majesty was
in the enjoyment of good health ; then followed the political
business, during which Tickel confronted the King, and,
holding up his forefinger, looked like Prospero dictating to
Caliban. " Report says, King, that you say one thing, and do
another unfriendly to English trade." Caliban roars out,
and it is interpreted, " Who says so he is a liar." Violent
roars were continued and echoed between the palace walls,
his large eyes rolled, and his forehead wrinkled. Go fetch
prisoner, quoth the King. A poor naked wretch was brought
in bound with cords tied in extraordinary knots, evidently
causing great pain; his head showed unhealed cuts, and his
arms and breast were lacerated. He trembles, he throbs
just below the region of the heart, he speaks low and indistinct with sheer mortal fright. Flog him, says the King,
and into his defenceless body pitch two members of government with their fists. At length the poor man told his
tale in broken sentences on his knees before that cruel
ruler of men, the worthy friend and ally of his next door

neighbour, the King of Dahomey. The prisoner's statement is interpreted to the captain. The King opens his wide mouth and bellows, " Now do you see I do what governor wish." Interpreting is slow work, but from the voice and gesticulation much can be gathered before the words are explained. King continues: " I shall now cut that man's head off," and he would have ordered in his executioner there and then, but our captain, with admirable coolness, told him that he would not, as the representative of Queen Victoria, allow it, and he gave Caliban distinctly to understand that he must not, at the peril of his own head, take the lives of any political offenders, but send them for trial to the Governor of Lagos. The palaver was then concluded.

This savage King, thus compelled to submit to the mighty name of England, assumed a sort of cheerfulness, and actually ordered in moselle and rum and water. Whilst the courtiers fell upon their faces, kicked up a dust, and snapped their fingers, we drank his health. I was seated on a chair behind the captain, looking as innocent as an old maid at a christening, with a soft felt hat resting upon my knees, and a piece of paper about two inches square, assisted by a stumpy pencil, quietly engaged sketching Caliban's head inside the hat. He observed me, and demanded to know what I was doing. I dropped the pencil and paper into my coat-pocket, and drew out of the same pocket with the same hand a bright Sheffield metal flask, with a portable drinking-cup to slip off and on at pleasure, the use of which I was about to explain ; but Caliban, seizing the bait, took off the screw top and placed his royal nose to the orifice and laughed, for the thing explained itself without the ordeal of interpretation. As the flask was empty, I gracefully presented it to him. He was highly delighted, and forgot to pursue further inquiries, or, as decapitation seemed to be his favourite

amusement, he might have asked for my head "on a charger."
In return for the flask, he "dashed" two large ducks and a
basket full of good yams, and I still wear my head.   So
much for Caliban !

We were not sorry to get away from the sun-dried brick
and mud built palace.   Walking through the town, Sheetah
met no end of his Mahometan friends, and he must introduce
us to each one.   They seemed to respect him very much,
and I do not wonder at it, for he is a very intelligent,
shrewd, and good man.   We asked him to take us out of the
filthy town, for the heat was great and the stench from
refuse was oppressive.   He took us uphill, and we rested
beneath a tree, in front of which was a well about fifty feet
deep.   Out of this well a woman kindly drew up for us, with
a long string, calabashes of cold clear water, and we enjoyed
it in quiet.   After becoming somewhat cool, we inspected
the markets, and found them exactly similar to those at
Lagos, with the addition of numerous pipe-head makers
working clay and turning out in an artistic manner red,
white, and black pipe-heads.   Other people were engaged
making good reed stems of various lengths to fit into the
pipe-heads.   Makers of fishing-nets were busily employed.
The nets are formed of tough cord—spun from vegetable fibre
similar to Irish flax.   But the calabash engravers attracted
the greatest interest, for with very rude instruments they
carved quaint ornamental designs upon gourds of every
shape, from that of a fat bottle to a fancy open basket.   We
were kindly invited into trading stores belonging chiefly to
French and Italian merchants, and agreeable conversation
resulted until a Krooboy announced that the gig had arrived
from the man-of-war and was in waiting; so we shoved off,
got on board, and rapidly returned to Lagos.

It is not often during the rainy season that fierce tor-

nadoes occur, as they are peculiar to the dry season ; but the
day after our arrival from Porto Novo we had a howler. The
forenoon had been very bright and very hot. We were
seated in the verandah after midday breakfast, enjoying the
sea-breeze and pipes and tea, when suddenly the rumble of
distant thunder was heard. On looking inland towards
Abbeokuta we observed inky clouds streaked with vivid
lightning coming up rapidly against the sea-breeze. The
sea-breeze ceases suddenly, and calm ensues—a calm that
you can feel by the sinking of your own spirits. Presently
all animals get under cover. English rabbits, in their protected enclosure, scurry into their holes. Lizards catching
butterflies flee out of sight. Land-crabs stop excavating
and go home. Pigeons, strutting before bits of looking-glass
stuck in front of their houses, and making love, speedily
go inside, those on flying visits hurry home with fright and
hide their heads ; several wobbling tails sticking out of the
same pigeon-hole indicate that internal discord is going on.
The fox-bats, asleep during day, clinging by their claws to
the branches of trees of dense foliage in the courtyard, with
their bodies suspended, as is their nature, may be observed
clawing a tighter hold. All labour is stopped, and everybody
takes shelter. The venetian doors and windows surrounding
the living rooms, usually wide open day and night, are closed
and bolted. Suddenly the sun disappears, and the ensuing
darkness is appalling. The theatre of heaven bursts into
tempest. Hiss, hiss, comes the lightning, flash after flash
dancing over ironwork like momentary blue flames of sulphur,
totally blinding you while it lasts ; whilst the thunder so
crashes that you cannot hear anything else.

> " The wind blew as 'twad blawn its last ;
> The rattling showers rose on the blast."

Trees are broken and branches fly through the air, and the

roofs of many houses disappear. The weather doors and windows rattle almost to bursting. The rain is driven nearly horizontally, and a deluge covers the country. In half-an-hour the sun returns with his silent beams, and all nature is once more calm and bright.

CHAPTER IV.

THE NIGER DELTA, MISSIONARIES, CANNIBALS, RIVER
PIRATES, AND THE YARN OF A CASTAWAY AT THE BENIN
BRANCH OF THE NIGER.

THE trading steamer for the Niger is ready to start.
She carries three hundred tons of cargo, her bunkers
are filled with coal, and she only draws seven feet of water.
It is said that she can steam thirteen or fourteen knots an
hour. The furnaces are so constructed that wood can be
used as well as coal, which is a very important consideration
in savage river navigation, where trees are abundant on the
banks and where coal is not to be had. The afternoon of
the 26th day of July is fixed upon for our departure, as the
river Niger is now sufficiently swollen by the rains peculiar
to the northern tropic to afford deep water and safe navigation. The deck is crowded with people undergoing the
grief of parting, which is very affecting to witness. It was
somewhat difficult—the crew using all gentleness—to clear
the ship; but at five P.M., as the last weeping visitor
jumped on to the wharf, we steamed from Lagos harbour.
The sight of Christian missionaries and their families surrounding Bishop Crowther, congregated in the after part of
the vessel, solemn, good-looking, and civil Mahometans
assembled forward, and friends on shore waving adieu as
they ran along the line of lagoon beach, a moving crowd
until we left them far behind, was pleasant to look upon.
We had in tow a small steamer to be repaired on the beach
inside the river Nun, where the rise and fall of the tide is

moro than at Lagos. Astern of her was also towed a boat laden with coal, and navigated by two Kroomen. Tho whole formed a nautical procession of three. After crossing the bar, the difficulty of steering caused us to collide with a brig at anchor; but, as we previously slipped the tow-rope and let our craft following drift and anchor, the damage done was slight. However, it was sufficient to compel anchoring, also to examine and repair injuries. It only took a few hours to do so; for, being most anxious to get to sea— especially not wishing to be observed from the shore when morning broke, and probably ridiculed—everybody set to work cheerfully, and during the night we proceeded on our voyage. As the steamer in tow was addicted to leaking, it was agreed that a gun should be fired if the leak gained upon her so as to apprehend sinking. A young but efficient white sailor was in charge, with a crew composed entirely of negroes. Fortunately, we were favoured with very good weather, considering that it was the rainy season, and naturally we expected the contrary. But yet the vessels rolled and pitched, hawsers stretched, and, rising from the sea, shook the water out like long wet dishcloths being wrung. When the hawsers slackened, the vessels in tow rushed violently forward; this necessitated careful steering so as to avoid collision.

The next day at noon we were only abreast the river Benin, about twenty miles from the land, which we sighted towards evening. Our course is now S.S.E., to keep along the shore at a moderate distance. Before sunset we stopped to change and " chop "—feed—the Kroomen in charge of the coal-boat. During the day we had exchanged messages and jokes with the commander of the steamer in tow, by means of blackboards and chalk, but one communication, about a pig, we could not make out. Whilst stop-

THE RIVER NIGER

TO ITS CONFLUENCE WITH

THE RIVER BINUE.

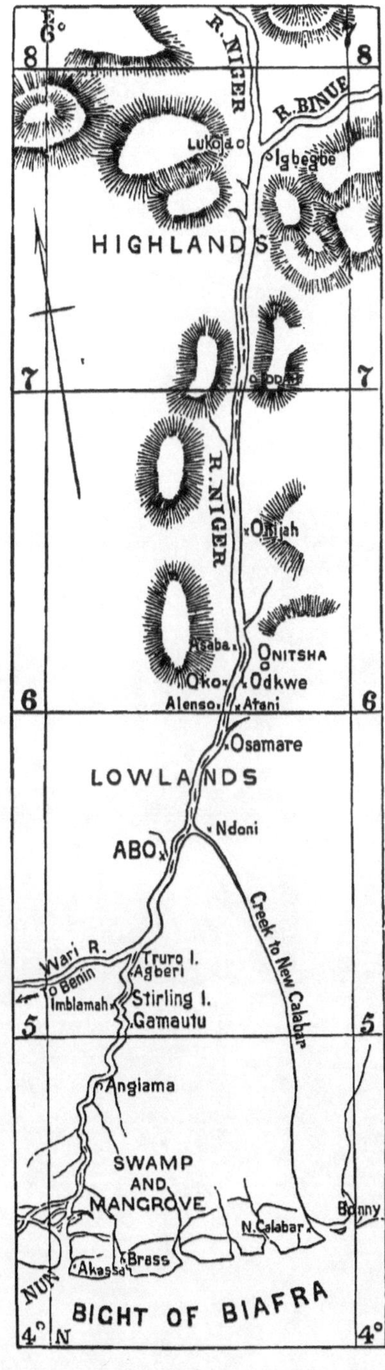

ping, he lowered his dingy, pulled alongside, and informed us that all his live-stock for the voyage was lost. His pig, observing the land through an opening in the bulwarks, was, by a sudden roll and jerk, pitched clean overboard into the sea, and within one minute disappeared, doubtless seized by sharks following the vessels.

The passengers are sorely afflicted by sea-sickness, with the exception of the' Bishop, who is well accustomed to the sea. They lie perfectly helpless on deck beneath the awning, rolled up in bundles, and huddled together for warmth. Luckily, the deck is roomy, and the steering-gear, being worked from the bridge, causes the after part of the vessel to afford the best and quietest resting-place for the temporary invalids. But yet the tops of waves frequently tip suddenly over the counter, drenching the sleepers, and the sudden immersion frightens the poor women and children terribly. The staid Mussulmans beneath the fore awning crowd close to the rail, on which they rest their necks and open their hearts to the deep. These are the times on board steamers filled with wealthy passengers most appropriate for the stewards to pass round rattling subscription-boxes, to collect bullion for the building and maintenance of lifeboats, and also to support the widows and orphans of sailors. If a sea-sick Dives will not freely contribute to these noble charities *then*, he never will.

The second morning showed us close to the mouth of the Middleton river. We kept near to the land along this part of the Delta, so as to be satisfied about the proper entrance, but a strong head-wind and current retarded our progress. At noon we steamed into the muddy water rushing out from the Nun branch of the Niger; a definite line, extending to a long distance, distinguishes it from the pure blue ocean. The same phenomena occur far out at sea, out of sight of land, off the mouth of the Amazon, the Mississippi, and other great rivers. The bar of the Nun extends seven miles from its mouth. Crossing it we experienced difficulty ; it happened to be ebb-tide and nearly low-water. The coalboat's tow-rope broke; so we stopped in three fathoms, with the eastern breakers not far distant, and, lowering the lifeboat, sent additional Kroomen, with orders to sail it into the river. That done, and the lifeboat hoisted up, we steamed ahead, but the violent jerking of our towing hawser threatened to snap it. The engine was reduced in speed, and we anxiously watched. At length the hawser snapped in two, and the small vessel's foremast, starboard anchor, and bulwarks were carried away in one instant by the destructive rebound of the broken rope. We at once stopped ; she ran naturally by the speed upon her when the rope broke to within shouting distance. The crew had, by piling wood into her furnaces, just managed to get up steam, although her cabin, engine-room, and stoke-hole floors were covered with water. Her commander—plucky young fellow—was loath to abandon the vessel, as some one suggested ; in reply, he simply sung, above the howling wind, " It will nebber do to gib it up so," and actually executed a nigger break-down on his bridge, which we expected soon to disappear beneath the waves. His dare-devil behaviour infused activity into everybody to do their utmost to save the vessel. She steamed very slowly, and we moderated speed to keep company ; but the ebb-tide was too strong, and we both drifted to leeward instead of making progress. Suddenly a gun was fired and her ensign hoisted, union-jack down, the signals of distress. We stopped and lowered boats for the purpose of saving life, and found that her fires were extinguished and that she was fast sinking. As a last effort we bent on a fresh hawser, and, putting on full speed, tore through the rough sea over the bar and anchored, with two hours' daylight to spare, above the village of Akassa, on the eastern bank of the Nun, four miles distant from the sea, in perfectly smooth water. We were in a state of frantic delight, and immediately beached the little steamer in safety close to trees.

From the river Benin to the foot of the huge Cameroon mountain there is hardly a vestige of land apparent above the surface of the sea. What does exist is alluvial mud and sand, swept down the various branches during ages past, and gradually forming delta. It is covered to the water's edge by mangrove-trees, the uniform height of which, at a distance of seven or eight miles, looks like the first lesson in pencil drawing, perpendicular strokes in close order. A break in the pencil strokes indicates the mouth of a river, and there are about twenty-four of these openings between Benin on the west and beyond Old Calabar on the east. These rivers are intersected by numerous cross-streams, called creeks, which are affected by the tides pertaining to the nearest sea-opening. The tides meet as in the Menai Straits, and create fierce agitation of the water and counter-currents, rendering navigation by canoes or boats tedious work. The creeks swarm with crocodile and fish. On each side the tendrils of the tall mangrove-trees, growing downwards, strike root in the muddy banks below water and form a network of darkness, the appropriate home of the crocodile and the python. Utter loneliness and terrible solitude are experienced in passing through them, and although apparently unfit for human residence, yet villages exist and traffic is carried on by canoes; but no through traffic as yet, for it is impossible to induce canoemen to go beyond the limits of their respective tribes. It is perfectly practicable for steamers of light draught, built on the American river plan, to navigate through creeks from Benin to beyond Bonny, and probably even to Old Calabar, and also far into the interior.

Shortly after arrival, the Bishop disembarked with his people to attend to the Church mission established at Akassa, and there remain until we should advise him of our departure. A few of the others visited a trading factory, an iron house two stories high, with the usual business premises below and dwelling rooms overhead, surrounded by a cool verandah. The jungle is cleared in the immediate vicinity of the house, a neat kitchen-garden formed, well-stocked pigeon-houses erected, and suitable sheds for palm-oil and coal. The house fronts the sea-breeze; in the background tall trees and thick underwood shut us in on that side like a high prison wall. It is impossible to penetrate the bush, as it only covers a tract of foul swamps. The white sandy beach in front of the house is only available to walk upon for a short distance. Trees, growing in many places to the water's edge, cause all local travelling to be performed by canoes or ships' boats. We spent a jolly evening ashore. Our host played upon a harmonium, songs were sung all round, and we felt sorry, when occupying mats and mosquito-curtains, that time had flown so quickly; but to enable one to get up with cheerfulness at five A.M., it is necessary to retire whilst the clock registers the previous P.M.

Early on the morning after anchoring, notwithstanding a persistent and heavy downpour of rain, two chiefs of Akassa came alongside. They were conveyed in separate canoes, larger than those in use on the sea-board, and crowded with retainers making rude music and acclamation. They came on board and wanted " big dash and plenty of rum." Each chief wore wide ivory bracelets, on which his name and rank were inscribed—"Opunuma, King of Akassa," on one, and

" Francisco, King of Akassa and pilot of the Nun," on the other. The monarchy thus appears to be divided and mixed up with pilotage. These two are most unclean creatures, and it is well to keep at a respectful distance to windward of them. A younger man accompanied the chiefs, with an unpronounceable name upon *his* ivory, distinctly announcing that he was a prince and the son of a " big gun "; he grinned at everybody and seemed highly amused. A staid-looking but filthy Ju-ju man, or priest, attended upon the royal party. They brought neither yams nor fowls, but, in the most overbearing manner, demanded tribute for the vessel. They asked for " plenty cloth, plenty guns, plenty powder, and plenty rum." Our trading agent told them that he would not recognise their claim to any tribute. They were, however, supplied with a bottle of trade rum and a tumbler. Each more than half filled the tumbler, and, disdaining the use of water, poured the raw spirit into his-capacious mouth. It is a very singular way of drinking, and is common amongst American Indians in the Far West. Each man when drinking closes his throttle-valve to prevent the liquor going down, then he rolls the strong drink round and round the gums to create intense smarting before swallowing. It is apparently a pleasant sensation, and not unlike the manner unconsciously adopted —but only as regards the first part of the performance—by ladies at home who roll about, until it reaches the right spot, a teaspoonful of brandy to relieve the toothache.

When the operation of gulping took place, their eyes sparkled with devilish, dissolute delight. The bottle was soon emptied, after which they temporarily fitted themselves on to camp-stools, and they looked remarkably uneasy. It was quite evident that they preferred squatting on deck, but knowing that that was not " white man fashion," and not wishing to appear undignified, they grinned and bore it. Opunuma then said, through Francisco, who speaks Nigger-English, " I own the land about here, and I only got dash from you one time; I want big dash every time every ship come." He understood customs toll. It was endeavoured to be explained—but, I must candidly admit, very lamely—that the present, or "dash," made some six weeks previously was sufficient, at any rate for the rainy season. They would not have it so, but called for more rum, which they got and concealed in the same manner, and then they wandered about the vessel on a tour of inspection. We had watch set upon their actions, and refused to allow their followers to come from the canoes on deck, as they bear the reputation of being expert thieves. As far as anthropology goes, Akassa people are qualified to compete with the most degraded members of the human race; they have villain, murderer, and cannibal stamped upon their baboon-like faces. As the lower classes stare from crowded canoes—there are from twenty to twenty-five stark-naked paddlers in each canoe—they jabber fiercely, their eyes glisten like those of caged wolves, and they seem to groan, "Oh! oh! give us human chops divine and good, washed down our hungry throats by lots of rum and blood." We gave them the rum—neat. The chiefs, when asked if they ate "man," denied it stoutly, and appeared highly offended; but, at the same time, they pointed to neighbours on each side higher up the river whom they accused of doing so. After enjoying a good dinner on deck, thereby laying an excellent foundation for more rum— meantime the canoemen being also filled with biscuits and good things—they at length got so "screwed" that their legs refused to locomote. Then the Ju-ju man, assuming command, ordered the bodies into the canoes, and had them covered with mats. I regret for the sake of the cloth, of which there was not much about him, to state that this royal chaplain behaved in a most extraordinary manner. He was not unable to walk, but he whooped loudly, danced wildly; and, when under way, howled forth unearthly Ossian-like anthems, joined in chorus by his congregation, as if to say—

"O let thy song arise in praise of those who fell."

There was no sorrow at our parting; we were, on the contrary, glad as they paddled away that "distance lent enchantment to the view."

Inside several mouths of the river Niger, for a century and a-half, sailing-vessels have been in the habit of anchoring for longer or shorter periods, sometimes extended to many months. These ships were carefully housed over with palm-thatch, to exclude the sun, and also to afford shelter during the rains. The masters or supercargoes traded with important chiefs and other clever natives, formerly for slaves, but latterly principally for palm-oil. Strange to say, the trading agents remained in ignorance that they were living at the entrance to the puzzling Niger. Mungo Park on his second journey, penetrating the interior of Africa, in 1805, was on his way in a canoe on the upper part of the river, having crossed from the river Gambia overland and enduring terrible suffering, which every schoolboy reads, and, even at this distance of time, sympathises with. He was actually coming down the stream, and felt assured that such a large body of water flowing eastwards—so he stated after his first journey—must have an outlet to the sea somewhere; and he would have arrived amongst the Liverpool vessels in the bights, but unfortunately he lost his life at Boussa, latitude 10° 14′ north, longtitude 6° 11′ east.

Clapperton and Lander, in 1826, travelled overland from Badagry to Boussa, where they crossed the Niger and

proceeded northwards.   Clapperton died at Soccatoo early in
the following year.   Lander marched from Soccatoo to
Kano, and from thence was making his way direct to the
confluence of the rivers Niger and Binue, and had nearly
succeeded in doing so, when he was overtaken by armed men,
made prisoner, and taken back, almost broken-hearted, two
hundred miles of weary land-travel to a place not far from
Kano.   Lander, thus stopped from prosecuting his journey
by the river, was obliged to return by the tedious land-route
to Badagry.   However, in 1830, he, with his brother, again
landed at Badagry, marched through the country, struck the
Niger, took a canoe, and came joyously down with the
October and November heavy rush of falling water, and
arrived at this, the Nun mouth.   Thus the outflow, which had
been as much matter of dispute and amiable quarrel amongst
travellers and geographers as, on the contrary, the sources of
the greater Nile are now, was ascertained by Richard
Lander.

In 1832, the late Macgregor Laird built two small
steamers, and, engaging Richard Lander to accompany him,
ascended the Niger from here.   The expedition was associated
with continued disaster ; both vessels got aground high up
the river when the waters were falling, and they were stuck
fast until the following year.   Laird and his party endured
extreme hardship ; they were ill-treated by the natives,
ill-housed, and ill-fed.   Their suffering in this pestiferous
climate reduced the number of white men by death
from forty-seven to eight.   Lander was shot by the
natives at Angiama, and died shortly afterwards at Fernando
Po.   The details of that eventful adventure are most harrow-
ing.   Anybody reading the book describing it * cannot fail
to appreciate the heroic conduct throughout of the people

---

* " Magregor Laird, and Oldfield's Niger Expedition."

under command of the first white man to ascend the Niger, to whom the honour is due of having opened up the vast trade of the interior. The marvel is that any one survived to reach the sea-coast.

In 1841 the British Government sent out three small steamers (the " Albert," " Wilberforce," and " Soudan ") to endeavour, by treaty with and presents to the native Kings, to abolish the slave traffic, and by a display of the results of civilization, and kind wishes duly and properly interpreted, to encourage legitimate trade with England. A tract of country opposite to the Confluence of the Niger and Binue was purchased and a model-farm established. The experiment, however, proved to be a complete failure, and the mortality amongst the white men—only a short time up the river, compared to the first expedition—was so great, one-third of them having died, that people at home naturally became disheartened. This caused the Niger to be abandoned, and the grand river rolled on in solitude, as far as white men were concerned, until 1852. Mr. Laird in that year established the African Steamship Company, and shortly afterwards sent out a specially-built steamer of light draught to ascend the Niger and trade during the rainy season. He also built factories at various points for the same purpose, and expended a large fortune to benefit dark Africa. But his death, in 1862, stopped the direct development of the resources of the Niger. Indeed, it was not encouraged by many of the palm-oil traders in the Delta, for they favoured the views of the intermediate savage tribes, who levied, and lived by and prospered on, tribute on produce one way, and goods the other way, as both passed their particular districts. A direct trade with the Niger meant brokerage ruin to the residents between the seaports and the producing countries ; hence it was, and is, strictly objected to by them.

In addition to this local opposition, wealthy firms at home, wishing to keep up the monopoly which they had so long enjoyed in the Delta, strongly objected also to direct trading up the Niger. For many years, by issuing suitable orders to their agents, they succeeded in driving away anybody presuming to oppose them, especially in their own particular rivers—just in the manner that Constantinople dogs fall upon and worry to death a stranger dog which may happen to want to pick up a bone amongst them. But, in the natural course of events, it was found that the regularity of steamers to and from England, and their gradual increase in size to accommodate extending trade, afforded small traders the opportunity of collecting produce, sending it home, and rapidly receiving goods in return ; and they availed themselves of the facilities. Whilst the old-fashioned firms kept their old-fashioned ships anchored in the unwholesome rivers for six or eight months loading and stowing palm-oil, the new men had sent home by steamer palm-oil bought at the same time as the oil still on board the vessels at anchor. That oil was in use in England in the form of soap or grease for railway axles, and the new men had received returns twice or thrice over before the unwieldy ships, so to speak, brought their pigs to market. The monopoly was then and for ever at an end. Several people in England interested in this branch of the commerce of the world say that the West African trade "has gone to pot, sir ; it is worthless, sir." But in reality it is not so. It is only changing into more modern hands, with ideas suited to the age, and it now bids fair to extend and expand properly, not only at the mouths but up the main river. At the present time six or seven trading steamers of light draught run for nine months of the year, making as many trips as they can to and from factories as far as the Confluence, and during the height of the rainy season they are enabled to proceed to factories established above the Confluence. They deliver goods and receive produce; but they are obliged to be well armed, for the savages in the Delta frequently fire upon them as they pass to and fro.

On the 1st of August, at 9.45 A.M., we steamed at full speed from Akassa up the Nun branch for the main river Niger. At 10.10 A.M., we entered Louis Creek, and in one instant lost sight of the Atlantic, the ocean which we all love, and which some of us may never look upon again. It was a moment of sadness to everybody on board. Although, from Akassa, we only saw the line of ocean fronting the river, yet we enjoyed the heaven-sent, life-sustaining sea-breeze, which we now lose. A rapid turn of the vessel swept her round a corner, and to all appearance we are land locked.

Louis Creek is about eighty yards in width; it runs between Alburkah Island on the left and Nicholl's Island on the right, leaving Clarendon Island astern. There are mangrove-trees on every side, but no land is to be seen. These trees, with their spreading roots springing from mud below water, and their numerous pendant tendrils, are so closely interwoven that we can only see into the thick, slimy thicket a few yards from the water's edge. The paddling of the steamer, echoed from the densely-wooded banks, is the only noise heard. It is terribly lonesome; no sign of life. It is a deep stream, and

> " So calm, the waters scarcely seem to stray,
> And yet they glide like happiness away."

But speedily we round into the main river, and, at 11.45 A.M., pass Sunday Island. We encountered heavy rain, but, to our great joy, rapidly got out of the dreary mangrove region. It is a remarkable fact that mangroves only exist in the vicinity affected by the action of the tide. Palm-trees of various sorts and lofty silk-cotton-trees begin to show abundantly. The first sign of life is a small plantation and a dozen mud hovels, situated one mile above Sunday Island, on the right bank. Fires are burning inside the huts, and smoke comes out of the doors, as these swampy residences are not provided with chimneys. Several small canoes creep close alongshore, paddling against the strong downward current. We observe occasional huts on the right bank, and large trees on each side, some of which are covered with beautiful flowers. If English oaks were studded with full-blown tulips instead of acorns, their resemblance to these trees would be complete. We rush past creeks, ferries worked by canoes, and occasional clusters of huts, until the land begins to show two feet above the river, and banana plantations appear. Canoes are being loaded with palm-oil in casks, for conveyance through creeks to Brass river.

Above the village of Liambre the huts improve in appearance, the banks are higher, and patches of sugar-cane, in addition to bananas, become more frequent. Palm-trees stick out of the sides, bending by the action of the current, until washed away. At every village the natives rush out and howl. Well-known Liverpool marks are observed on the casks of palm-oil getting leisurely filled. Low fishing-stakes jut out at various places, and here and there fishing-scaffolds are erected, from the top of which a man, sheltered by a little roof, with a line in his hand, watches the fish swimming. The line is attached to a mat-net sunk between stakes run out into the river. From his elevated position he can, at once, see the fish over his net, then he hauls the line sharply, and a companion below takes out the fish thus cleverly captured. At 3.45 P.M., we passed the village of Opuhpuroma, where the river is about three hundred yards wide. Here, in addition to palm-oil, we see the first animals in the Delta—sheep—and they are not bad-looking. The river now increases to half-a-mile in width. At 4.15 P.M., abreast of Angiama, where they shot poor Lander, we counted twenty-five canoes laden with palm-oil, and two hundred casks on the bank ready for shipment. About a thousand people shouted, wanting us to stop. When abreast the north end of the town we did so, on observing which, by our steam-pipe roaring, the multitude cheered. Canoes came alongside, containing big men of the town, accompanied by an intelligent boy, who spoke Nigger-English, as directed by the chiefs. "People want you to stop for make trade." We told them to cut plenty of wood, and that we would call and pay for it upon our return. They doubted our doing so, and the boy quaintly and laughingly remarked, "Ah, you tell dam lie!" That naughty boy had evidently not learnt English at a mission. He said that the people wanted "plenty salt, plenty powder, plenty gun, and plenty, plenty, plenty rum," and that all the oil in casks was going to traders at the mouth of Brass river. We gave our visitors a few bottles of rum, and, on the order to go ahead, they shoved off, splashing up the water fantastically with their paddles.

During the stoppage, and it lasted for only ten minutes, the steamer drifted from the north to the south end of the town. The cheering of the spectators was pleasant. Lifting our hats to them, in return for the compliment, disclosed our "bare-footed" heads—shaven for comfort—which caused them to laugh and chuckle like other folks. We steamed ahead, passing villages, creeks, and ferries, until 6.15 P.M., and by that time it was quite dark; so we anchored in the middle of the river, not only to give the mosquitoes from each bank a fair chance of drawing our blood, but also to protect ourselves. The dinner had to be hastily eaten, for insects got scalded and drowned in the soup, and covered the plates and dishes. Armed sentries were appointed, instructed to quietly call all hands if canoes approached. A dozen breech-loaded rifles were at hand, and our four six-pounders were properly charged with grape-shot. After completing these warlike preparations, there was nothing else for it but bed. Mosquitoes, flying beetles, and unknown insects filled the candle-lanterns. They flew at the light, and, getting singed, dropped around the candle until the quantity of wings and bodies rose higher and higher and threatened to put out the light ; so we had a couple of ship's lamps swung beneath the awning, and, creeping below mosquito-curtains, sought repose, assisted by tobacco-smoke.

But going so unusually early to bed, added to the strange change from open sea to a sort of canal navigation, kept us awake. We sung songs and spun yarns, as seafaring people invariably do, to create happiness, drowsiness, gentle sleep, and oblivion for the time being.

"Jack," called out one of the company, "send us to sleep about your being at sea in a boat off this blessed coast, without grub or liquor. It will soothe us to know that on getting up hungry in the morning we shall have plenty to eat. I can understand your being without food, but how you went without—call it water—for four days in this climate gets over me."

The individual alluded to remarked, "Get out !" but, removing his pipe, commenced :—

"Well, it's a long time ago now. We were anchored off Lagos, homeward bound. Two boats, loaded with over-carried cargo and some Sierra Leone emigrants' luggage, stuff which we were not able to land on the outward voyage, were sent towards sunset to the beach. I had been two days in Lagos town hunting up cargo, and arrived at the beach

with the mails for home just as the boats were shoving off.
I must tell you that we were short-handed on the steamer,
but Captain Gardner, of H.M.S. 'Waterwitch,' kindly lent us
Krooboys, fellows who know how to work boats in surf.
They and I were in the gig towing the empty launch, but so
much water came over us on approaching the bar that we
got swamped and scrambled into the larger boat. Just as we
got safely over the bar pitchy darkness set in, and a fierce
tornado blew us off the shore."

"Why didn't you anchor?" asked one of the listeners.

"Anchor, eh? Yes, we would have anchored, but we
had no anchor, so we pulled hard toward the steamer's lights.
The lights, instead of getting bigger, grew less and vanished.
We knew that she was only waiting for us to be off, but we had
to give up pulling and take to baling with our hats, to keep
ourselves from drowning. The boat had never been in the
water since it was born, and the heat during two voyages
had so opened the seams that, as it was hung to the davits, a
pleasant breeze blew through, keeping the vegetables cool.
Stewards always stow vegetables beneath boat-covers even in
these modern days; *that* is partly the reason why. It looks
pretty to see snow-white canvas spread over boats, and it is
pleasant in dock to describe to lady visitors the action of
lowering and hoisting, whilst their gentle voices exclaim, 'Oh
my!' and 'Dear me!' especially if you are spoony on one
of them; but when the water is up to your calves in a boat,
on the open sea on a dark night, it's no joke.

"Well, the first night passed, all hands baling. We
drifted straight out to sea, driven by the tornado. When
that was expended we drifted to the eastward. When
morning broke we could see nothing but sky and ocean, and
presently the hot sun arose. I was one white man with
nine strange Krooboys. I sang every song that I knew, and

lots that I didn't know, to keep ourselves jolly. I divided my companions in distress into three watches; one man to steer with an oar—we had no rudder, it was left on board with the anchor in the hurry of lowering the boat—the other two to look out for land or vessels, and trim our lug-sail, which alone saved us. We ran in for the shore, thinking that the steamer would come to rescue us. Towards evening we sighted the breakers, ran through them, and landed. The Krooboys begged of me not to attempt running through the surf, but the boat did it, and was at once hauled up clear of the water.

"We wandered over the beach, across the land, to the margin of a series of shallow lagoons, covered with flowers and reeds. I thought that we might shove the boat over and into the main lagoon if we could find it, but these limited lakes led nowhere. Some beautiful large white lilies, floating on their surface, attracted my attention, and I collected a few. But we found nothing to eat, and that was what we wanted. Not a shell-fish on the beach, not a nut or plum on the trees, nothing but beautiful desolation. We drank the lagoon-water eagerly, but it was brackish, and it made us very sick. At length I expressed to the boys my determination to abandon the boat and walk along the beach to Lagos. I sat for some time looking at the lone ocean, thinking of Robinson Crusoe, and longing to wander somewhere and get something to eat, if it were only a snail or a frog nicely cooked. After a while the Krooboys crowded round me. They were attired in the becoming man-of-war costume—wide rolling collars to their serge shirts and the usual nautical trousers; so that added to the value of their words.

"The spokesman said, 'Massa, suppose them bush-men lib here catch we—they no be we countrymen—they eat we, and take white man, gibe him lille chop, and you die too.

Suppose you no die, they make big palaver, get plenty cloth
and rum from white man for you, but they chop we all same,
or they take we for bush and sell we for slaves. More better
we take them boat and go for sea. Massa, we beg you.
You no fit for walk for Lagos. You sabby them place
white men lib. We sabby which way work boat. Come, we
beg you come to sea. Sea be good for we, all same for you.'

"I was fairly knocked over by their argument, and, as
they said truly, I was not fit to walk along a desolate beach,
beneath a hot sun, without food or water, for several days.
So we launched the boat into the briny, and kept it sailing
off and on to avoid drifting past the river Benin, which, had
we passed, there would have been little or no hope of our
being saved. Without a chart or compass, I did not know
exactly where Benin was. I only knew that we were to
windward of it, and that, by keeping as near to the same
spot during dark night, we must come to it. In the middle
of the following night, whilst standing in too close, we
grounded on a sandbank. It must have been some distance
from the land, for we could see nothing through the darkness but the froth of the sea. We jumped out to lighten
the boat and get her off. I was up to my arm-pits before
climbing in again. All helped to shove her off, and I kept
her afterwards further from the shore. On the third day, at
early dawn, feeling shivery after sleeping half in the water
swishing in the bottom of the boat, and dreaming of hot-
pot and awakening finding it not, I took off my clothes to
dry them, but the sun blistered me so much that I had to
resume the damp clothing to dry as it would. Thinking of
the hot-pot, I bit at the boat's gunwale to employ my teeth.
Oh, it was dreadful agony to be without something to cool
our parched lips!

' Water, water everywhere, but not a drop to drink.' "

" Now, Jack, that's poetry ; draw it mild," called out an old friend.

" Two Krooboys went mad and fought. One tore an eye out of the other, and it hung upon his cheek. I felt like going mad also, and howled out, ' Go it, Sal! I'll hold your bonnet.' Now, you know, no fellow in his senses would say that, for fortunately no Sal was there. Well, after a little, we calmed down, and I said, ' We want to catch Benin ; suppose we no catch them ship live for Benin we all die. Now keep good look-out, boys, and no drift to leeward, and to-morrow morning we sabby catch Benin.' They did keep good watch and order. I slept in the water and cared not to awake, but prolonged misery makes you awake, if only to look around.

" The head Krooman—Jim George—said, very pathetically, as if all hope had fled, ' Massa, you got daddy ?' ' Yes, Jim George, I got daddy.' ' You got mammy ?' ' Yes, I got mammy, Jim George.' ' All two be sorry and cry plenty to hear you done die.' ' Oh, Jim George, Jim George,' I said to myself, ' I did not want to think of that.'

" Whilst day lasted my spirits kept up wonderfully, but when the sun went away my heart sank with it, and that night I cried, and it makes me sad to tell it to you fellows now."

" Well, finish it, old fellow, and let us go to sleep," shouted a chorus of voices.

" On the fourth morning, to our intense joy, we saw the river Benin to leeward of us, and still further to leeward, but eight or ten miles at sea, were three vessels at anchor. I did not like to risk making for the vessels, for fear that, in our weak condition, we might not be able to fetch them, or that we might drift further to leeward unnoticed by them ; and, as the river was near, we put the boat straight over the foaming bar, running before the strong morning sea-breeze into the river, the water of which we eagerly drank, dipping our hands over the boat's side as it glided along. There was a bamboo-built factory on each side some miles up the river. We steered for the nearest, that on the left, which was occupied by Dr. Henry; the other, Sam Cheetham traded in. For many days all that I could comprehend was that they were good Samaritans. Their kindness saved my life, and restored the man-of-war's Kroomen to health also. I'll shut up now, boys, and tell you the rest some other time, if you care about it. Good-night."

No answer. Everybody was fast asleep. Jack chuckled, relighted his pipe, and thought, " Well, ' shiver my timbers,' I have been as good as a dose of morphia to you fellows; and the beauty of it is, that you don't know it."

No canoes came off to disturb our rest during the dark hours of night, and just as day broke on the 2nd of August, steam being up and the anchor weighed, away we went. Sunrise was glorious. The " rich father of the day " shed upon the river and its banks and the country beyond, hues which made our progress a vision of delight, and we suddenly awoke to enjoy it over early cups of coffee. When abreast the lower part of Tuesday Island, the man heaving the lead announced that the water had suddenly shoaled to nine feet; so our engine went slow, and, steering across to the right bank, we found safe navigation in three and three and a-half fathoms. The morning was very calm and pleasantly cool. Light clouds floating high up in the sky gave promise of a fine day. We passed several large trees covered with flowers looking like full-blown orange-lilies, but different from those observed yesterday.

When opposite to the village of Ekebro, about three hundred people appeared in front of their houses, just as

British villagers would turn out to see a waggon-load of live monkeys go by. We were highly amused at the chief, who was adorned with anklets and ivory bracelets. He gracefully made salaam, placing both hands upon the top of his head, bending his body low, and extending his hands to his feet. Being corpulent, evidently this polite movement was attended with difficulty. He had a white shirt on, but, as soon as we went by, he calmly took it off, and, assuming the character of Adam, handed it (it was his only garment) to an attendant, to be ready for the next steamer. The huts look very miserable. Above the town granaries are erected on props above the earth, with fires smouldering underneath to keep the contents dry.

The banks, increasing in height to nine feet above the river, are ornamented with very large trees, and the water becomes deeper, as we find no bottom with a five-fathom lead-line. The left bank above Ekebre sweeps gracefully round, and from the opposite side a long, white, sandy spit projects, plentifully dotted outside with fishing-stakes. One mile higher up, at another turn on the left bank, several large trees appear, with the land partly washed away from their roots. These trees are about to fall into the river. Others have recently dropped into it, and they form dangerous snags; so that, to save our paddle floats from destruction, we had to avoid them. The river is now three hundred yards wide, and it curves so very much that we are obliged to steam from one side to the other to get into the deepest water, generally found close under the steepest bank. In fact, whichever bank is most recently washed away, indicates, by the silent but swift current, the best channel for navigation.

We are now in the midst of what are termed, on Glover's excellent chart, and properly so, "hostile villages," from

which the natives fire and occasionally kill people on board
steamers passing to and fro. We are prepared, not only
with our four six-pounders, but with loaded rifles at hand, to
return smoky compliments on the instant. As the banks
increase in height we elevate the guns, so as to sweep the
line of human bodies in front of the villages. As certain as
we pass the village everybody turns out to gaze. At 8.50
A.M., we passed a creek which was once mistaken for the
main river, both being about 350 yards in width. The
steamer that went up this creek for a long way had to
return, so we profit by her experience. At Sabogrega, on
the left bank, about two hundred inhabitants were on view,
and several other villages, on both sides, declared the census
in the same manner. At these places we observed palm-oil
casks firmly jammed in canoes, bung upwards. Through the
round hole, the bung being out, the oil is poured from jars
to fill the casks; this saves hard labour in re-shipping heavy
puncheons. Ivory appears more abundant. Women wear
anklets made of it from four to six inches in depth. These
ladies wobble ungracefully as they come to the front.
Cripples and other invalids hobble out quite as fast, and
exhibit in many cases painful glimpses of unnaturally
swollen legs and breasts. Most of our shore audience make
signs as if they wanted something else to drink than the
refreshing river-water, and they jump and shout, evidently
inviting us to stop. Others throw sand towards the vessel.
But we pass on.

The forenoon turned out very hot, so we exposed our
clothing, railway-rugs, and boots, which were thoroughly wet
with yesterday's rain, to the sun, and they speedily became
comfortably dry. At noon we enjoyed a delightfully cool
breeze from seaward, and it was unexpectedly pleasant,
because we fancied that we were out of its cooling range, and

it proved more especially welcome as, half-an-hour after eight bells, our engine became heated, so that we were obliged to anchor to allow it to cool, and the breeze dispelled the hot calm.

The natives to-day are not so ferocious and wicked in appearance as those at the mouth of the river, but still they are very doubtful-looking customers. Everybody having experience of this river reports them as not to be trusted. They are tattooed, as most African tribes are, and the patterns vary according to prevailing custom. During infancy females are cut with sharp knives upon the face, body, and back. In many cases both sexes exhibit ridges of unnatural additional flesh, which rise from their smooth skin and quite disfigure them to our eyes, but to their own, perhaps, add beauty. Tiny hats placed upon a pile of coloured jute, towering above the heads of white girls, might not meet the approval of negresses.

The ladies sometimes appear attired with a pretty coloured cloth folded neatly round the waist, and it looks very coquettish; but, when suddenly called out from household duties to look at a passing steamer, many of them forget their garment, and stand gazing, unconscious that they are conspicuous figures in the landscape. Some are hideously ugly, with the strong limbs developed by hard work, which should pertain to man only. Others, on the contrary, are remarkable for their extreme beauty, perfect innocence, and attractive features. The absence of clothing is compensated for by the presence of anklets, armlets, and bead necklaces. Most of the beads are imported from Venice, but the country beads, which cannot be imitated, are highly prized, so much so that one bead is often worth more than the price of a slave.

Ascending the glorious river affords continual interest and

excitement. We are comfortably seated upon camp-stools beneath the bridge awning, before a table upon which Glover's chart is pinned for our guidance. Occasional refreshments are laid upon the table, but care is taken not to moisten the chart. The swift steamer steadily, in the smooth water, sweeping round curves, opens out new and brilliant views of tropical scenery, and, in a very happy and contented state of mind and body, we admire everything. It is like listening to a description of travel with a piano playing whilst machinery unrolls the panorama. But the absence of Irish potatoes, as in America that necessary accompaniment to any good dinner is called, also joints of British beef or mutton, and, on the other hand, the presence of mosquitoes and a few other trifles, recall the actual Niger. However, we cannot have at all times what we want, so must make the best of existing comforts. Butterflies and birds, in great variety, afford us pleasure. Stakes, nets, reed-cages, and other sorts of ingenious contrivances to catch fish, delight us. We know all about palm-oil, but we know absolutely nothing of other valuable products lining the banks of the river, and abounding in the country on either side of us far inland, which it will take at least one hundred years of extending commerce to appreciate, and, to the eye of a trader, properly ferret out and take home to pay.

At 4.30 P.M. we were abreast Stirling Island, and, keeping close to the right bank, swept round an extensive curve. Quantities of fern showed at the water's edge, enough to drive a fern collector out of his senses with joy at the variety. On many of the tall trees the nests of ants bulged out like lumps upon the heads of some folks. Myriads of ants in battalions, going to and from the nests, form black lines on the trunks 'of the trees. At one of the numerous villages, past which we steamed swiftly, they scolded us violently, making the instinctive and well-understood signals for rum. But we could not afford time to stop, so simply lifted our hats to the savage ladies and gentlemen and smiled. Many of them jumped, and gave vent to their feelings by swearing heartily. I am inclined to think so, because their actions appeared similar to those of white men given to that evil habit.

The natives of these villages attacked a steam-launch on its way from Onitsha to the sea. It was a small but handy vessel, about twelve tons capacity, and was navigated by two white men, assisted by seven negroes, and propelled by double screws. She grounded below Truro Island, and by doing so lost one of her screws. On the next day, whilst proceeding down the river, working her remaining screw, she ran foul of a snag. This happened at the upper end of Stirling Island. Collision with the snag bent the shaft in such a manner that the engine was disabled and the vessel rendered unmanageable. She then drifted to the lower end of Stirling Island, where she was hauled alongside the west bank, for the purpose of endeavouring to repair the shaft. The natives on the east bank, observing that a vessel was disabled, crossed the river in canoes with the object of capturing her. They landed on the west bank, and, sheltered by trees, commenced firing upon her. One Krooman was shot in the arm, and the bullets rattled upon the iron like hail. To escape from certain death they immediately shoved off from the bank, and the hapless vessel drifted by the current out of the range of fire. But, upon working the engine, the bent shaft caused the remaining propeller blade to cut a hole in the hull, the consequence of which was that she immediately filled with water, and in three minutes sank to the bottom of the river. To save their lives the people on board had to jump into their boat and cut it adrift, lest they should be taken under water with the vessel. Then the savages showed their true nature and gave chase. Rushing from their jungle fortress, and jumping into their canoes, they yelled and paddled after the little boat, as sharks swiftly swim, exhibiting only their black-fins above water, after a man overboard. It was a period of intense excitement to the wretched castaways. They had only saved bare life, had suddenly lost personal effects, their floating home, and everything to render life endurable. But the white men had each saved a modern rifle and suitable ammunition, and they knew how to use them. They blazed away at the canoes and kept them at a respectful distance. But the natives of each village, as they passed it, also opened fire upon them, and launched other canoes in pursuit. However, the two white warriors kept them at bay, until savages lower down the stream put off in canoes to intercept them. In this dilemma, hemmed in on every side by ferocious pirates, the white men made for the village of Gamautu, where for a short period an English factory had been established, but was abandoned. They naturally thought that the Gamautu people, being acquainted with the nature of white men, would certainly afford them protection, so they landed. But, to their intense disgust, they found they had jumped out of the frying-pan into the fire, for they were at once made prisoners and were very badly treated. Fortunately for them, a determined liberator was not far distant.

Captain Stott, in charge of the "Sultan of Soccatoo," bound up the river, happened to meet the launch coming down, near to Agberi, before the disasters commenced. Nine days afterwards he heard a native rumour that his countrymen were in trouble, and he instantly sent a black messenger with some brandy and biscuits, and, in case the report might only be a ruse to capture himself, he also sent

a sheet of paper and a lead-pencil to know the real state of
affairs. The messenger returned in forty-eight hours with
the same sheet of paper, on which was written in pencil—

"Gamautu, May 31st, 1875.
" Four A.M.

"Dear Stott,—Your messenger arrived at 1 A.M. this day, and is to
leave again at midnight. We are in a sad state here, these savages
threatening to kill Osborne and myself if we are not ransomed by another
day. I have sent you two letters before, but they tell me that the Kiama
people captured them, and have made the canoemen prisoners until the
Gamautu people give us up to Kiama. For God's sake come to our relief,
for there is no saying how far these savages will carry out their threats.
Many thanks for the brandy and biscuits and candles; they have quite
revived us. Hoping to see you down on receipt of this, I remain, yours
truly, in trouble,   " RICHARD CLIFF."

And underneath that was the following :—

" Midnight,
• " Gamautu, May 31st, 1875.

" Dear Stott,—Hearing that your messenger is still here, I take this
opportunity to let you know the state of affairs. The king and chiefs
have just ended a palaver about killing Osborne and myself. We are to
be killed in two days if not ransomed, according to the wish of Ju-Ju.
Your messenger has just come in and says he is going away now.
Hoping to see you to-day, as I am afraid it will be all up with us to-
morrow. The launch is sunk just below Stirling Island. Look out and
don't run foul of her, as she is laying almost in the channel.—I remain,
yours truly, in trouble,   " RICHARD CLIFF."

Captain Stott, taking the faithful messenger on board,—
who was an intelligent old man belonging to the village of
Agberi—to act as interpreter, steamed back seventeen miles,
and anchored off Gamautu. He found that the successful
pirates gave the black crew of the launch nothing to eat, so
he took them on board and fed them. He found, also, that
the two white men had received nothing during their long
detention but a few miserable plantains; so he sent them
by the interpreter hot meals from his own table. The
negotiations for ransom lasted for two days. The chiefs and

natives assembled in council demanded and got from the steamer each day before the palaver began three demijohns of rum, containing twelve gallons, with which they wetted their whistles. Then they shouted, foamed, and excitedly argued, as is customary with African savages. They demanded £400 in rum and goods as the price to liberate the white men. Captain Stott offered £200, but that amount was indignantly refused; however, on the second afternoon it was accepted. One half had to be landed on the beach before one white man was handed over. On landing the remaining half, the other white man was set at liberty, and he was coming off by the same boat in which he had landed, when the Gamau-tuans demanded the boat. However, he got on board the "Sultan of Soccatoo" in safety. The goods paid for our two countrymen consisted of matchets (rough cutlasses), cloth, and rum in demijohns. They took the largest payment in rum. The invoice price of the lot, £206 7s. 3d. Captain Stott hauled his vessel a little further into the stream, and at daybreak he opened fire on the town with four six-pounders, and each white man handled a Winchester rifle. The demijohns were in rows where they were landed, the natives being too drunk to remove them. The rifle practice at them was good. They were all smashed, and any savage trying to save one got properly potted. The pirates made a great orgy during the night; their drunken shouts of joy were heard on board the steamer; but they awoke to receive just and immediate punishment. At one P.M., the village being destroyed, the "Sultan of Soccatoo" proceeded on her voyage.

There is an excellent channel on the west side of Stirling Island affording shorter run, but we preferred the sweep round with certain deep water, and accordingly steamed so close to the east bank that if one of the big trees occasionally falling did so as we were passing, it would not be pleasant. Falling trees are rapidly swept away by the strong current, but sometimes they stick fast in the muddy bottom and form dangerous snags. Occasionally the snag creates a bank by accumulating alluvial deposit, and in time, perhaps, forms au island, and thus the current is changed.* We observed two canoes laden with something rolled in palm-leaves at a distance ahead ; they were paddled with unusual velocity, and apparently the paddlers were afraid of us, for they roared lustily. We quietly overhauled them, and shortly passed close to the canoes, quite deserted. The crews had jumped overboard, and, landing, disappeared in the bush. The people in the next canoe overtaken in a similar manner, were rather more civilised. There were about twenty-five men and women in it. They had a house forward and shade aft. These worthy savages ceased paddling and calmly stared, wondering, as they all do, what on earth can possibly induce white men to visit their country.

Two miles above Stirling Island, on the left bank, is Imblamah and half-a-dozen other villages, with short spaces between each. This part of the river is densely populated, and the inhabitants are most eager that we should stop ; but, on account of the hostility shown by their immediate neighbours, we do not present them with the rum elixir of African life, for which their mouths water as we appear in sight. Destroying their villages and stopping their supply of grog are the only known means of reprisal for brutal attacks upon friendly steamers, and the only way to inculcate lessons tending towards civility and civilisation. The signs for rum are ludicrously made the same at each place. The affection for such terribly fiery stuff as trade-rum is certainly an acquired taste, but I have heard it seriously argued that,

through its exciting, but sometimes softening, spiritual
influence, Christianity may eventually be introduced.   At
home it is generally believed that if a bottle of rum and a
Bible were offered to African savages to choose for " dash,"
out of simple pure-mindedness, they would eagerly grasp the
latter.   There may be a rush for Bibles in other savage
countries ; but here, alas ! it is really not the case.   Would
any white or black child prefer a work on algebra to a lollypop ?   Upon mature reflection, I am inclined to think that—
bless its little heart !—it would vote for the lollypop.

Large canoes lie alongside villages, ready to convey palm-
oil through creeks to ships at the mouths of the river, but
the owners have got no idea of industry beyond supplying
present wants, nor any notion of the value of time ; so that
frequently residents run short of rum, and then, as Toole
truly remarks, they "are not happy."   Rum is reported by a
native on board, who is evidently a connoisseur in the
article, to be well watered and coloured by the infusion of
tobacco-leaves by intermediate piratical brokers.   But the
wary old gentlemen who appreciate strong fiery stuff with no
nonsense about it, shake their grey wool as they enjoy it,
and descant upon the honest direct trading steamer from
which it was obtained ; exactly in the same way that sensible
middle-aged, and even veteran, Christians wag their ears
over good old port.

At ten minutes past six, when darkness approached, the
leadsman announced three fathoms, but the moment afterwards we suddenly struck upon a sandbank.   The shock
caused everybody to cling to something for support, or, failing
that, to fall flat upon the deck.   The deckhouses creaked and
threatened to dissolve partnership.   Working the engine hard
astern got us off into deep water in twenty minutes.   We
sounded the compartments, found no water rushing in, so we

anchored at once, and dined hastily by candlelight, on account of the terrible but usual invasion of insects. Meantime a boat was lowered and soundings taken across the river. The energetic sounders proved that the channel had altered. The river is one mile broad, and, as before remarked, the alteration of the channel, common in all large rivers, may be traced to a snag. Stoppage to cool the heated engine, and getting aground caused a general depression, and we felt snarlish, uncompanionable, and totally disinclined to talk. The leadsman blamed another nigger, whose duty it was to shout orders from the captain to the engineer, for getting the vessel ashore. Lies were told on both sides; but they are not uncommon whenever there are two sides to a question, and falsehood excites as little attention here as at Board of Trade inquests on wrecked vessels at home. Discord of any sort, on board small vessels, is naturally known to everybody and heartily disliked; so, creeping underneath our mosquito-curtains to our really happy beds, we listened to the sound of concertinas, penny-whistles, and mouth-organs, practised upon by our negro students; also to the merry talk and laughter of the people who had been sea-sick, but who now rejoiced in good appetites, steaming over smooth water and enjoying perfect repose at night. The music, however, did not soothe the savage beasts residing in adjacent jungles, for they set up a variety of interesting howls. We turned over on our mats, and felt so glad that their voices only could reach us. Gradually most of us fell asleep, and the only noises then heard were the eternal chorus of bull-frogs and crickets, varied by an occasional roar from a crocodile or loud snore from a sleeper. But a missile thrown by the nearest awakened "sleepist," at the head of the "snorist," caused a mild "cuss," and subsequently silence reigned in the court.

On the next break of day, crossing to the east side, we

steamed over what was marked on the chart "dry." The first villagers turned out rubbing their eyes. We had woke them too soon—they must slumber again. They did not utter a word, and we laughed at their not being sufficiently lively to ask for rum, as with limp limbs, like truants from school, they went to bed again. At Agberi and other places they acted differently. Having had more time to observe our approach, they shouted for rum, but we simply looked at the canoes loading palm-oil, and passed away, like time. Taking the channel to the west of Truro Island, we found shallow instead of deep water. At the north end of it the navigation was so difficult that we had to anchor and take soundings. We ascertained that we must either go back and take the channel to the east of Truro or shove through a very narrow passage between a bank and the island. Nobody likes to go back, and we succeeded at the latter, and shaving trees, broke off overhanging branches. Our deck was so filled with oak and mistletoe-looking stuff that the ship appeared like "Birnam wood moving towards Dunsinane." In the most exciting moment sit is impossible not to admire the beautiful or the comic. Our chief-officer shouted to all hands, "Here come along, all you beggars, and clear away this 'Christmas!'"

The east side of Truro Island affords the best navigation now, but it is liable to change. When within two hundred yards of the east bank we got stuck aground again. For a long time the engine backed, and the passengers, as requested, rushed to and fro to shake the little ship, and she did shake off. But there was muttered swearing amongst the crew—"oaths not loud but deep"—at our grounding so frequently. However, when from two to three and a-half fathoms were announced, they apologised for rudeness unduly displayed under moments of excitement, and they politely asked each other to partake of coffee, and related short but amusing anecdotes, so that cheerfulness was restored.

Shortly after leaving Truro Island we opened out on our left the Wari branch, leading to Benin, a most important navigable stream.   Beecroft ascended it in 1841.   James Pinnock, an enterprising young merchant, who had established factories on the Benin, was the next to ascend it in 1872, thus not only establishing direct traffic between Niger trading places and the sea at Benin, but saving time and avoiding the risk of running deeply-laden river steamers at sea.   Cultivated farms now appear.   Villages are more numerous, well adorned with devil-houses similar to those at Porto Novo.   At dark we anchored below the celebrated town of Abo.

During dinner one of the missionaries stated that *he* was not asleep the other night when one of the white men told about being adrift in a boat and landing at Benin, and, as he was to leave the ship at Onitsha, he would like to hear the story finished.   It was put to the vote and carried.   After pipes and coffee in cups, with the saucers reversed to keep suicidally-inclined insects from drowning themselves, we arranged our grass sleeping-mats, hard leathern pillows, and, rigging our "skeeter" bars convenient for discourse, the yarn was resumed.

"Well, my Christian friends and brother sinners," said Jack, "I told you that I and nine faithful Krooboys landed in a starving condition and nearly dead at Benin, and that the two white men, trading there kindly supplied all our wants.   We were thankful to Providence for preserving our lives, and also for restoration to the delightful society of our fellow-men.   I stayed with Dr. Henry and learnt trading with the natives.   Those were the days when ' palm-oil ruffians,' as they were called—and sometimes with good reason—made money hand over fist. Henry wanted me to stay for a couple of years as a paid clerk, but I did not like Benin ; it was too lonely. We could only play 'all-fours' at night before bedtime, and slap our faces as we felt mosquitoes alighting to feed thereon, unless when I crossed the river to see Sam Cheetham, and then we had a jolly time together. Cheetham had a schooner, and, as I wanted to get away from the river to join any mail steamer, he kindly offered myself and the nine Kroomen cast away with me a free passage in her to Fernando Po, which offer I thankfully accepted. I shall never forget his kindness as long as I live. Meantime, during a prolonged stay, the Kroomen, sailing or pulling our English-boat, took me long distances up the river and through the creeks, taking advantage of the tides. I visited Jebouffu and Jerry, venerable chiefs, and true friends to white people. They were highly-delighted to possess long malacca-canes, gold-mounted, with their names and titles inscribed on the tops, which had been sent out to them from the Queen. These sticks acted as good as written letters, for the bearer delivered by word of mouth messages from his master, whose stick in the hand of the proud messenger constituted his authority as envoy-extraordinary. Jebouffu and Jerry welcomed me heartily as the white man who had crossed the bar of the river in a boat when the water was 'sass' (saucy). I visited another chief up the river on the right bank, who sent by his 'stick' an invitation, and also a canoe. I took the Krooboys with me, who really enjoyed fun, and, with their pretty man-of-war dress, formed an escort fit for royalty. They carried me over the mud around the canoe right into the presence of the chief. He was seated hammering upon a piano, and, jumping up, gave me a hearty welcome and commenced to talk. He was very gracious, and, like a good fellow, intimated inquiringly the nature of fluid. He said,

'You like-ee champagne?' 'Yes, I do like champagne—when I can get it.' And then he continued, 'What be good for white man, be good for black man? No be so?' 'Be so,' I replied vigorously. The retainers, as usual, fell upon their faces and snapped fingers whilst we liquored up, and a lot of girls behind us, separated by a screen, giggled and laughed at our friendship. They were uncommonly curious, for several pretty ebony faces peeped through the folds of the screen, but, as the chief did not introduce them, I avoided asking him how he liked a Mormon life. Suddenly he desired me to try the piano, which was a good one, but it looked very much out of place stuck unevenly upon a mud floor. I could only play 'In my cottage' and 'Yankee Doodle' with the right hand, but, fearing no criticism, I went blind at the low notes with my left hand, and the effect was electric. All hands turned out and danced like mad. I never saw such a sight, and I rattled away like 'old boots.' 'Yankee Doodle' 'knocked' the courtiers and also the girls. The piano wanted tuning, and there was no tuner nearer than Europe, but the nearest approach to time was sufficient, and it was jolly. The Krooboys rushed in; I don't know why they did so, but, faithful fellows, they perhaps thought that I was being executed. However, seeing what was going on, they joined in the merriment, and we were all well fed on delicious palm-oil chop and yams, until Jim George, the head Krooman, stated solemnly, 'Sun only lib one hour, massa; come home before day done gone.' We shook hands all round, and the Krooboys, laughing all the time, carried me over the mud into the canoe, after the manner of Toole in 'The Artful Dodger,' and the beauty of it is, that it was at her Majesty's expense also.

" Well, at last we went on board Cheetham's schooner,

but for two days, as the weather was bad, we anchored at the mouth of the river under the north side abreast Fishtown. The king of this place was called 'Suffolk'—christened, I believe, by Sam Cheetham; but why 'Suffolk' is a mystery. However, he was proud of the name, and, although only a poor man, existing upon tribute levied upon fish—which trade is precarious everywhere, as fishermen, like farmers, always plead poverty and bad seasons when taxes have to be paid—we made a festival out of seabiscuits brought from Cheetham's schooner, and palm-wine supplied by royalty, and we enjoyed a pleasant interchange of ideas. At length we put to sea, and four days afterwards arrived at Fernando Po. I wrote a letter to the commander of H.M.S. 'Waterwitch,' describing the brave conduct of the Krooboys and their faithfulness to me, and as the flagship H.M.S. 'Penelope,' Admiral Bruce, was at anchor in Clarence, I went on board and told the kind-hearted admiral what good fellows they were."

"Did you never see them again?" inquired one of the listeners.

"Oh, yes. I was out on the coast again as jolly as a sandboy in less than six months afterwards, and brought each boy a good sailor's knife with his name engraved on a little metal plate let into the haft. Let me see ; 'Headman Jim George' on one, 'Second headman Ben Jumbo,' 'Jack Andrews,' 'Tom Tobin,' 'Tom Walker,' 'William Walker,' ' Prince of Wales,' ' New Prince,' and ' Bottle of Rum.'

"The Admiral had heard of my being adrift, and told me that H.M.S. 'Polyphemus' and the mail steamer, on the morning after our being driven out to sea, had both steamed at parallel distances forty miles down the coast, and then, giving us up for lost, had returned to Lagos. We were much further out at sea at the time. I stayed ashore

at Clarence—now St. Ysabel—at the invitation of Mammy
Matthews, and went with her and her family and friends on
picnic excursions whilst waiting for the steamer from England, which happened to be broken down, so that two
months elapsed.   We had a happy time of it, visiting pretty
retreats on farms growing pineapples, as common as turnips
at home, only the fruit of one is below and the other above
the ground.   It was too happy to last.

"One day, returning from a distant farm in a boat, a
tornado came on, and it thoroughly drenched everybody, but
the sun soon dried us again before landing.   That night, as
I walked up the steep hill home, I felt that my backbone
ached and my head was inclined to wobble painfully, and,
never having felt anything like it before, at ten I told Mrs.
Matthews, and she said, 'My dear boy, you have got your
first fever, and I will nurse you,' and she did, faithfully and
lovingly.· She had nursed Richard Lander when she was a
young girl.   Weeks elapsed, and all that I can recollect is
the great kindness of Mrs. Matthews and her daughters, and
also a habit I got into of shutting one eye to take a good
aim and shy medicine bottles at my attendant, a negro boy
asleep on a mat close to my sofa-bed, to ask him to give me
a drink of water.   The sofa was close against a window, and
when the window was opened at daybreak the branch of an
orange-tree, laden with ripe green fruit, overshadowed and
revived me.   Admiral Bruce very kindly offered me a
passage to Ascension in his ship, but a mail steamer,
sweetly baptized the 'Hope,' conveyed me home.   Off
Cape Palmas we met an outward-bound steamer, and
from her we got a newspaper containing a short notice of
my death, and that of the nine Kroomen.   'All drowned.'
It is not often that epitaphs are read by the defunct.
Home, eagerly looked for, was reached at last.   Mourning

parents clung fondly to the messenger from the sea, and

> 'The pleasure of that moment hath sufficed
> To sweeten all my life with its remembrance.'

Good-night boys." "Gur ni—" responded drowsy mates. But the missionaries were awake, and they warmly returned thanks.

CHAPTER V.

WHEN we steamed up towards the creek, which leads to
the town of Abo, a large canoe met us, containing
a young savage of influence. He induced us to anchor, as
the chiefs ashore wished to make arrangements to re-estab-
lish trade ; and, as Abo is the most important and central
part of the palm-oil region, we were equally desirous to
ascertain their views. They came on board with droves of
attendants, and a long palaver ensued, rendered pleasant to
them by frequent potations. They offered fair promises of
protection if we would land goods to barter for palm-oil.
But, on the strength of similar promises, other factories had
been built, filled and supplied with goods, and in course of
time they were duly plundered ; so all confidence was
naturally lost in the Abo people. Trading factories were
afterwards started on the opposite bank of the river, higher
up, at a place called Ndoni. The Abo people now know
that prosperity results by steady trading with white men,
and the time has arrived to give them another trial by establishing a trading-post in charge of a determined agent,
backed by well-armed servants.

We informed the chiefs that we should consider the
matter, and, placing in their canoes a few bottles of the
popular beverage, told them to clear out, "hook it,"
"vamos the ranch," or other words to the same effect. We
had lost nearly a whole day over their drinking palaver.

They lingered as long as a drop of rum was on view, and would not budge ; so we up anchor and steamed ahead so rapidly, that some of the canoes, not having painters sufficiently strong to be towed, broke adrift. Upon this the chiefs and their retainers on board yelled, and we bundled them into other canoes. A few minutes afterwards two canoes shot out from the opposite bank of the river, and made towards us. The paddlers gave utterance to unearthly guttural sounds intended to express joy. We stopped, and the smaller one, containing a live prince of the Akassa stamp, came alongside. He climbed on board, just as if he were entering his own house, and ordered the small canoe to go home and the larger one to follow the steamer.

We stopped at Ndoni. The factories here are excellently situated, convenient to the mouth of a branch creek which leads to New Calabar, from whence traffic is carried on to Bonny, inside Breaker Island. Bonny river is not a branch of the Niger, but the river westward of it, called the New Calabar river, is. As we had a little daylight left, we proceeded. Meantime we entertained the prince on the bridge with champagne, but he appeared to think it hardly strong enough. I cannot spell his name, and to pronounce it properly requires a cold in the head and a violent sneeze to jerk it out.

> " I am not good at Niger names,
> And so I call him Simple James."

Simple James was dressed in a naval engineer's uniform coat, with bright buttons, and blue cloth trousers rolled up over his bare feet, exposing a string of cowrie-shells on his left ankle ; a blue silk-velvet cap, with gold band and tassel, completed his costume. He is related to the royal family of Abo, and appears a harmless imbecile. Just after leaving Ndoni rain descended in torrents, so that darkness set in earlier than usual, and we anchored in the centre of the stream, here about a mile wide. Simple James dined with us and enjoyed sherry amazingly, but he pulled a long face over half-a-glass of beer, given for trial. A few of the last of our potatoes—"white man's yam"—he managed to bolt without an observation. We conversed through two interpreters. A telegraphic message might be sent round the globe and a reply received long before we understood what was meant. Our interpreter spoke Houssa and English. The young savage of importance who boarded us at Abo, and who came on in the steamer, was Houssa by birth, and spoke Houssa and Abo; and so we slowly comprehended.

As dinner was about finished, Simple James produced a small parcel rolled in paper containing faded letters— "books"—from white men, stating what a good fellow he was, and christening him "The friend of the white man." Just then the noise of a horn blown violently was heard; it came from the large warlike canoe which had followed us from Abo. Up jumped Simple James. He rushed on deck, shouting at the top of his voice, and presently ushered in his favourite wife. She walked into our small saloon as ungracefully as a brewer's horse would enter a drawing-room, "by rayson" of the heavy lumps of ivory worn above her ankles, which clanked together at every movement, sounding like the noise of clogs and pattens made by Lancashire witches upon stone pavement. Close at her heels was a man attired in scarlet cloth, and also a hideous-looking Ju-Ju-man. These courtiers took their places, standing behind Simple James and his wife. Several attendants of lower rank squatted on the deck, and the windows were crowded with eyes. To say the least of it, the place was warm.

The moment that the princess seated herself she dropped her silk robe—her only covering—below the surface of the

table, and thereby revealed a remarkably handsome plump
bust. We had no Solomon to sing a song in her praise ; but
failing that, everybody helped her to the best that we had to
eat and drink. In addition to the remains of dinner, tins of
preserved meat were opened, and the table strewn with
good crisp captain's biscuits, and all speedily disappeared.
She occasionally, in the gentlest manner, handed a glass of
sherry to the Ju-Ju-man, and also to the man in red. But
those eminent worthies intimated, by making wry faces,
that sherry was far too mild for their courtly discriminating
palates. Rum was produced, and, whilst each professor
imbibed the first glass, he made a subdued noise of delight, a
sort of "umm," with closed lips and sparkling eyes. We
had found out their favourite vintage, and they laughed
and made merry, and everybody else was merry also to see
them merry, as *their* poet-laureate might remark (wonder
if the scarlet man were he ?). They literally " walked " into
the rum, without water, glass after glass, and enjoyed it.
The table was soon cleared of eatables. After the select
guests were filled they handed scraps to the yeomanry.
Knives and forks had been placed before Simple James and
his consort, but fingers were preferred. After the buxom
young lady had eaten what she wanted, she kindly handed
her plate to the Ju-Ju-man, and he made the platter clean.
She then called for a pipe, and her husband and the others,
thereby acknowledging her as the "grey mare," did the
same. Through the interpreter it was intimated that they
were sitting over a large quantity of powder, so that smoking
would not be advisable. They laughed heartily, understood
the danger, and all adjourned to the bridge deck, where pipes
and tobacco were produced and enjoyed by the light of
lanterns.

The heavy rain ceased during dinner. The atmosphere

11

became clear, and the moon shone brightly, with its wide and tender light illuminating the river. And the lovely stars (only to be seen to perfection in the tropics), those beautiful "forget-me-nots of the angels," assisted the moon, and brighter silvery light robed that "Ethiope night." But look upon that picture, and then glance beneath the farthing-candle-lighted awning upon this.

I filled my largest wooden pipe with cut cavendish, and, smoking it until the ventilation was correct, wiped the amber mouthpiece, and gracefully presented it to the princess. She was charmed by such delicate attention, and blew clouds like a cottage chimney in a wood. The united tobacco-smoke in the still night drove the smaller insects away. Camp-stools were occupied by our visitors, excepting by the Ju-Ju-man, who stood steadying himself behind Simple James. I never witnessed such a hideous old savage as this Ju-Ju-man. He was covered with large yellow spots, and had actually raw places upon his hands and arms. He wore necklaces, armlets, leglets, and a browband made of cowrie-shells. A heap of mystic-looking packages, mixed up with horns, leopards' teeth, leathern cases, and feathers, suspended from his neck, positively weighed him down. He certainly is the most heavily-endowed incumbent of my clerical acquaintance. His clothing consisted of a rich garment, rolled round his waist, and a fancy cap upon his head. He evidently ruled the scarlet man and the retainers with proper severity, but was kind to the lady and attentive to his prince. He inquired, through the interpreters, whether I was in his line, and the question was put to me. The stern, searching eyes of Satan were fixed upon me demanding the truth, and the truth is I should have liked to have sold Satan, but, as the Bishop was there, I dared not assume a virtue which did not exist; so I simply held up my hands, after the manner of the Apostles over the Church of the Lateran, which might mean anything, but did not present him with a Bible and beg of him to read, mark, &c., it; for rum, at that period, was his soul's sincere delight. He is an artful old dodger, and as full of flattery as the courtiers in "Barbe-bleue." Whenever Simple James said anything, he yelled out something like "Ha! ha!" or "Ho! ho!"—evidently meant for affirmative or negative jerks to chime entire approval of his master's taste. "Ha! ha!" said the prince. "Ditto," echoed the Ju-Ju-man. "I will not-ta!" roared the prince. "Don't-ah!" shrieked the Ju-Ju-man, and "Right you are!" (translated from Abo freely).

Simple James told the agent, whom he had seen several times before, that he knew that he was coming, for his Ju-Ju-man told him so. He asked for a "book." "Yes," the agent replied, "I will give you a book when I come back; that is, if you will make your people cut plenty of wood for the steamer's use; but now you do nothing to assist us. You do not even bring a single fowl or a yam, and we have got neither on board. If you want English people to bring plenty of cloth and salt, guns, powder, and rum, you must make your slaves collect palm-oil to exchange for those desirable things." Simple James, if he had had any manly feeling about him, would have felt ashamed at being lectured, and promised amendment; but he changed the subject adroitly by pointing to his coat. Between the two brass buttons behind, a slight slit was observed by a sailor, who said that "A stitch in time would save nine;" but it was not stitched in time. The coat was buttoned in front, to exhibit within range of his own vision, as well as to the vulgar crowd, two rows of brass buttons shining like stars up and down his "buzzum" and stomach. But the slit had suddenly burst, either by sneezing or by his getting *tight,* and extended up to

the back of his neck, exposing his epidermis to the moonshine.
He was at once presented with an overcoat, one of the
patent paletots warranted by an extremely polite "counter-
jumper" not to shrink in rain; but didn't it?   It was dry,
and, although now too small for the owner, was the very
thing for Simple James.   A signal was made to his wife to
mend the other coat.   She took no notice of the rudeness,
but sat enjoying her pipe.   She was much above that sort of
thing.   She was beautiful, was prized for being so, could
command slaves to work, and knew her position. It gradually
dawned upon us that Simple James was a mistake.   He
showed no wish to develop trade.   His love for white men
was for what he could get out of them; and his instinct only
showed superior to the Akassa monarchs in having a more
brilliant retinue to accompany him, leaving to his Ju-Ju and
scarlet men the arrangement of details.   But these detailers,
wandering about the deck, appropriated everything that was
loose, and calmly stowed things away in the canoe.   A sailor,
seeing campstools thus stolen, stopped them in transit.
Simple James, when informed of it, told the scarlet man to
"look to it, look to't, ha, ha!" and the Ju-Ju-man echoed
the sentiment.   This official, with zeal too excessive to be
genuine, thrashed some of the paddlers, made them howl
properly, and restored a few articles from the canoe.   Our
chief engineer facetiously pointed to the funnel and told
them to take *it*.   The steward, disgusted with their conduct,
remarked, "Hif this is the vay the royal femly do 'ere, wot
the doose is the lower horders and the vorking-clawsses
like?"

The princess so won upon everybody by her natural good-
nature and by her kindness to her servitors, that she was
presented with a piece of thick silk.   Without saying a word
she opened it out, got a couple of her servants to extend it

before her, and calmly, but with brightened eyes, felt the texture, exactly as ladies do in Bold-street. Female love for soft raiment and refinement all the world over! Scissors, fish-hooks, a looking-glass, "*Punch* his Almanac," a bowie-knife, and other useful articles of feminine attraction were also given; sailors, firemen, and even missionaries contributing. I ventured to hint to Simple James—through the medium—that, for the benefit of European society, in case white ladies desired to adopt the fashion, it would be well to measure the size of his wife's ivories. He readily accorded permission. There was no "green-eyed monster" about him —quite the reverse. The anklets measured twenty-seven inches in circumference, were eight inches long, averaged two inches thick, and weighed at least ten pounds each. I could only estimate the weight by balancing them in both hands. They had been slipped on when she was a growing girl, and would be buried with her. They must have been sawn from the lower ends of tusks, once belonging to a gigantic elephant, but the fashionable young lady had invisible pads fitted inside the lower edge of the ivory, to prevent its hard substance hurting her ankles. They looked like the white tops of boots peculiar to grooms, worn loosely over the ankles, with all the leather below cut away.

Simple James had a severe headache. This melancholy fact caused no surprise; for if sherry, beer, champagne, and about an equal quantity of the total in rum, did not create internal discomfort, why the Highlandman's "aqua-fifty" in a bucket would only represent a mild beverage. However, it is well to bear charity to all men, and make every allowance. Perhaps the potatoes disagreed with him; so blame the potatoes. Do not geese and plum-puddings, at merry Christmas gatherings, act as scapegoats for overflow of spirits, subsequent depression, and "tapering off?"

The Ju-Ju-man now came to the front, and, respectfully taking off the cap covering his chieftain, solemnly muttered a prayer to Ju-Ju ; he then spat upon that aching head three times, alternately blowing gentle but rummy zephyrs, like the hiccup of a fallen alderman who had "loitered in a wine vaults." What will not faith in your pastor do? Simple James was speedily himself again, and loudly called for more rum. But our trading agent had had enough of the lot; he ordered two demijohns of rum into the canoe in charge of the scarlet man, who seemed to act also as lord-chamberlain of the rum pantry. "The friend of the white man" called for more liquor. The steward suggested that the letter "har" omitted from this title would render it more "appropriater." Meantime the mediums were busy translating the list of presents which other steamers had given him. It had no effect; so at last they went into the canoe, solely to prevent the two demijohns of rum being "spiled." The young and really beautiful princess was overcome. A missionary said that "it was sad;" and a sailor remarked that she was "three sheets in the wind, and the other one fluttering." But she was only showing her good-nature and jollity. Several decent people wished fervently that they had only got half the complaint of the pagan prince. Attendants, representing clouds, wafted the princess, like Guido's Aurora, through the air into the canoe, and placed her tenderly and lovingly beside his royal "tightness," Simple James, who tried with maudlin affection to steady the procession, but it was too much for his nerves. He had to be carried first to his place of honour, when he commenced to take his clothes off and wildly "chuck" them to his attendants, who folded up each article to be ready for the next ironclad.

The canoe left the vessel's side with drums beating and

horns blowing. Presently we heard, wafted through the balmy night, the sweet voice of "Aurora" leading the choir to a hymn. Hark! Is it "Flow on thou shining Niger?" No. It is! it is!—the beautiful Abo version of "We won't go home till morning!"

> "And so let Simple James take wing,
> No more of him I'm going to sing."

As trading steamers run to and fro upon this river, hostile natives become gradually acquainted, and appreciate each other's good qualities. These folks are as much strangers now as the natives of England and France were only a few centuries ago. Improved means of navigation, free-trade principles, and personal knowledge of foreigners, gradually obliterate ancient prejudice handed down from nursery to nursery. Many of our esteemed and sage ancestors firmly believed that Frenchmen lived entirely upon frogs. Onitsha people, with a similar notion, think that natives of Abo and all tribes on the river below their elevated position eat nothing but man. Wherever sheep and oxen abound, or antelope jump, or monkeys skip from tree to tree, or rats and mice are to be had, man-eating is not practised. In addition to an infinite variety of animals, the land above the Delta yields cereals in abundance ; maize (Indian corn) is the principal staple of life; so, on this river, cannibalism naturally ceases at Onitsha.

On the morning after Simple James left us, we were so "seedy" that it was nearly six o'clock before anybody but those on watch awoke. But, as the furnaces were banked, the fires only required stirring up and fresh fuel adding to make the steampipe howl. No one but a very sound sleeper can lie unconscious with boilers "diddering" beneath, shaking every bone in the drowsy body, destroying the peaceful tenor of pleasant dreams, especially about "Aurora."

It is better to awake to real life and calmly observe the dew, like heavy rain-drops, sparkling everywhere outside the awning, and also to glance at the galley coffee-pot. "Not boil yet, san." Closer inspection of the galley shows that the cook has only just awoke; he is putting a few sticks underneath the coffee-pot, and applying a match warranted only to light on the box. He had dreamt about "Aurora," as well as other Christians, Mahometans, and Pagans; so he was loth to be torn away from his idea of the beautiful and the true, and suddenly resume the scullion business. It is not wise to kick up a row with a dreaming cook, for he manages the most important part of earthly joy, and can make the coffee strong or weak as he is treated well or ill. Another short snooze has to be worked off in a chair, until the sun over the trees and the coffee from the galley announce real day. Meantime, as the vessel moves, it becomes apparent that the banks are not so thickly wooded. The river increases in width, becomes deeper, and at eight o'clock we stick in mud abreast the centre of Bullock Island, near to the northern point of a smaller island, but only for a short time. At half-past nine we stopped off the town of Osomari to land stuff to traders. Here we observed canoes, about seven feet long, just able to carry one man and a few yams, paddled more easily and swiftly than the "Rob Roy" coffin playthings dotting our home lakes and rivers.

A low point of yellow sand extends into the river from Osomari, on which, being convenient for canoes, markets are held until the still rising river overflows it. Natives crowded, both at the town and market, to look at the steamer. We saw herds of speckled cattle, and the sight caused us tenderly to long for beef-steak. The country looks like Eastham on the Mersey, and the river is about the same width when the Mersey is at full tide. Groves of palm, sprinkled with a few tall silk-cotton-trees, are only wanted at Eastham to complete the resemblance. We now come to beautiful islands, plentifully adorning the grand river, increasing in grandeur and width the higher we ascend the Delta. At every village the natives assemble in front, as usual; but, as we steam further from them and out of reach of their voices, we can only admire their improved dwellings, their extensive farms, and their brilliant country, gradually rising upwards into wolds like those of happy Lincolnshire, but better covered with timber.

Trading factories have sprung up at Alenso and Oko villages, and their situation is the prettiest that we have yet seen; for, from their pleasant verandahs, delightful views of highlands extend in a north-easterly direction. The adjacent villages, or any suitable position on the bank, afford sites for any number of traders. Young men possessing good strong constitutions, combined with a knowledge of Manchester, Sheffield, and Birmingham goods, able also to handle a rifle, cook food, or do anything rough and enjoy doing so, as well as eating heartily, might do worse than try to settle here. If they understood the baneful influence, but productive nature, of trade rum, guns, and powder, and, in fact, comprehended simple, ordinary requirements to render life happy, they could start from the Nun, Brass, or Benin mouth in their own steam-launch laden with sawn planks, uprights, nails, and sheets of corrugated iron, to form a roof covering, a dwelling, and a shop. Selecting their location, freely granted by chiefs owning the soil, upon presents being made, they can easily create a new village and christen it what they please. Whilst the house is building the steam-launch plies to and from the ocean steamer. British goods are received, shop opened, and produce purchased on such remunerative terms, that in a few years original squatters will be well able to retire into private life and leave the hard work and exposure to an unhealthy climate to others equally ambitious but better able to endure climate and fatigue. These pioneers should be relieved by other white men, one year in England and the next on the Niger. But if they "greed" too much after wealth and stay too long in Central Africa without change, Nature steps in, and allots them a permanent tenancy of "six feet of earth." But, nevertheless, the trade by such means extends, and will continue to do so, far into the unknown country on either side the river, and also far above the Confluence, to partially unknown districts, and, in respect to the upper waters of the Binue, to places really unknown. All these regions yield valuable produce, which is eagerly bought up at home and turned to a thousand good uses. Thus remunerative trade develops and flourishes. The same may be said of any navigable river in Africa, excepting the Nile, of which the Khedive, assisted by his bondholders, enjoys the benefit.

We see before us high land, and presently stony banks appear. We have cleared the Delta, and anchor off Onitsha during daylight on the 5th day of August. In addition to the anchor, we take the turn of one hawser round a huge silk-cotton-tree forward, and another one round a tree aft; so that the little vessel is perfectly moored close to the shore convenient for business. She is hauled into a sheltered embowered haven, as snug as if berthed in dock. The straight outlines, a picture of modern skill in shipbuilding, relieved by the graceful trees, create a feeling of happiness to everybody, and, having perfect confidence in the good intentions of the natives, we rejoice and go comfortably to sleep.

Onitsha is the northern limit of the palm-oil trading region, and it is the first town on the river built upon rising ground. Higher up the country Shea butter and ivory are the principal articles of trade, but still palm-oil is extensively cultivated as an article of food. The town is very pleasantly situated on elevated land at a distance of two miles from the east bank of the river. A romantic wide lane runs north of it, sloping southwards. On each side of this beautiful lane silk-cotton-trees grow. Some of them, starting double from the roots, rise two hundred feet into the air, and are abundantly furnished with wide-spreading branches. Trees of shorter growth, clothed also with thick foliage, exist below the giants of the soil, thus affording a double shade, and springy mossy banks about their roots yield grateful rest to the weary traveller. Varieties of palm, banana, paw-paw, long grass, and other rapidly-growing vegetation, cover all the land, excepting what is occupied by dwellings and enclosures surrounding residences, or tracts of bush-land cleared of trees, exactly in the same style of North American backwoodism, to create Adam-like farms. From the great number of houses in ruins, which are partially covered over with jungle—dangerous and snake-abiding looking places to explore, in some parts of the town extending over many acres—Onitsha has evidently been a larger place than it is now. Cultivated gardens and bush-trained arbours are plentiful, forming deliciously cool retreats during the heat of the day. But for the squalid dwellings, a stranger, dazzled by the bright scenery, might fancy being suddenly transported to one of the gorgeous scenes in the "Arabian Nights Entertainments." A wall covered with vegetation surrounds the town; the entrances to it are artificially constructed by training straight trees, closely planted into screen-work. At each side of these trees, like portions of the Maze at Hampton

Court, a narrow passage introduces you into a dark arbour, and passing through you enter the town. All about these entrances, and in all places of public resort, rude images of their favourite evil spirit appeal to the generous public. These 'images are carefully housed over, and their well-known drinking habits are abundantly supplied from the Niger. But, in addition, surrounding every house, garden, arbour, road, lane, or farm, articles of fetish are abundant. exactly as at Porto Novo and many other parts of the coast; and thus good or evil habits extend by permeating instinct.

A few years ago our agent obtained permission from the King to open a factory, and through the Rev. C. Taylor, a Sierra Leone missionary, who kindly interpreted, the king intimated what particular sort of beads, colour of silk-velvet, and other articles would be acceptable to him. It was arranged that his personal presents should be sent to the palace after dark, and not given along with inferior gifts to the head people, lest their envy might be prejudicial to his happiness. The time for audience was fixed two days before it took place, as the King had to consult his magicians on the subject. Silk-velvet robes, bright cotton prints, turkey-red chintz, razors, powder in kegs, bars of iron, guns, swords, knives, looking-glasses, and demijohns of the darling rum, were divided; so much for seven chiefs, the same for the old women who constituted the Board of Trade, and about a similar quantity, but less of the rum, for the young dandies about the court, who were too full of natural vigour to require any stimulant. Twenty Kroomen and a lot of native volunteers carried the presents upon their heads, and a procession naturally formed. As we approached the town a great crowd followed, not only composed of men, women, and children, but also of that invariable accompaniment to all festive proceedings—dogs. The road to the palace winds and doubles; at length a long, hard, mud-carved wall looms in view. Heaps of spears, guns, bows, and arrows are deposited resting against the wall, for the visitors are compelled to enter the palace without their deadly weapons. A hole in the wall is the way in, and the next moment we see King Obi Akazua, a living effigy of Guy Fawkes, a thin, wiry old man of light bronze colour, conspicuous amongst the congregation of black faces around him. He is supposed never to leave his palace, and is reputed to be an influential man amongst his neighbouring Ossian-like chieftains.

As the palace is only furnished with mud seats, the Bishop very kindly sent chairs and forms from the mission for our accommodation, so that we are comfortably seated on the left of the mud throne. The dais is concealed by bright patterned mats and soft leopard skins. A hard, leathern, elbow-accommodating seat, like a double Mexican saddle placed sideways, affords grateful rest for the royal arms. In one hand the King wields a long black horse's tail fixed into a handle, with which he smites at insects. Convenient to his other hand is a bell about the size used by British bellmen in remote villages. He has frequently to use this bell and ring it violently to obtain silence in the court. The reception place is 120 feet long and 50 feet wide; it is open in the centre, and the sides, about six feet wide, elevated above the centre, are sheltered by palm-leaf thatch. The seediest barn in Yorkshire would be much more suitable for debating state matters. But the climates differ. On the right of the King are assembled chiefs, profusely decorated with wide cowrie tiaras; and feathers, once belonging to brilliant birds, stick out of their wool. Below them are a few sensible old women representing trade. Beneath the shed on the left are the commons, and in front, like the crowded tiers in the gallery of a theatre, are a lot of boys, and, just as other boys do, they make fun of what is going on ; but they get terribly wolloped for doing so. It takes several lords-in-waiting to keep order. The sheds are crammed with spectators, two or three rows standing against the wall, and those in front squatting. Through an opening on the right, the women of the royal household peep, but they are driven away by the King's brother, who roars like a bull at them. They go away, but stealthily return, when the interest in the debate causes them to be partially unnoticed. But as they converse in loud whispers, like ladies caged in the House of Commons, they are again and again driven away and still return ; until at last the Onitsha " Dook " of Cambridge gets tired of remonstrance, gives up abusing the ladies ; and so they remain mistresses of the situation, and very properly so, for it is good to see their bright eyes sparkle anywhere.

The King's favourite son, a tall handsome youth of the same bright colour as himself, sits at the foot of the throne, armed with a dagger. The King's clothing consists of a red cloth sugar-loaf cap, a few brass rings upon his arms, coral necklace, and a yellow silken loose robe. His wrinkled forehead shows that he has had trouble in his time. He is very civil to his chiefs, sending to each, after they make obeisance, a piece of kolah-nut. He sent to each of us the same. All who approach the throne, the moment that they enter the open space in front—rigidly kept clear—double their right hand into a fist and shake it at the King. This signal of assault and battery here is correct court etiquette. It means—"I hope that I see you strong and well, oh, King, like unto my fist and my arm." Then they fall upon their knees, and, bending down, touch the ground with their foreheads, and some of the Falstaff chiefs and corpulent ladies of trade have considerable difficulty in getting up again.

The agent, through the interpreter, stated that if the King would protect his clerk, he would at once open a factory, but that the King must encourage his people to grow cotton and bring to the factory plenty of palm-oil, otherwise it would not be worth while to trade. He also said that should any plundering take place, he would at once shut up shop and remove elsewhere. It took three hours to arrange this. The King consulted his chiefs on one hand and the commons on the other. Committees of each left for private consultation in another part of the palace. Speeches were made, some of which were very loud and angry in tone. One old woman came forward, and, keeeling before the King, stated her views. At length, in a few brief, but effective sentences, a very ugly little old man, wearing a sensible head upon his shoulders, spoke out, and he was cheered loudly, by sudden bursts of acclamation at each period. So that it was settled to allow trade with white men.

The distribution of presents then commenced. The articles were produced and laid upon the ground, but the difficulty of dividing them caused great confusion. The recipients were dissatisfied. If the vessel's entire cargo had been placed before them, the feeling would have been the same. Envy, hatred, and malice came out strong, and I fully expected that blood would have been shed. In the midst of the excitement we retired. The King whispered to the interpreter his command to have *his* presents quietly sent that night. We were not asked to drink anything. The young prince rushed after us with his father's love, and kindly invited us to go back and try some palm-wine, but we were too glad to get away. The pressure of the crowd and the high Stilton flavour about the palace generally induced

us politely to decline, and, in return for the compliment
paid us, to ask the Prince of Onitsha Wales on board
ship to a banquet without words.

Gins to clean cotton, a hydraulic press to squeeze it into
the well-known bales, were landed and fitted up.   Several
thousand pounds' worth of goods left the ship, and the store
was opened.   On the first day it was crowded with people
urging claims for presents, from the wet-nurse to the
Prince of Wales, to the fisherman overlooking the store from
his perch cockloft near the big cotton-tree, who had descended
and assisted in making a hawser fast, and was thereby entitled
to remuneration.   But trade was started, and it flourishes.
Other stores flourish also, and they will continue to do so
until time is no more.

Bishop Crowther kindly invited all who could be spared
from the ship to attend divine service on Sunday forenoon at
the Church of England mission.   The morning, as Sunday
mornings generally are, was delightful.   The sun was not
shining too strongly, and the pathway led through tall grass,
somewhat resembling the mustard-grass abundant in Lower
California.   White men in strange countries always preserve
some fancy articles to decorate the person on the Sabbath of
welcome rest, and we presented a tolerable appearance as we
walked one mile from the river-side inclining upwards to the
mission.   But the creases and mouldy spots on coats
indicated too long familiarity with closely packed sea-chests;
however, the wrinkles speedily smoothed out by exposure to
sunshine.

The mission is a collection of thick mud-walled houses
with verandahs fronting inwards, forming a pleasant garden
square, in the centre of which is a belfry.   The church-room
is about eighty feet long by forty wide, with open window
spaces for the free admission of air.   It is roofed with palm-

leaves, and contains seats constructed of mud, conveniently built round the edges of the wall, and eight solid seats of similar material front the pulpit. The missionaries are all coloured men educated at Sierra Leone, and are under the direction of Bishop Crowther. One of them read prayers in the Abo language. The lessons were read in English. The Bishop delivered a short but very appropriate sermon, each sentence of which was translated into Abo. The missionary interpreter stood on the left of the pulpit. The congregation, numbering about one hundred, was chiefly composed of children. The missionaries did most of the singing and responses, only a few of the children instinctively joining, and it was really wonderful how soon they adapted their voices to, and picked up, the tunes. About a dozen adult males, some of whom carried bows and arrows or guns, looked on with open mouths. The front seats were occupied by very small children, nearly all of whom were naked; but some of them were clothed with flaming kerchiefs, and they evidently caused envy on the part of those less favoured. All had brass or ivory rings on their little arms and legs. During the Litany I counted on one girl twenty brass rings, like ordinary stair-rods curved to suit the proper size, fitted over each ankle. These infants looked very pretty, but during the service several of them fell fast asleep, and, as the mud seats have no backs, their little bodies bobbed to and fro until they lost their balance and capsized clean over, backward or forward as Nature prompted. Then they were carried out howling, just like other early Christians. A sexton, rejoicing in the costume of one sheet of white calico big enough for a respectable shroud, was kept fully occupied tapping old and young sleepers with a very useful wand-stick about ten feet long. He smote the sleeping heads with cracks which sounded like the noise of a hammer upon a cocoa-nut, but his smiting did not appear to hurt. Several spare missionaries, who were our fellow-passengers, being present, the service, with the exceptions I have named, somewhat resembled home.

The Bishop told the natives that it was wrong of them, because their children were taught at the mission to read " book," to expect payment for the privilege. This is what natives cannot yet comprehend all over the West Coast, and also up here. They are under the impression that they ought to receive payment for their children attending school, instead of gladly embracing the advantage of education. He also informed them that if they wanted to live with greater comfort, and enjoy the pleasure of wearing clothes, it was their duty to work during six days the same as white men. He urged upon them the nature and the palpable results of industry, and begged of them that, instead of idling away their time, making fierce war, tribe upon tribe, they ought to cultivate the beautiful country which the Great Architect of the Universe—known to all people who on earth do dwell by various names, as languages differ, and here by the name of " Tshuka-Tshuka "—had caused to exist around them a land overflowing with everything that the heart can desire, supplying their every want and tending to enrich other countries not so highly favoured. He informed them of northern lands where white rain fell and where cold was so intense that the plantations and houses were covered by a thick white pall for many months during each year; that the natives there were naturally white, and had to work hard to make cloth and all sorts of useful manufactures for the benefit of countries like Onitsha, from which they wanted cotton and palm-oil in return. The good Bishop urged them to grow yams, cut wood, to cultivate the growth of cotton and palm-oil, and, by bringing the result of their labour to white traders, they could get cloth or whatever else they wanted pertaining to civilised or semi-civilised comfort. They would then be enabled to throw away their present filthy garments, and, instead of leading useless lives, work for six days and rest on the Sabbath. He illustrated his discourse by parables, delivered in such clear and concise terms, that the most savage and untutored intellect could easily appreciate the good advice and common sense, probably never heard before.

Historical incidents related in Scripture are more easily comprehended by Central African savages than by uneducated people in England. The manners, customs, and traditions of Central Africa naturally assimilate greatly to those of Egypt, Syria, and Arabia. Washing the feet after walking; anointing the head and body with oil; the worship of idols; the influence of magicians or Ju-Ju-men; presents of changes of raiment and other useful articles; polygamy; human sacrifices; circumcision; the form of obeisance to superiors; the salutation of friends; the universal custom of women assembling at wells and rivers to obtain water; and also illustrating common conversation by parables. Thus, as negro boys become able to read the Bible at mission schools, they rapidly and naturally develop Eastern tastes, and they can appreciate Holy Writ' far more than the youth of cold Britain. These boys are intensely interested in those glorious narratives which add romantic but dim brilliancy to the history of the Jews. Many traditions have been promulgated which science has proved to be untrue; but still it is delightful to listen to perfect innocence relating the narratives of Joshua and the sun, Jonah and the whale, Pharaoh and the Red Sea calamity, as established facts.

We have got a young negro on board, acting as assistant-steward, who has been educated at the Old Calabar mission, and he can recite from memory in language so simple and touching that it makes everybody listen and wonder at his ability with pleasure.   He is full of Bible-stories, and, amongst others, relates all about Joseph being sold as a slave by his brethren.   His native habits are introduced throughout each tale, and his remarks about the deceased Mrs. Potiphar are not complimentary to that " free-lover " lady.   This boy may be taken as a sample of boys educated at Christian missions in Africa.   As they arrive at the age of maturity, it is a well-known fact that they combine the "muchly " wedded life of David and Solomon with the tenets of Christianity.   As Dr. Watts truthfully poetises, " For 'tis their nature to."

It appears very strange to white people, upon entering Onitsha market, to see the general clearance which takes place.   The women rush away, screaming to their children to do likewise, and not even the allurement of tempting pieces of cloth, constituting the loose money in the pockets of a white man, will induce many of them to shake hands. In the bush the natives are equally shy.   When wandering along the usual paths existing everywhere about the country, with a faithful attendant Krooboy carrying a gun and suitable refreshment to be taken when needed, large bodies of armed savages are frequently met with, and it is very difficult to make friends with them.   Some run away in affright ; others come like dogs of uncertain minds, balancing between whether to fawn or bite.   But a piece of tobacco or a twopenny looking-glass presented, brought out their good points.   They would put down upon the ground the invariable shooting-iron accompaniments, and freely allow me to inspect their long trade muskets, with the old-fashioned flint locks, covered carefully with the dried skin of some animal to keep the priming powder dry. Nearly every man carries an iron spear or a dagger-knife in addition to the musket. One man had a small elephant's tusk hollowed out, with a hole about the middle, through which he howled, and he appeared proud that, by my strongest orchestral exertion at blowing, I could only produce a hissing sound. He intimated that he had got a bamboo harp at home to suit my voice; so I went to his lair, got the harp, and afterwards took him on board ship, and adorned his untutored legs with a pair of trousers, and, as he landed again, a crowd collected, and he was as much a source of attraction as the Vatican Venus would be walking down Regent-street arm-in-arm with the Lord Mayor.

I do not like to call these people savage friends, for some of them were very civil and polite, and, in return for kindness, took me over extensive yam farms. The vines of the yams are trained to sticks, giving to yam plantations the look of dwarf hop grounds. They showed me where guinea-fowl were to be had for shooting. The flavour of guinea-fowl resembles pheasant, and we had many good dinners in consequence. They also brought tender monkeys and parrots, and doves of wonderfully bright plumage. Everything eatable was transferred to the ship's galley, and excellent pies were made by our black cook, and no questions asked.

The presence of the steamer induces crowds of men, women, and children to come and sit down to look at us. At the foot of the huge cotton-tree, round which we have a sort of "hawser" claim, the multitude bathe from morning until evening. The river runs swiftly, so that their native soap-suds are not lasting, else the fish perpetually caught by the scaffold-managed trap would not employ two men constantly. One day, during a bathing lull, I noticed that

the fishermen gave up work. One man went into the bush; the
other retired to his high cockloft and disappeared. Waiting
until the latter was asleep, I landed in a canoe and quietly
climbed up the bamboo poles, shaking the structure as little
as possible as I ascended. Upon getting my neck over the
lower edge of the little cockloft roof, I observed my gentleman
coiled round a mud fireplace, with charcoal burning. He was
fast asleep, enjoying the warmth. Mischief suggests itself
naturally at times to some wretches. I tickled his big toe
and howled like a lion or a tiger, as children do when playing
at nursery menagerie. But I had no idea of the *dénouément.*
His whole nervous system, suddenly recalled to activity,
plunged his body over my head into the river, and he swam
to the vessel. I was very sorry for behaving so badly, but
really could not help it. A change of raiment, consisting of
a good sized pocket-handkerchief, and a couple of glasses of
rum, a good feed, and a daily repetition of kind treatment
whilst we sojourned at Onitsha, made that fisherman one of
my best friends. Like Caliban, he showed me every fertile
inch at Onitsha. A missionary very kindly interpreted the
practical joke, and I believe that man now is a promising
Christian, and sings—

> " No more dams I'll make for fish,
> Nor fetch in firing
> At requiring ;
> Nor scrape trenchers, nor wash dish.
> Ban, Ban, Ca-Caliban,
> Has a new master.
> O, brave monster! lead the way."

Although on friendly terms with the monarchy, the women
of trade, and the ragged people about court, still we had to
complain of injustice. One of our Houssa passengers,
wanting to come on board from the shore, and not finding a
ship's boat at hand, but seeing an empty canoe convenient,

quietly jumped into it, and, paddling alongside the ladder, came on board, making the canoe fast by a fibrous thong which served for a rope. But the man was not a sailor, and did not know how to make a rope or a thong fast, so that the canoe beeame loose and drifted down the river. It was, however, picked up a few miles below Onitsha, and the salvagees made a claim through the King for twenty pieces of eloth and a case of trade guns; but this demand was so extravagant that our trading agent indignantly refused to entertain it. A war-eanoe, crowded with armed men making a big noise, eame alongside the steamer and demanded the eloth and guns. Now, the value of the eanoe, when new, was about the tenth part of the demand for its salvage; in faet, under the eireumstanees, one shilling's worth of goods would have been ample payment for reeovering. it. The Houssa passenger offered one piece of eloth and one gun as compensation, but his offer was deelined with derisive seorn. One of the missionaries got the demand redueed to fifteen pieees of eloth, and reeommended payment being made, but the agent sent word that he would re-ship his goods and abandon all idea of trade if this sample of outrageous conduct constituted their poliey. After three days' palaver the Houssa man arranged the matter by giving ten pieees of eloth, but after doing so he kept quietly coneealed on board the ship; for had he ventured again on shore, his person would have been confiseated and sold into slavery.

We found great diffieulty in obtaining wood for fuel. Our ehief supply was got by picking up trees floating past the vessel, and sawing and haeking them up into billets. I strongly reeommend that all steamers going up this river be supplied with a eireular saw, worked by steam. One apparently respeetable native agreed to proeure wood at a eertain price, and, bringing it on board, reeeived payment by instalments as it was delivered; but finding that we urged him to become more industrious, and knowing that we were most anxious to proceed higher up the river, he doubled his price and struck work. We served this savage out properly by refusing to take his driblets of wood, and trusted to obtain supplies elsewhere.

. The green wood brought on board and piled in bunkers brings centipedes, scorpions, and other unpleasant creeping things with it. When stowed below, in proximity to the furnaces, the heat kills these creatures, and no doubt renders their rich bodies useful articles of fuel; but, unfortunately, some creeping things get amongst the deck passengers, and one girl, bitten upon her heel by a scorpion, cried bitterly all day long and suffered great agony. Her ankle was very much swollen, and, as we had no doctor on board, we at once opened the medicine-chest, examined the book of directions, applied what was recommended to relieve pain, and she recovered.

We steamed from Onitsha at ten o'clock on the 12th day of August, and half an hour before noon passed the romantic village of Asaba, pleasantly situated amongst shady dells on the left bank of the river. The inhabitants assembled, blowing horns, and politely shook their fists at us. Just before leaving Onitsha, our chief engineer, coming up from the stoke-hole reeking with perspiration, and engaged mopping his countenance with a piece of dry cotton-waste, as is the custom of engineers in hot climates, was accosted by a chief shaking a huge fist in his face. The next moment the chief was knocked down, and it took some time and several glasses of solid rum to explain to the injured party that the engineer did not know that shaking the fist in close proximity to the face was a sign of friendship instead of hostility. The bank of the river is high at Asaba, and in many places it is overgrown with trees right down to the water's edge. In one of the little bays we observed about fifty women bathing and washing clothes. The waves caused by the steamer's paddles, almost shaving the trees, so frightened the ladies that they scampered into the bush like so many Whitby jet, dripping, but beautifully made, and active samples of Venus rising from the river. At two o'clock the steamer grounded for a few minutes in the channel south of Lake Island; there was only one foot of water forward, and yet four fathoms aft. We were obliged to lower the boat, and after two hours' detention, found the navigable channel near to the left bank. The river then showed a long straight reach forward, looking like an inland sea. After passing several villages, at dark we anchored below Onijah, in latitude 6° 33' north.

The following day was Sunday, a beautiful calm morning. Before sunrise the river, spread out like an unlimited mirror, reflecting the dark foliage of the banks which overhung its quietness, showed the shadows of the trees, together with the brilliant variety of colour, distinctly in the water— Nature's grand photography. After steaming fourteen miles we got aground above the village of Ojipo Majare, and stuck there for three hours. We had to work the vessel off by the tedious process of kedges and hawsers, taking the kedges out in boats and bringing them back again after floating the vessel. Church-service should have taken place at eleven o'clock, but it was unavoidably postponed until the afternoon. 'In the midst of it the vessel again struck, and the Bishop quietly concluded the service, for everybody that could assist to get the vessel afloat again was required to do so. Our chief officer, exasperated at the forenoon's hard work, was in a very bad temper, for he rudely broke in upon the congregation, shouting at the top

of his voice, " Here, all you blessed missionaries, come and
lend a hand to get the ship off." It was amusing to see our
passengers forced to run fore and aft, and to and fro, to make
the vessel vibrate whilst getting her off, and everybody able
to pull a rope was, by the force of circumstances, compelled
to lend a hand on the kedge-hawsers. Most of them worked
very unwillingly; it was quite evident that they did not
relish it at all.

At four o'clock the cliffs of Iddah loomed in sight, and at
five o'clock we anchored off the landing-place in ten fathoms
of water, the current running at the rate of six miles an hour,
caused by the great river sweeping round the front of steep
cliffs. We were obliged to let our second anchor go, to secure
the ship from drifting, and we paid out forty-five fathoms of
cable.

The light-red sandstone cliffs of Iddah extend for about a
mile along the right bank of the river, and rise perpendicularly
from the water to the height of one hundred feet, forming an
extensive plateau of healthy highland, on which, in the midst
of long grass and trees, are three or four villages forming the
town. Between the villages, and also far outside them, the
land is cleared of grass, and the cultivation of corn, yams, and
cassada is extensively conducted. The inhabitants appear to
depend very much upon agricultural pursuits for a living.
The trade consists of ivory and slaves, bartered to natives
of the lower countries in exchange for brass rods, guns,
powder, salt, and Manchester and other goods, which are
again forwarded further into the interior for other ivory and
other slaves. The people are happy and contented. In fact,
we find that the higher we ascend the Niger the more
civilised and better dressed the natives appear. Each district
has a fancy for distinct sorts of goods. Here they wear blue
baft sheets or country cloth robes, in which the indigo dye is

prevalent, for they grow indigo and have indigo dye pits, like our tanners' pits, in abundance. These cloths are about the size of two good-sized table-cloths sewn together, and are worn folded loosely round the person, and they present a graceful oriental appearance.

At daybreak the view from Iddah of both sides of the river is most enchanting. Distant mountains stretch across the horizon from north-west to north-east. Between, are great plains rising into tableland. The flat smiling level country abounds in forests, bounded by the far-away hills. Quiet villages, consisting of round mud huts, cluster picturesquely over the landscape, with their conical thatched roofs showing like collections of beehives; the blue smoke arising from them suggests the idea of railway trains spinning along the vista and skimming latitude at the rate of a degree an hour. A small stretch of imagination is only required and you have porters calling out "Iddah—Iddah—tickets ready." "Take your seats for the Confluence, Timbuctoo, and the North." "Change here for the Nyanzas, Gondokoro, Magdala, and Cairo." "Ladies with the big ivories, get in, please."

English Island is a sandbank fronting the cliffs of Iddah. It is submerged when the river is at its full height, but at other times markets are held upon it. It is more convenient as an exchange mart than landing at Iddah, and carrying goods or produce up and down hill. The water-mark on the cliffs shows that the river has yet to rise ten or twelve feet. The current drives our engine at half-speed, and when the engine is blocked the water rushes through the paddles like a cataract.

Canoes came alongside with plentiful supplies of wood, fowls, eggs, and corn. Some tusks of ivory, or, as traders call them, "teeth," were offered for barter, but the goods

demanded in return, being above the value of the ivory at
home, did not justify our trading agent in purchasing. We
experienced great difficulty in keeping the crowd of natives
from coming on board. They swarmed on the deck and
bridge, explored the cabins, and made themselves so much at
home that we were obliged to arm our sailors with country
grass switches, somewhat like pliable bamboo canes, which,
when applied with force upon the naked body, causes a
lengthy swelling, like that created by a healthy mustard-
plaster, wherever the cane momentarily rests. But so very
many natives claimed to be kings' sons and members of the
aristocracy—exempt from thrashing, as they thought—that,
having driven the bulk of the mob away, and having given
unto the noblemen rum, we found that the Iddah peerage
was too many for us, so we had to threaten them also with
switches unless they cleared out. But they laughed at and
mocked us, and would not leave the ship. Observing this
bad example, the lower classes again climbed on board from
their canoes. We might have chucked a few of them overboard, and did think of doing so; but the thought ended
in thought, for they might have taken it as an insult.
However, we appealed to the Attah, and speedily he sent off a
messenger in a royal canoe; and from its raised platform,
first striking a hollow iron instrument to call attention—and
it made a jolly row—he announced that anybody coming on
board our steamer without having business thereon, should
instantly receive the royal order of Eunuch. Upon hearing
this proclamation the rush of negroes to canoes was wonderful. It was exactly like the sensation caused by the cry of
" fire " in a crowded building. They left us, and we had
room to breathe.

Bishop Crowther established a mission here, but abandoned it. During its existence we visited the Attah, or

King, taking with us a large piece of red silk velvet, which was neatly packed in a pictorial box. We also took several pieces of bright Manchester prints, a few jack-knives, razors, scissors, and other useful articles, forming a tolerably good present, intended to obtain the goodwill of the Attah. We walked from the river's bank about two miles through corn-fields and villages. The sun shone out intensely hot. As we passed through the markets, the women and children, as usual, commenced to howl and run as if to save dear life ; but, upon making signs of friendship, some of them remained and stared hard at the strange white faces. Many of the young ladies were in full dress costume, consisting of the usual well-worn "necklace;" but they were lost in wonder at our appearance, and we, in wonder also, returned the compliment. We had the Krooboys to carry the presents, and naturally a crowd of men, boys, girls, and dogs soon collected and followed us. Upon arriving outside the palace several chiefs came out to us and wanted to look at the presents. We refused their request, and, considering their conduct rude, treated them accordingly. Presently we were ushered through a series of mud-hovel approaches to a small open space and told to wait. We waited and got tired of waiting. Our long walk had naturally created thirst ; so indignation arose, as in a theatre when the curtain lags beyond the time for rising. We told the retainers by signs to tell the Attah that our name was "Walker" unless he came forth, and forth he came.

The Attah was a very stout, good-looking, middle-aged man, and he shook hands warmly all round ; after each shake he placed the palm of his hand against the region of his heart for one moment, thus affirming the sincerity of his welcome. We did not bring an interpreter from the ship, trusting to persuade a missionary to accompany us ; but, although we called at the mission on our way to the mud palace, we could not induce anyone to come with us. I think now that they were afraid to do so. We managed pretty well by signs. The Attah actually got up a smile over his presents, and, observing his good humour gradually increasing, I lifted my elbow, with the right hand approaching the mouth, and he instantly ordered in calabashes of palm-wine, beautifully fresh. It was delicious fluid, and had the bouquet of the finest Liege Burgundy with the strange appearance of skim-milk. We were satisfied that it was good, wholesome stuff, and thoroughly enjoyed it. During the drinking part, one of our deputation laid down a sketch-book, and out of native curiosity the Attah desired to look at it; he did so, and was evidently highly amused at the sketches of canoes, his own cliffs, the mountains in the distance, and the heads of some of the ugliest of his subjects. We sadly yearned for beef-steak on board, but how to tell the Attah was a puzzle. A sketch was made somewhat resembling a cow; and it was intimated, by a visible penny, that more money or goods existed on the ship to pay for whatever we wanted. The Attah laughed at the bullock sketch until his good-natured sides shook again, and he bellowed loudly " Buu-o-uu;" and correct he was. He instantly ordered two of his courtiers to go and catch one and take it on board our vessel with his love.

Before daybreak on the morning of the fifteenth day of August we steamed from Iddah, and at three o'clock in the afternoon we came to anchor off the town of Igbegbe, within twenty yards of the rocky landing-place. Igbegbe is a town of considerable importance, and, from its convenient position at the Confluence, it will naturally increase. It contains now about six thousand inhabitants, and is situated on the east bank of the Niger at its Confluence with the river

Binue, or Chadda. The natives pronounce the name emphatically "Bin-way."

The surface rock at Iddah, and also at Onitsha, consists of heavy red ironstone, similar to that at Sierra Leone ; and no doubt granite exists immediately beneath it, as is the case at Sierra Leone. Above Iddah granite breaks out on the surface in the form of the most extraordinary rugged hills that it is possible to imagine. The total change of scenery is very striking. You pass from foul swamps in the Delta to a grand bold mountain district, truly like transition from the fens of Lincolnshire to the Highlands of Scotland. The hills observed at a distance from Iddah line each bank of the river. There are grassy slopes and cultivated valleys, above which immense rocks grandly tower, some of them shaped like pyramids of solid granite, about one thousand feet high. The pyramids of Egypt are dwarfs compared to these grand natural specimens. It appears as if we are threading through forests of enormous cities of the dead. The granite peeping everywhere out of rank vegetation, not only from the bank in front of either side, but right away up the slopes to the tops of the ranges of hills, shows out like cathedrals, castles, and vast mansions. The growth of huge trees, wherever nature affords means of taking root, adds to the idea of the vastness of the imaginary buildings. Many of the lower hills, studded with great granite boulders, piled one upon another, look like the cemeteries of giants. Those who ascend the Niger for the first time are lost in astonishment at the grandeur. The results of a terrific convulsion of nature, extending as far as the eye can reach in every direction, are so marked that wonder merges into awe of Him who created earth from chaos. In many puzzling-looking places villages appear, generally built upon gentle slopes between impassable rocks. But elsewhere lonely jungle, inaccessible cliffs, and fearfully wild scenery suggest the appropriate residence for lions.

A great crowd of people welcomed our arrival with shouts of joy. We fired our guns, depressing the muzzles of those facing the town, so that the hard wads, which sailors always will ram and jam home over the top of the powder, to increase the noisy report, should prove harmless. At the din caused by the guns, the natives rushed towards their huts, but they soon flocked back again to gaze at the " white man's big canoe." Several young lady passengers have now arrived home. Some belong to Igbegbe, and others to Lukoja, above the Confluence. We missed the girls, but underneath the awning aft they were gaily clustered, concealed by a screen, engaged in changing their travelling clothing and donning gorgeous attire. They came out at last with bright bandanas on their heads, like small turbans, neatly tied at the back; they had clean new dresses, in which yellow and Turkey-red came out violently, but their scarves were meant to, and did, astonish the natives. Screaming with pure happiness, they jumped into a canoe and took naturally to the paddles, in haste to reach the shore, although we were so near to it that a " shove-off " from the ship was sufficient for the canoe to glide to the landing. The moment that they got into the canoe the yells of pleasure, and the dancing by the people on the bank, were something to remember. Those bare-footed and dark, but comely, angel-looking, light-hearted girls sprang from the canoe, and fairly flew up the incline, right into the fondly-extended arms of their mothers. Then the hugging began, and it brought happy tears to several eyes to witness their ecstacy. They do not kiss as British mammas and daughters under similar circumstances would do; but the old lady lifts the young one off her feet and bends backwards, and for a

moment you imagine that they must come to the earth, but
they do not. A short space of time is tacitly allowed for
breathing, and then the lifting is reversed. Then they clap
their hands and laugh and cry alternately. It was very
gratifying to observe this great and happy touch of truthful
nature.

That night the mosquitoes had such a feast upon " white
man " that, if they publish an almanac, the fact will be
noted as an event. After breakfast we went ashore, accompanied by two European dogs belonging to the trading agent.
One of them, called "Boatswain," a very large tailless French
poodle, and a very quiet animal, soon became the lion of the
place. The skeleton curs fled in terror of our " Boatswain ;"
they even forgot all about canine etiquette, which ought to be
prevalent, and generally is, all over the globe. Boys, girls,
men, and women, laughed and ran away shrieking. The
smaller dog raced at everybody and barked so much that,
fearing it would take fever, it had to be consigned to the arms
of an attendant Krooboy, and its excitement kindly controlled.
We visited the mission (it is closed now), a collection of
squarely-built, grass-thatched mud-houses, similar to the
Onitsha mission-house. In the spacious square, fruit-trees
are abundantly planted. The usual mission-bell is in the
centre, the sound of which to the natives is a most important
feature of the Christian religion, as the numerous volunteers
who take their turn at ringing it testify.

It happened to be market-day, so we wandered about to see
the sights, and were perpetually hemmed in by good-natured
people. Their perfume was certainly rather objectionable ;
it was somewhat like walking about a badly-ventilated stable
suddenly opened after having been closed for a week during
the summer season. Women squatted, standing underneath
sheds or in the open air, surrounded by baskets, have spread

out for sale heaps of corn, small pyramids of salt, native soap
in balls, small white beans, and a variety of seeds.   They
also sell native-made razors, of very rude workmanship, but
uncommonly sharp; native-made iron shovels, country cloths
woven of grass-fibre and cotton combined, cotton reels, raw
cotton in bags, palm-oil and Shea butter in jars, and very
good honey; English goods are likewise offered.   There is a
great abundance of fowls, ducks, and goats, and at the
butchers' stalls rough joints of elephant and hippopotami, so
hacked that they look as if they had been bitten off by some
huger animal, instead of being neatly cut and sawn for
human consumption by a professional butcher.

The breweries are worth inspecting.   They appear to be
managed entirely by women.   The vats consist of earthenware jars, each holding about twenty gallons.   Five of these
jars are clustered together and plastered over with mud.
Charcoal fires burn underneath them, and other large jars
appear to receive the fluid in its different stages.   The
women kindly handed us samples of their beer in calabashes.
It is extremely mild and cloudy in colour, but not at all
a bad substitute for English beer.

The barbers' shops, as in Eastern countries, are evidently
also an institution here.   They are crowded with customers,
who sit down upon mats.   The barbers stand bending over
them and shave their heads.   Beards, being very scarce
articles, are carefully preserved, but the thick woolly heads
submit to be shaven in a variety of interesting patterns.   In
some cases ridges cross the cranium, in others the wool
appears in little squares like the ground plan of a newly laid-
out American city. Others prefer a solitary top-knot, sometimes ornamented with cowrie-shells, or beads, or feathers at
the ends. Some gallant gentlemen wear a bristly ridge of wool,
extending from the forehead to the back of the neck, standing

up and looking like the hairy appendage to the old-fashioned dragoon helmet. The barbers use no soap; they simply apply water plentifully, and then work away with the razor. It would yield a pleasing but very ticklish sensation, to those natives who retain their wool intact, to start a rotary machine armed with wire instead of bristles, properly to comb the Ethiopian wool straight without injury to the skull; but then again, on the other hand, objectors to all mechanical improvements might with good reason produce statistics to show that it would throw a vast number of interesting insects out of employment.

During our short stay at Igbegbe, the river-bank in front of the vessel was crowded day and night. Early in the morning, women came down in troops to bathe, and some of them were capital swimmers. They played a variety of mermaid antics. We appreciated their free and easy manners as interesting samples of dark-complexioned Venuses on the loose water. All day long strings of women came for water with earthenware jars upon their heads, holding from five to eight gallons each jar. These they fill by wading into the river, and then carry them away upon their heads, wriggling their agile bodies beneath the weight, just as the Arab women do on the banks of the Nile. They linger, too, over filling the jars; and, from their confidential conversation, evidently the place to obtain water is their school for scandal.

Here are some magnificent specimens of the baobab, or monkey-bread-fruit tree. This tree abounds all over the coast above marshy ground. The fruit hangs from it in plenty, about the size and shape of bladders of lard, but elongated at the ends. One remarkable specimen measures twelve feet in diameter, and grows out of the centre of a cluster of granite. It has moulded itself to the form of the rock, but it is quite evident that shortly the granite will split in all directions and the still growing tree become free.

Igbegbe was bombarded in October, 1874, by three trading steamers. It appears that Okiawa, the King, objected to wealthy Sierra Leone and Lagos immigrants, established at Lukoja, trading up the river Binue. Now, these people are the most suitable to trade, for they are far better fitted by Nature to traffic than white men, as they can stand and enjoy the heat of the Central African sun, and, in addition, they are partially educated; whereas white men soon subside beneath the sun and die. The black traders purchase goods from the white men, which they take to various markets and return laden with ivory, benniseed, raw cotton, and lubi. Of lubi anon. The Lukoja traders were not powerful enough to fight Igbegbe alone, so they requested the trading steamers to assist them. They complained that the savage chief of Igbegbe intercepted their canoes, and not only confiscated their cargoes, but, in addition, sold the crews into slavery. The English steamers agreed to inflict summary punishment upon Igbegbe, or "Bebbe," as it is pronounced, with a guttural sound previously, but "Bebbe" is near enough. There is another hard name connected with this affair—Omarue, King of Beda, a neighbouring petty monarch, subject to the Sultan of Soccatoo. Omarue's predecessor was called by his friends Massaba, a contraction of Mahomet Saba; he commenced to sleep with his fathers in 1873, but during life he was a good sort of Solomon, and was really fond of white men and their doings. Well, Omarue wanted to have a hand also at the pounding and bombardment of "Bebbe;" but, like a sagacious man, he kept his armed canoes behind the white warriors until he saw how the battle "wented." If they failed, he might probably have deemed it wise policy to assist in plundering them.

But the white men went in and won, and then Omarue landed his forces, and, well knowing where the "Bebbe" monarch kept his stores of powder, salt, guns, and goods, to use a very expressive American phrase, he "euchred" his English allies and collared the "swag," whilst the English steamers were bombarding the town for an idea.

Lubi is dug from the earth in large cakes three or four inches thick ; the cakes are broken into sizes convenient to carry. It presents the appearance of rock-salt, and is offered for sale in moderate quantities. It tastes like saltpetre, but burns with a feebler flame, more like nitrate of soda. Natives bring it both from the Upper Niger and the Binue, and say that it comes from a long distance inland. Wherever found, it doubtless exists in large quantities, similar to the nitrate of soda in South America, and it may ultimately form an article of export to England. At present it is doled out, probably to keep up the price. It is used extensively as medicine by the natives, and also given freely to horses. It is worth 2d. per lb. here, but at Lagos and other places it fetches from 9d. to 1s. 6d. per lb. Lubi is preferred by the coast-town inhabitants to the nitrate of soda or saltpetre sent out from England.

The native-grown tobacco-leaves are plaited and rolled in coils similar to ropes upon the deck of a man-of-war, but fastened together by means of long wooden skewers. This tobacco is preserved by the application of a solution of lubi, and is very mild in flavour, like Turkish, but coarser. The natives of Africa everywhere prefer the stronger flavoured and better American leaf-tobacco, but when we had smoked all our bird's-eye and cavendish we were obliged to try the native article, and found it not at all a bad substitute. Whilst consuming it, occasionally a small, but not annoying, eruption takes place in the pipe, and this only shows that

too much lubi has been used to preserve the flavour. A coil
of this tobacco, fifteen pounds in weight, costs about two
shillings in cowries. It is so unknown in England that the
Customs pass quantities of it amongst passengers' luggage,
under the impression that the coils of tobacco are innocent
door-mats. However, the revenue does not suffer, for they
are only taken home as curiosities.

CHAPTER VI.

JUST as the order to "go ahead" from Igbegbe was given, and before it could be countermanded, a canoe, managed by stupid Lukoja-men, got underneath the paddles and was smashed to little bits; but the people in it escaped drowning by jumping clear of the paddles and swimming on shore. Two hours' steaming took us past the debouchure of the river Binue—the Confluence—into the Upper Niger, where, on the west bank, a little way higher up, we anchored off Lukoja in close proximity to trees. We had passengers for Lukoja, and the excitement caused by their arrival home was as great as that at Igbegbe. One young man, who had been away for a year in Sierra Leone, was almost pulled to pieces by his lady friends, who welcomed his body and estate. He was engaged to be married at the Church mission, and the ceremony was speedily performed.

Commencing in 1857, the British Government had a sort of consular agent residing here, subject to orders from the Governor, or administrator of British rule, at Lagos. His duties were to foster trade. The first man appointed was Dr. Baikie, R.N.; and he—as they term it of African travellers who stick to one place—"sat down" for seven long years, studying the language and compiling a grammar. But, unfortunately, when on his way home, in 1864, he died at Sierra Leone. His successors were generally young naval officers; and, as the life was horribly lonely for a young fellow accustomed to spend evenings with civilised beings of his own colour, a white man was paid to keep him company, and during his illness, or absence upon duty or excursions, the companion acted as consul. Every year they were changed by similar men, generally volunteers from the navy, landed from a small man-of-war bringing presents from the Queen to the various chiefs about. They laughed, told stories, read, and kept each other in use of the mother-tongue, which Dr. Baikie, after his long exile, had well-nigh forgotten, as far as speaking it was concerned. In 1865-6 white men commenced to trade, and then stores were erected and became settled institutions. The traders, with the assistance of the consular agent, managed to pass away pleasantly their otherwise solitary time. It is a dreadful thing to experience solitude in the midst of half-savages, even with the addition of brilliant surrounding scenery and good food. There are three British firms now trading, besides well-to-do Sierra Leone and Lagos merchants, and, by judicious presents to those in authority residing about them, protection is freely accorded; so that the consular agency, having been reported to have done its work, was withdrawn in 1869.

Before the traders came, the lonely Englishmen were sometimes without news from home for a whole year, and naturally they gladly welcomed a stranger-face speaking English, whether he were black or white. In those days we visited Lukoja. The acting consul and his white chum came half-way from their dwellings, towards the river-bank, to meet us, dressed as native chiefs do; nor is it at all extraordinary that white men sometimes adapt themselves, especially where there are so few of them, to the favourite aristocratic ideas of the people amongst whom they live. Our new friends had head-dresses of fez, surrounded

by extensive white turbans, according to the true Arabian
style. They wore "tobes" made of the finest Central African
home-spun cotton cloth. Their heads protruded through a
hole in the centre of the garment like those in the smock-
frocks of brewers' draymen, with the addition of a loose
burnoose hanging negligently over their shoulders, handy to
cover the face should the sun prove too strong. The fancy
cotton "tobes" were finely embroidered by the dark
beauties of the land, and trimmed with red silk, which the
lonely ones thoroughly appreciated and considered extremely
"high" and striking to the eyes of European-clothed
visitors. The embroidery resembles Madeira fancy needle-
work; but, as there were no white women about to admire it,
the artistic display was lost. However, our countrymen had
large hearts beneath their "tobes," and welcomed us heartily
to the best that their temporarily adopted country afforded.
They also wore, underneath the "tobe," large inexpressibles,
very baggy above, but very tight about the ankles—and
sensibly so—to prevent ants and other biting insects
exploring foreign districts. On their feet were sandals,
which are certainly proper to complete the Mahometan
Central African costume, but in walking over sandy or light
soily substance sandals are not a success. The lowest made
shoes, admitting ventilation over the toes, or else light leather
ample-sized long boots, like those depicted upon Oliver
Cromwell, to allow air also, are much better adapted for
any hot climate. We had brought with us from Lagos a
mail-bag containing their English despatches; so we left them
undisturbed to read the written speaking from their far-away,
but never for one moment forgotten, relatives at home.

The remaining cargo of our steamer was landed and
housed in a long shed connecting two round mud houses, and
in four days the vessel was despatched to the sea to bring up

a fresh cargo of goods to trade with up the Binue and higher
up the Niger. A wooden house in pieces was also landed.
Natives were set to work clearing the site for it, and enclosing
a large space around to form a plantation, and carpenters
were employed to make a proper trading store of it. Meantime, the agent, in addition to superintending everything
himself, planted with his own hands, amongst other existing
trees, Avocada pear trees, mango, lime, and orange trees. In
the vicinity of a little stream he sowed lettuce, mustard-and-
cress, onions, carrots and turnips, peas and beans, and a
variety of other seeds. Potatoes he also planted. He landed
and enclosed with wire-work a dozen rabbits from St. John's
Market. It is doubtful whether they will be allowed to live,
for snakes abound, and they are partial to rabbits, as may be
seen in the cage of the sleepy pythons at the "Zoo"; but
here big snakes are wide awake and lively.

After the steamer took her departure for the seaboard,
trading commenced. Each white man left behind had a mud
hut to reside in, and, to my very great delight, I became
tenant of the hut which had been so long the home of Dr.
Baikie. The enclosure organised by Dr. Baikie consists of a
dozen solidly-built (for the country) circular mud huts, each
with a conical thatched roof; also, separately built, other
huts, suitable offices for kitchens, and so forth. Each building
is constructed so far apart that, if one takes fire, the people
rushing from the others can easily extinguish the flames
without danger to the rest. This is the safest and simplest
way to build trading-places or residences where land is of no
value. The whole is surrounded by high mud walls, and,
being situated upon an incline, open drains readily carry
away the floods peculiar to the rainy season. The walls
constitute right angles, and form a parallelogram, with only
one gateway entrance at the front, which is situated upon the

lower level. Looking eastwards is an island, and beyond that a point of land separating the two grand rivers. Another mud house is built over the entrance, where a watchman is supposed to sleep, but a beautiful donkey resides there. I never saw anybody else watching.

My hut leaks literally like "old boots." It is separated from another hut (in which sleeps the trading agent) by the long shed where our English goods, in bales and casks, are piled high. We can shout to each other during the dark hours of night, and that is comforting. My outer door consists of a mat lowered, but I clear away the mat to allow the entrance of pure air to breathe. Are we not enclosed by high mud walls, and cannot the donkey within the gate bray if an enemy approaches? We sleep in peace. But the roof wants new thatch. It is the rainy season, and drops are perceptible from the face to the feet. If you pull up your feet too suddenly, the knees naturally project through the mosquito-curtain and admit the unwelcome guests which it is intended to keep out ; so that the only wise plan is to grin and bear it, and in the morning enjoy a tub and a dose of quinine to keep fever at a respectful distance.

We have about two days of fine weather to one of heavy rain, accompanied by thunder and lightning, not so violent as during tornadoes at the beginning and end of the rainy season, nor during the dry season, but still uncomfortable, unless beneath a waterproof roof. One night the down-pour of rain was really fearful. I slept and dreamt about the house built upon sand, and was awakened by something bobbing against the mosquito-curtain, but was too sleepy to bother about it, deeming it to be some eccentricity of the rain or wind blowing through the open doorway ; but presently—bob—bob—went something against the person, like a supernatural warning to "get out." I

tried in the pitchy darkness to seize whatever it might be,
but failed ; and then a strange subdued noise, quite different
to that caused by wind or rain, aroused me thoroughly.　I
did not like to disturb and fire the revolver sleeping below
my pillow, for fear that the noise might have been made by
one of the odd boys belonging to adjacent huts, and that he
had crept quietly for shelter into the nearest hut, having
missed his own, and was afraid to speak his mind.　So,
getting up and striking one of the "Ark" matches, I found
myself in a puddle of water, but before burning fingers, as
the match became expended, I laughed outright and awoke
the nearest residents.　All the goats and Muscovy ducks in
the limited colony had assembled for shelter, and it was the
noses of the goats that had bobbed.　I was too sleepy to
drive them out and get wetter feet, and, feeling ashamed of
having awakened anybody else, turned in again, rubbed soles
dry against the mat, and let the goats and ducks enjoy
themselves.　They gazed with such pensive eyes at the
lighted match that pity for them was but natural.　In the
morning, I found that the rain, by inefficient surface-drainage
outside the hut, had swept a hole through the wall on the
hill side, which caused a stream of water to rush beneath my
bamboo bed, soaking a portmanteau and gun-case, and
eventually it had forced a hole through the wall to leeward.
The pent-up flood then rushed out, and in doing so carried
away a shoe with a sock neatly placed inside to keep
ants and beetles out.　It floated like a small canoe for about
one hundred yards, and then grounded until the next rush of
water took place.　When getting up, and observing only one
shoe, the wonder was whether I really had a wooden leg.
But an honest native, who was also blessed with not having
a wooden leg, picked up the derelict shoe and sock on their
way to the Niger and Atlantic.　He restored them conscien-

tiously, like the honest finder of only one half of a Bank of England note, because it was of no use to him.

On the day of our arrival we gave the lonely ones a dinner on board, and set our freezing-machine to work cooling the requisite liquors. Actually they could not bear the cold, which to our palates was most refreshing and exquisitely delightful. We reduced the temperature of beer, claret, and water 45°. From 15° to 20° below the ordinary heat of the atmosphere is our usual standard at daily meals, and that is quite sufficient to render drink enjoyable; but on this occasion we wished to please and likewise startle the Central-African-Anglo resident. Both our guests complained afterwards of inward chilliness caused by their not being accustomed to take their liquor so very cold. After dinner, beneath the awning, we imparted general news from home, for lonely residents in out-of-the-way places, who seldom receive newspapers, do not care about wading through details; they like better to be informed of results. We varied the entertainment by singing songs; but, as we were anchored close to the rankest kind of vegetation, the insects fairly swarmed into our candle-lanterns to such an extent that we were compelled to break up early and retire to rest. Our guests invited us to dine with them on the following day, with the proviso that each man should bring his own camp-stool, plate, knife and fork, and glass. This we did, and enjoyed a most sumptuous entertainment, consisting of buffalo meat, Muscovy duck, and palm-oil chop. Our hosts had only one of each article required for eating, so that, in packing up to travel, their luggage should be as limited as possible, compatible with individual comfort.

Imagine the bright, clear blue sky without a cloud. Flat-topped mountains, sloping upwards from fertile plains, immediately behind us and in every other direction, and in the distance across the waters similar hills and valleys, all

yielding pleasing variety of light and shade ; and the whole
landscape covered with woods, forests, and grass-land, rising
from which, like land-marks, are huge trees, strangers to our
eyes.   Before us are the two great rivers, stretching out here
in rippling waves and there with a smooth silent current,
dazzling, re-reflecting, and lapping up the warm sunshine, as
if it were their food and they enjoyed it.   Such is Lukoja, at
the Confluence of the Niger and Binue.   It is impossible to
describe the joy felt in rambling up the hills during early
dawn and sunrise, and the eye feasting upon the ever-changing
panorama.

The island opposite to Lukoja is fast becoming covered by
the rising waters.   A fortnight ago a dozen hippopotami with
their young migrated from it higher up the river.   In walking
along the simple well-worn paths which connect village with
village, doves, guinea-fowl, and a small sort of partridge rise
from before the feet in every direction.   A sporting man can
range from a humming-bird to an elephant.   Slain buffalo
and antelope are frequently brought into our village, and,
after having eaten the very thin and tough fowls and lean
goats on the coast, their tender joints yield a most welcome
change ; and for awhile, with Nature in all its savage glory
surrounding you, you think that you would like to live and
die here, where the whole country teems with animals, birds,
insects, fruit and flowers, and the rivers swarm with fish.

Whilst the steamer was discharging her cargo, consisting
of bales and casks containing various kinds of suitable
prints, also rum, gunpowder, brass rods, and so forth, to
store and barter for produce, crowds of natives from distant
villages came to look on.   These spying bumpkins were
so curious that many of them built temporary thatched
dwellings on the river bank, and ate, drank, and slept, and
gazed, and chattered.   Our interpreter informed us that

they were lost in astonishment at the enormous quantity of
goods coming from the ship, and they decided that " white
man " must keep a devil on board to supply anything
required. When it came to trading, they were too anxious
to get more beautiful things than we could afford for the
produce that we wanted. We found that the best plan to
develop commerce was to expose only a few bales of Manchester prints, and merely samples of Sheffield and Birmingham ware, guns, brass rods, German looking-glasses, and
Venetian beads, so as to keep down their envy. Then, the
vision of what they coveted being limited, their ideas
followed suit ; but still they higgled over the price for tusks
of ivory. The first operation in buying ivory is to weigh the
tusk, then ask the vendor what sort of goods he wants to
select from the samples before his sparkling eyes. It is cal-
culated what we can afford to give so as to make a
good profit, and then the representative quantity of goods is
placed before the seller ; but he is dissatisfied, and stickles
for more, and to get more sometimes they whine piteously
and clutch garments, like the lepers of to-day on Mount
Zion for alms. Such childish conduct in trading matters is
undignified, and we express our contempt, through the
interpreter, and they frequently do " a weep " and promise
amendment. We place a few looking-glasses, fish-hooks, and
jack-knives over and above the merchandise offered, or, as
they have quaintly learnt to say, " for top." Yet still more
articles are asked for. We then refuse to trade ; so the tusk
is taken away and the goods replaced for the next customer.
But day after day the same tusk appears amongst others,
and finally it is purchased.

We exhibited too great eagerness to obtain ivory, so they
got it into their heads that we wanted the large tusks to
make ivory anklets for our wives and daughters, like the

heathens lower down the river ; and, although the interpreter violently gesticulated and endeavoured to prove that English ladies would never dream of wearing ten or a dozen pounds' weight of ivory over each of their delicate ankles, yet they would not believe him, and when he assured them that we made knife-handles and numerous other articles in common use out of ivory, they simply said "pooh" in their own language, and laughed him to scorn. It would be a grand harvest for cabmen should our ladies take to wearing such anklets ; but what then would be the state of the footwalks now so efficiently swept by long dresses ?   In this land, abounding with elephants, strange to say, ivory anklets and bracelets are not at all appreciated as they are at Iddah, Onitsha, Abo, and other places where elephants are not ; here they wear, instead, smaller-sized, narrow-rimmed circlets made of molten glass and beads mixed, or heavy armlets carved out of dark-veined marble.

Each morning at our individual huts we hold a compulsory levee.   Visitors come singly, in pairs, and also in half-dozens.   They gracefully bend one knee and snap fingers with you.   It is a sort of slipping grasp of the fingers only, not a regular hand-shake.   After the quick slip the noise made by the snap of the fingers follows.   At the same time they say, "Saanu," "Saanu," "Baturie," "Baturie," which, being interpreted, means "Good-morning, white man," repeated twice with emphasis.   Massaba has sent two huge canoes to receive his portion of the cargo, and, along with the paddlers, are several chiefs, ostensibly to protect us. These are fine, tall athletic fellows, well dressed in fez, turban, tobe, baggy continuations, and sandals, and they look extremely well with their long straight swords suspended over the shoulder by red-coloured woollen ropes and pendent tassels.   The sword-blades are stamped, some with the figure of a crescent, others with a resemblance of a lion. The blades come from the Mediterranean by caravans of camels across the desert from Tripoli, but the scabbards and handles are home-made, the former of beautifully-embossed leather, mounted with brass, and the latter of solid brass, inlaid with fancy ornaments and engraved with rudely-carved designs. Massaba's chiefs are fierce-looking fellows, and capable of doing mischief if on bad terms with anybody.

The bulk of our morning callers overhaul everything which we have for our toilet or daily use. They are so delighted with each article that it is a pleasure to observe their delight ; but, unfortunately, some of them are given to stealing, for trifling things are missed, of which we deem it policy to take no notice. One morning, returning from a bath, I met a young lady called Fatima gaily attired in a suit of light clothing which I had selected from my portmanteau for that day's decoration. She had even put on a collar and necktie, but the shoes she could not get into. The congregation laughed and clapped hands, and Fatima strutted like an Ancient Briton, and it was a fine sight. Remonstrating with her, more in suppressed fun than anger, I requested her to " peel," which she did, and the laughter of the spectators was turned against poor Fatima. They quizzed and bantered her, and no doubt she blushed. The downcast expression of the eyes is the only way to detect the blushing of our dark sisters. However, I presented her with a good looking-glass, and then she was envied, and other ladies might have aspired for other looking-glasses in the same manner ; but after that I received my morning-callers seated in the doorway, and barred the entrance with a long " churchwarden " clay pipe, and told the natives that that long pipe was my " fetish," and they respected it accordingly, and did not step over it.

During early morning and up to breakfast-time—say

14

at about eleven o'clock—whatever hard work required to be done had to be done then. One forenoon the basement floor of our new house had to be properly made, similar to the excellent, smooth, hard floors of the most ordinary circular mud huts. A lot of industrious women assembled for the purpose, and three or four lazy, good-for-nothing-else, men-minstrels played drums; but the women appeared to like the arrangement, for they worked all the harder, and their every action kept time to the enlivening noise made by the music. The women did all the work; they brought water, gravel, and earth, and, stooping low, handled pieces of flattened wood, with which they slapped the splashing mixture until the floor was like asphalte. It was then allowed one clear day to dry; afterwards another musical entertainment took place whilst the women coated the surface with cow ordure, and subsequently they polished it, and then it was as hard and shone as brightly as the palace floors of Versailles. The women are very industrious, and as a rule the men are exactly the reverse. At pounding green corn in a strong wooden mortar two women take hold of a long wooden pestle and work away with a will, and all the joints in their flexible bodies have full play. They also crush corn between two hard stones. One stone is round, about the size of a sixty-eight-pounder cannon ball, to suit the size of the hands; the underneath stone is large and concave like a hollow basin. In many cases, when working, women have their babies fastened behind them by means of a cloth twisted in a peculiar but safe manner in front. The flexibility of the body tends to keep the cloth tight around both mother and child. In every operation where women work in numbers they require musical entertainments, and the lazy fellows who supply the music pass the hat round previously for a collection of cowrie-shells. The material which

hardens mud floors is also applied to the walls of the circular
mud huts, to prevent, as far as possible, the accumulation of
nests of wasps, blue-tailed flies, centipedes, scorpions, and
other objectionable fellow-tenants. Our huts are full of
these holes, all well tenanted, and it is interesting to watch
the insects flocking in and out. Rats are friendly visitors;
they are much smaller than the British rat, are lighter in
colour, and wag longer ears.

During the middle of the day, when the thermometer
registers 98° in the shade and 120° in the sun, it is not good
to take your walks abroad. Sleeping in a hammock, and
dreaming of the man who supplies us every afternoon with
gallons of fresh palm-wine, is better. One day, when taking
a siesta, I suddenly fell to the ground; upon jumping up, I
found a madman belonging to the village standing over me;
he had cut the hammock nettles. He saw that my temper
was ruffled, so took to his heels, and I ran after him with a
stick to administer a lesson; but the poor fellow tripped,
and in falling his head came violently in contact with the
chime of a cask, its sharp iron edge inflicted a serious wound,
and blood flowed. I sponged and dressed the wound, and
spoke in a comforting tone to him: his gratitude showed
itself in daily visiting me and bringing a piece of hot yam or
anything that he happened to be eating and offering me a
bite. The women of this village, as they do all over God's
creation in pitying the distressed and afflicted, take great
care of those of unsound mind. All readily offer this man
food and shelter, so that he has the run of the town and his
own choice of residence.

As the heat is too great for white men to wander abroad
with impunity, there are hunters able to stand the climate.
We supply them with modern rifles, first teaching them how
to handle them; and these men are really great benefactors,

for they kill buffalo, antelope, elephant, and hippopotami, and assistance is soon rendered to secure the carcasses. As the meat only keeps good for one day, we feast the village upon the remainder, after selecting what we require for daily consumption. One day, one of the hunters, called "Coco," got cornered by a fierce buffalo. The trading agent and I, according to our usual custom during the cool of the afternoon, were taking a quiet walk, when we heard a rifle-shot, and saw, close to the river bank, that "Coco" had fired at a buffalo and missed. The enraged animal charged at full tilt with its head lowered to toss "Coco" into atmosphere, but "Coco" threw his rifle at the buffalo, and, jumping into the river, swam round a corner, and thereby deluded the game. The buffalo not being accustomed to shoulder the rifle, it was found subsequently, and the animal respectfully retired into private life, and, no doubt, in its own language, described the event, and became a hero amongst its own cows. We tried several dodges to preserve the good meat, the most successful of which was cutting it into long strips, soaking it in brine, and then hanging it over wood fires in the heat of the sun, and both appliances shrivelled the meat quite dry, but still preserved its nutritious qualities. We felt very proud of our success, and when we walked our "chalks abroad," took pocketsful of dried meat, and it proved very refreshing to eat, especially when in the vicinity of a creek, from whence we satisfied the wholesome thirst naturally engendered by the pleasant salt flavour.

Some of the consuls collected the bones and heads of elephant, antelope, leopards, and various other animals to send home as trophies or specimens. To clean these, all that is required is to place the flesh-covered heads or limbs in the open air, when speedily millions and billions of ants assemble and consume every atem of flesh, leaving the skulls and bones perfectly clean and white ; but when the consuls go home they forget the specimens, and our enclosure, therefore, resembles somewhat the dried heap of bones mentioned by Ezekiel. If only these bones would resume life, as Ezekiel's did, we should have some good handy shooting without wandering.

After sunset, when the air becomes pleasantly cool, hilarity, song, and rollicking fun come forth from the conical huts. Young men and maidens assemble, and, with their arms as Nature formed them, twined around each other's necks, they softly breathe the old, old story which Adam and Eve first told in the Garden of Eden. Mothers troop into the balmy air with their children gathered about them as a hen gathers its chickens. The minstrels, beating the noisy drum and twanging the eloquent tom-tom, soon attract a circle of admirers, for music is natural to all Africans, and dancing, as a matter of course, follows ; and, as Nature and music prompt dancing, the most grotesque imitation of the actions of human beings are comically depicted, to the intense joy of the spectators, and the laughter, music, and jollity is kept up with the greatest excitement. The old men and women, forming the critical portion of the assembly, are provided with seats placed in a circle ; but, as they look on, gradually remembering the days of their youth, they take places in the dance, to the intense gratification of their children and grandchildren. This out-door exercise lasts until midnight, by which time everybody is fairly tired out, when all retire to their respective huts and enjoy a grand gorge of good food, washed down by calabashes of palm-wine, and after that they fall asleep. Verily, the natives of luxuriant Central Africa are very happy and contented in their natural state.

One bright moon-light night—it was so brilliant and clear

that you could see to read large print—the white men, trying vainly to go to sleep, at last got up, dressed, and went out to see the fun. It must have been some anniversary noted in their pagan almanac. Apart from the professional bards, there were a lot of young girls who evidently had organised a dance upon their own account. One of these dark but comely beauties, who was endowed with an excellent and sweet voice and good time, sang a song, the rest clapping hands at the proper periods, and all joined in a chorus at the end of each verse. Please to picture them in your vivid imagination as they stand in a curved row, beating time with their feet. The lady on the right advances with a graceful wriggle, cuts a few capers, whirls round, and falls into the united arms of the column of singing, clapping, feet-time-keeping girls, who jerk her up again instantly and push her forward. The same capers, wriggling, falling into arms, and jerking up again, is repeated over and over again until the dancer, becoming exhausted, drops on to the left flank. Then the next right-hand lady advances, and goes through the same performance. They keep it up for hours, the perspiration rolls from them, and their lively gestures and " accidentally on purpose " dropping their only cloth induce belief that they are coquetting extensively. When the moon is not to be had, palm-oil lights placed upon the ground act as a sort of substitute. How is that for high life amongst the jolly heathen ?

The table-land rising immediately behind Lukoja is marked on the chart " Patte," which in the Nupe language simply means "hill." The ascent is steep and difficult, yet elephant manage to climb it. One of our hunters informed us, on returning from the chase, after a hard day's exercise, that he had seen a herd of buffalo, and also four elephants, close to the village. These animals had been observed visiting the river for a healthy drink, and afterwards jogging along leisurely towards the nearest highland.   At five o'clock on the following morning we made up a party and started for the mountain-brow.   We were well armed with breech-loading rifles and revolvers, and a *posse* of negroes carried spare arms and refreshments.   The path up hill runs zig-zag for about two miles, and the latter part of the journey is simply scrambling up and over steep rocks, but the ascent is materially assisted by laying hold of the springy overhanging branches of trees.   The dew from the five to ten feet high grass soon thoroughly soaked our clothing.   At length, seated upon rocks upon the flat top, at an elevation of 1,200 feet above the level of the river, we were amply repaid for the fatigue of climbing by the glorious sight.   The sun, as it rose over the Binue, flooded the broad expanse of the river with beams of golden hues, illuminating the eastern heavens and driving away the misty dawn with its first peep above the horizon.   It reminds one of the nearest earthly resemblance to it portrayed by Turner's grand pictures.   The Binue gradually unfolds itself through fertile plains, with slopes on each side tapering upwards to far-distant and indistinct highland, and winds, shining like a vast mirror, amongst islands, until in front it joins the Niger coming from the north-west—another mighty body of glassy water also interspered with islands.   No confluence of two large rivers can be more clearly defined, nor a better view obtained.   It is literally a full-sized chart spread out for admiring inspection, and we viewed it at the best time of the day to enjoy it.   The sides of the table-land are covered with trees growing out between the fissures of rock.

We traced buffalo and elephant in most inaccessible-looking places for those animals.   Trees, bent by the trunks of elephant, showed how they had progressed, and bare branches notified that as they journeyed they fed upon the tender leaves. The table-land bears traces of villages desolated by Massaba, and artificial mounds of earth indicate the remains of yam plantations. For three days' travel westward no human habitation now exists in this magnificent region. We saw numbers of small trees torn up by the roots and the foliage carefully peeled off by the trunks of elephant, but we failed to meet with anything beyond deer. They were almost as large as English. cattle, and every few minutes we fell in with troops of monkeys. Some of the monkeys were very large and had manes like lions. These chattering animals crowd in the trees bearing stone-fruit. On our approaching they jumped from tree to tree, making them bend with their weight, and then they disappeared over the edge of the surrounding precipice into dense jungle and great caverns. We could not get nearer to them than two hundred yards. _These cunning creatures have outpost sentinels, that give timely warning of impending danger. One of those on watch, rejoicing in a respectable but ferocious-looking mane, showed fight. It stood right in our path and howled. The agent really thought that it was a small lion, and, as it stared hard and did not appear inclined to budge, he knelt, took aim, and fired a Whitworth breechloader, but missed. Upon the bullet whizzing past our inspector, it turned tail to flee. Then the monkey habits were apparent, and the lion-like attributes vanished. Whatever berries or plum-fruit monkeys eat, man may with safety do the same ; and wherever we saw them feeding we enjoyed the same fruit and noted its nature for further use.

The climate on this table-land is very mild and cool, and, as the gentle breeze was inhaled with satisfaction, we experienced the same happy sensation as that caused by winter residence in Madeira. In every direction we gaze at mountains, and most of them are flat-topped, looking like inverted wash-basins on a large scale. The flat top of each mountain is a distinct plateau of rich land, extending for several miles, and well-adorned with trees. Here and there amongst the fertile soil are beds of granite rock. In some cases Nature has formed hollows in the rock, as if spread out for our use, where are tiny pools of water fresh from the clouds, selected in pleasant shady retreats. We thoroughly enjoyed kneeling down and drinking it like horses, and then rolling to and fro with pure happiness at having found cool water in hot Africa, after the manner that donkeys spend their Sabbath of rest in green pastures. When traders become more numerous they will, no doubt, live on the hill-tops instead of on the banks of the rivers. It is quite easy to get carried to and fro in hammocks, and the difference in the temperature is so great that residence above or below actually means life or death ; but at present white traders are very stupid in this respect. Bountiful Nature has provided in many places in Africa healthy hilly districts convenient to get to, but the white man clings to the low-lying lands, really as if he wanted to be handy to jump into a grave convenient to his trading store.

The Bishop, who accompanied the unfortunate Government expedition of 1841 up this river, came up also by every other odd steamer running, with intervals of years between, until steamers commenced to run regularly, since when he ascends the Niger every year. He informs us that during his time on this beautiful table-land, and also on the bank of the river above Lukoja, there were many thriving and populous villages, but that the late Mahomet Saba, or Massaba, King of the Nupe country, wantonly and wickedly destroyed all the villages and rendered the fruitful country desolate. Massaba also overrun other happy rural districts, sold the inhabitants into slavery, and retired to his capital, called Beda; but shortly afterwards he was driven from his throne. However, upon obtaining assistance from the Sultan of Soccatoo, to whom he was subject, and to whom he paid tribute, he was enabled to put the usurper to the edge of the sword, and the edge did its business and worked death. He was a powerful King, and although at first sight undue severity appears, yet he understood the way to rule savages. His great virtue was his attachment to white traders. He gave them every accommodation, encouragement, and protection, to facilitate the establishment of trading factories on his part of the " Kwara "—the native name here for the Niger; higher up the river it is called "Joliba"—and if Massaba's successor, Omarue, has only got the good sense of his predecessor sufficiently to continue goodwill and succour to traders, a great future of wealth to all concerned will be developed in this part of Central Africa.

The kings and chiefs on this portion of the continent are accustomed to live in barbarous luxury by the sale of their slaves, who form, like cowrie-shells, a medium of exchange. Massaba would have bought any quantity of guns, powder, and goods with slaves, and he innocently offered them to us. The consequence was that a deputation had to be sent to him to explain that Englishmen do not traffic in human flesh. We obtained produce instead of slaves, and all white traders do the same. As chieftains make their slaves collect oils, gums, ivory, and seeds to barter for goods, then they will find out the true value of keeping labour in their own countries. They cannot be driven to abandon their ancient customs, so that it is only by means of promoting legitimate commerce that they may be induced to reduce or to limit the number of slaves sold. We see continually in this village gangs of strong men

attired in iron chains, of a lighter pattern than those represented on the Liverpool Exchange monument, but attached
in exactly the same manner. These poor creatures are
Massaba's slaves on their way to Iddah, to be sold to the
Attah for gunpowder, at the rate of a big man for a small
keg. He sends them also to other neighbouring monarchs to
exchange for goods from the Mediterranean or Atlantic
seaboard.

Dr. Baikie used to redeem slaves at the rate of from
three to ten bags of cowries per head, the younger people
fetching the higher price on account of probable slave
progeny. Each bag is worth 12s. 6d. His successors found
that they could not prudently continue to do so, because
cunning people made a trade of the mercy meant; so they
redeemed horses and asses instead, costing about the same
amount per head as slaves, and they found by experience that
animals worked more cheerfully than liberated slaves.

The lower classes here appear to be formed by Nature
dependent upon the cleverer people. But, upon reflection,
this seems to be the case all over the world, whether in the
most highly-civilised or the most outrageously savage country ;
whether *employés* in the former or slaves in the latter ; and,
in more cases than people like to acknowledge, the term
"slave" and "servant" are synonymous. It is a grave
mistake, though, for one moment to entertain the idea
because African slaves are so called that they are any
worse treated than people of every grade in civilised society
who, not possessed of independent means to enable them to ·
live "free," are obliged to work for somebody else. Occasionally a stupid African freeman, not properly appreciating
the priceless boon of glorious liberty, sells his very own self.
He receives the price of his own body, and, upon the strength
of that, he liquors up until not only his birthright, but also

his manhood-right, vanish like the evaporation of the trade-rum which he has swallowed. This is a very sad thing to contemplate, but it not uncommonly happens. To weak minds, it may appear that it is of greater advantage being under the protection of a powerful master than ·existing perhaps in a poorer manner as a free man. It is extremely hard to believe this doctrine, but human nature is verily a strange compound of contrariety and puzzle. It is well known that some highly-educated business men, becoming so very nervous about responsibilities and possible disaster, frequently give up all battling with vexatious life on their own account to become the servants of others. So we must not be too hard upon the poor untutored African who sells himself in a somewhat similar manner.

Women and men are frequently kidnapped on the paths between villages and sold into slavery. Mammy Peters, a very agreeable old lady who lives in comfort with her husband on a thriving farm, and who frequently sends us grateful and most acceptable presents of dishes for dinner—too good for aldermen—composed of pepper-pot, palm-oil chop, and palaver-sauce, relates, with much and deep heart-spoken feeling, that when a girl, with an earthenware jar getting water from the river, she was captured by cruel men from a passing canoe. She was simply stolen from her dearly-loved home, from her mother and her family, and disappeared like a dream. The canoe took her down the river, and she was passed through the hands of various savage tribes until she ·arrived at Angiama, where she was sold for the purpose of being eaten by the luxurious cannibals of that infamous village. The human-meat purchaser, acting according to the popular "fetish," had the girl's hands dipped into boiling-hot water. If her hands, as she quaintly remarks, holding them out to view, came out "proper," she was to be killed and cooked.

But, fortunately, her hands did not come out "proper." So she was again sold, and, duly arriving on the seaboard, became the property of a celebrated Lagos Portuguese slave-dealer, who shipped her with a crowd of other human beings forming an entire cargo. That cruel export of slaves does not now exist, thanks to the persistent bravery and watchfulness of our gallant navy ; but *export* slavery must not be confounded with *domestic* slavery. The former, as far as the west coast of Africa is concerned has been stopped ; but the latter, as before remarked, flourishes. Well, the slave-vessel containing this tossed-about girl was captured by an English cruiser, and taken, as was customary, "prize" to Sierra Leone, where, along with the others, she was set at liberty beneath the protection of the British flag. She was able to earn a good living ; everybody willing to work there can do the same. In course of time she married, and embraced Christianity, and gradually industry was rewarded by means of comfort for declining years. But she always hankered after the place of her birth, and, when trading steamers commenced to run up this river, she induced her husband to come here to spend their old age in her early Niger highland home. She is a blithe bonny old negress, and it is good and refreshing to listen to the sad and happy events of her life related in simple and deeply-pathetic language.

Leopards sometimes steal cat-like into this village, even in the middle of the day, when they are very hungry. They, probably, instinctively know that then the inhabitants are resting inside their huts ; so they quietly levy tribute, and leisurely walk off to their lair with ducks, sheep, or goats, and woe betide the little child who crosses their hungry path.

One of the white men, a few days after our arrival, showed me a very fine collection of butterflies, beetles, scorpions, and other interesting insects—especially so after death—pinned in light boxes and preserved with camphor. He also exhibited to my selfish and admiring gaze about twenty magnificent leopard-skins, and, with regard to them, he casually remarked that he had—ah—shot—ah—the original wearers. I naturally felt the deepest respect for such a talented and yet bashful Nimrod, and wanted to know how he did it; whether he sat up at nights in a hole dug in the earth, as other African travellers have done, and watched his opportunity, or whether he killed them in the jungle ; but he was very reserved upon these points, as all truly brave men are. One night, as it approached towards dawn, I was awoke by terrific, wild-animal, zoological-garden shrieking, and, further sleep being out of the question, I quietly dressed and waited for daybreak, and, as soon as the grey dawn dispelled the darkness, I sallied forth to discover whence the noise proceeded. At a distance of about one hundred yards from the compound, I observed a large rat-trap looking affair, constructed of stout limbs of trees stuck deep into the earth, and fastened together by strong fibrous thongs, the whole construction being about the size of a very small mountain-side cabin in Connemara ; but so closely were the uprights and cross-pieces placed, that once any-thing above the size of a cat got inside and partook of the bait—which upon biting released a very heavy falling con-trivance, enclosing the "feedist"—it could not escape, and wild cries, and violent exertion to get out, were, therefore, naturally expended in vain. Inside this trap was · a roaring live leopard. It had eaten the bait (a living bleating kid) as the uneaten trotters and portions of skin lying about plainly showed ; and although it had the advantage of being alone and undisturbed by other animals, still that blessing was counterbalanced, and more so, by captivity and confiscation. The leopard enjoyed the early breakfast, but the banquet proved expensive, and it had to pay for that last meal, and did so. I approached the cage, the animal flew round and round it and scratched, and there I saw the beautiful wild beast in its native purity. Soft speech only made it show its teeth fiercer and fiercer, so 1 returned to the compound, awoke the eminent hunter of wild beasts, and quietly, but sarcastically, suggested that he might add one more skin to his collection, and he went "like a bird" and coolly shot the leopard through the bars of the cage, showing the sportsman-like manner that he had been enabled to collect the other skins.

During this, the rainy season, the paths are at times almost impassable, and it is very unpleasant and difficult to walk through the long grass and drooping branches of trees laden with moisture overhanging the narrow way. In deep gulches, where streamlets gently babble and meander as you cross them by jumping from boulder to boulder, upon returning you perhaps find a deep, fierce torrent rushing towards the river, sweeping great stones before it, and washing away earth from each side. In this case, as it is raining "cats, dogs, and pitchforks," figuratively speaking, so that it is perfectly impossible to ford the turbulent body of water, you are prevented returning home, and you are obliged to hie to the nearest village and accept the friendly shelter, rest, and refreshment which are always cheerfully accorded, and remain there until the waters subside again to the rivulet condition.

The dry season commences in November and ends in July. During this period the river falls here thirty-five feet from its highest point in October to its lowest during June. The river Nile at Cairo has the same rise and fall, occurring at about the same time. The mountain torrents are then changed to deep dry ravines, plentifully strewn with huge boulders. As the waters fall extensive islands appear, upon which natives flock from the highlands and dwell. These wandering tribes cultivate the rich alluvial soil, planting various sorts of grain and tobacco; and frequently they succeed in collecting two crops before the river again rises. Sometimes, however, the second crop is lost by the premature appearance of the rainy season. Wild duck, pelican, and crown-birds in great numbers flock to the islands to earn their living by picking up their particular sort of food, as do hippopotami for the purpose of feeding upon tender vegetation. On the islands at the Confluence, temporary houses are erected and markets are held, where traders from high up the Upper Niger and from distant parts of the river Binue conveniently land produce, ivory, and slaves from their large canoes, and, meeting traders from Lukoja, Igbegbe, Iddah, Onitsha, and other places, exchange them for manufactured goods obtained from the seaboard. On the mainland the long grass becomes dry and is burnt up—sometimes intentionally, but often accidentally. The flames from the burning grass, licking high up the trunks of trees, destroy dry ones; the parched, light, jungly bush, crackles, and in a few minutes only ashes are seen upon the surface. After this the arable land is ready for tillage. Occasionally fire sweeps towards a village; the inhabitants thereof turn out instantly, and with branches of trees try to beat it down. Should the dwellings take fire, they have sense enough to pull surrounding houses down to limit the conflagration, and by so doing save a portion of the hamlet.

The ears of the women are pierced, or rather punched with holes, and through these holes they insert and wear cylindrical long beads of bright patterns, composed principally of opal or bright blue transparent stone, or of cornelian

and agate in various tints. On their backs, bosoms, arms,
and faces, fancy patterns, tattooed during infancy or child-
hood, expand with their growth, and exhibit to view pictures
something like ornamental crochet designs, just as if antimacassars made of whipcord had been pressed back and
front by steam power, breaking the tender skin, and then
gunpowder or Indian-ink rubbed over the bleeding samplers
left. This seems an unholy way of disfiguring the human
body, subjecting it to unnecessary torment. It is considered,
however, the correct thing to do. The Arabs are given to
somewhat similar tattoo-work; and it may, therefore, be
fairly assumed that natives of the intermediate countries
adopt the same custom. A bright, black, sparkling, but
brittle metal, darker in colour than lead, and said by some
people to be antimony, is freely used, in the shape of fine
powder, to dye the eyelids of the ladies and throw the whites
of their eyes out wickedly. The same custom exists in
eastern countries in other forms. The ladies here also stain
their finger nails with henna, as Turkish and Egyptian
women do. A redwood dye is used also by some women, and
with it they rub their nearly altogether apparent persons.
It forms a dull brick colour on the skin, and quite spoils
the pretty and naturally glossy black appearance; but it is
the fashion, and must be followed, like the modern civilised
dresses so tightly fitting to precious forms that, on a front
view, the graceful contour is delineated; but, as the sailor
said to the judge, "abaft the binnacle" hangs useless appen-
dages. I am sorry to say that, as the dark daughters
of the land wax ancient, the most sensible of them are
sometimes accused of witchcraft; and, exactly as some of
our plum-pudding-headed ancestors acted with the wise-
women of bygone periods—*they* burnt them as witches—
here they appeal to Ju-Ju, which prescribes doses of poison

to test witchcraft or guilt of various sorts. If the old woman recovers from the effect of the poison, all right; but sometimes the reputed witches are cruelly beaten to death by sticks and stones, and the bodies are then cast into the great river, food for crocodile.

Women here, as elsewhere, get wonderfully excited over a wedding. The young man who had been absent for one year, and who came up with us to his home at Lukoja, was married by the Rev. Mr. Johns, at the Church of England mission. After the Christian portion of the ceremony was over, then commenced the Pagan festivities—latent amongst all African Christians. The whole community—Christians, Mahometans, and Pagans—"went in blind" for a week's carnival. So frantically wild were they with joy that they appeared to have taken leave of their intellects. The young girls found supplies of cowries from somewhere, with which to fee in advance the professional drummers, and also the tom-tom and stringed instrument performers. These eminent worthies are wide awake enough to get the money before they strike a note, and they subsequently make frequent collections as people become lively and their cowrie-bags become loosened.

We had music and dancing day and night. Even solemn old men and withered ancient beldames shook their legs about wildly under the influence of *fermented* palm-wine (which is very intoxicating) and frequent potations of the more potent trade-rum. Mothers of families, with a child clinging straddled sideways upon their hips, or else tied behind their backs, went in for the dissolute life, and so neglected their household duties that not a few of them were summarily recalled to reason by their hungry and forsaken husbands breaking in upon the orgies and punching their heads and beating them, as some of our glorious, free, and independent electors do with their generally sensible helpmates. Lynch law is justifiable when husbands beat wives, and it gladdened me to see that these cruel husbands were summarily punished upon the spot. Indignant and stalwart youths fell upon them and nearly killed one or two of them. They will not readily forget that wedding. It was truly a " rum scrimmage ; " but little incidents of that sort only caused a temporary cessation of the carnival. The musicians struck up, and away went their constituents at it. again. The white men looked on for one or two evenings, but the novelty soon wore off, and it became exceedingly monotonous, especially as we could not readily fall asleep with the noise of the drums beating, the women shrieking with delight, the men shouting with boisterous joy, and the madman of the village intensely happy, and, becoming blind drunk, uttering those terribly disagreeable noises peculiar to idiots. But gradually, beneath the mosquito-curtain, the unearthly sounds became familiar and toned down to some well-known home tune; " sleep, gentle sleep, Nature's soft nurse," acted a kind part, and in oblivion, in that pleasant happy dreamland which is one of the most precious gifts of the Creator, our souls were wafted far away, forgetful of the present, anticipating with dull joy a happy future, mixed up with delightful but misty recollections of past pleasant days fled for ever. In those round mud huts, with open spaces on each side allowing the cool night air to waft through, our rest came as calmly as to the effigies in Westminster Abbey, with this difference, that they do not turn, but yet they have the advantage of being mosquito-proof; however, we have a better pull in another direction, for when the soul returns from happy dreamland we turn out in the morning ready for the day, and, as a rule, they do not.

Until the new trading store was erected, the bale goods

and casks were stored in the long shed connecting the agent's
hut with mine, through which was a sort of thoroughfare ;
but, to secure better protection, and to keep from the gaze of
the public, we housed the more valuable goods—which were
in small packages handy for thieves to pick up and run away
with—such as silk-velvets, good umbrellas, beads, and so
forth, in a conical mud hut similar to mine, and at ten yards
distance from my bed. This hut was selected because it had
a very strong door, which was fast locked by one of Chubb's
big brass padlocks ; but one morning we found the door wide
open, and a cunningly-devised, but not successful, Lukoja-
made brass key, to imitate the real key fitting the wards,
stuck in the lock, which it had vainly been applied to open.
Although so close to me, I heard no noise ; and, being most
tenacious of disturbance, would have awoke had any noise
occurred. The burglary must have been performed with great
sagacity and quietness, yet the round top of the padlock had
been filed through. It was evident that one of our confidential
servants had done this. We could not observe anything
missing, but, when comparing the inventory with the goods
remaining in the hut, it was discovered that a box of genuine
coral beads, costing in England two hundred pounds sterling,
and for which about five hundred pounds return in produce
was naturally expected, had been stolen. One of our educated
nigger clerks had applied for a week's holiday only a day
before, and the boon was freely granted by our always kind
trading agent ; but, as the clerk never turned up again, and
as we heard that he was "high-falutin" and leading a prodigal
life in adjacent villages, we naturally concluded that he had
collared the coral beads and was revelling upon the strength
of their value. Meanwhile, Massaba's chief sassured us that
they would find the thief and cut his head off. Well, if
they gave us the head of the thief without the missing coral

beads hanging from the lying lips of our special Autolycus, what satisfaction would that be ?   Those clever fellows traced footmarks in the soft sandy soil from the plundered hut to a drainage hole at the lower corner of the high enclosure wall, sufficient for a slender thief to wriggle through, and they arrested several innocent people, and wanted very much to cut their heads off before we made inquiry as to their guilt or innocence.   They acted so fiercely, and drew their swords so readily, and flashed their eyes so wildly, that we were obliged to insist upon their clearing out of our court of inquiry, and appearing as witnesses or not at all.   We began to suspect these fellows of complicity with the thief, but now think that zeal for their chieftain's protection to us caused them to act with great energy, lest their own heads, upon return to Beda, should be rendered loose by Massaba, if, like Sairey Gamp, he felt "so disposed."   They wanted to try several suspected people, and in their own summary manner execute such, but we would not allow them to do so ; so they sent special word to Massaba, and his reply, in good Arabic, was that they were to " cut off the head of every person suspected."   He also stated that the missing coral must be found and restored.   This was all very flattering to us, but, entailing as it would have done the slaughter of innocents, the agent, who, from being one of the principal capitalists in the venture, had also the most to say in the matter, calmly allowed the affair to drop. But had we caught the missing clerk we would have talked to him in a fatherly sort of way, pointing out to him the error of his ways and so forth.   Oh, yes ! we would have done so, especially the " so forth ;" but he avoided our pleasant society.   Peradventure, when that benighted negro thief visits England, dressed in broadcloth, and rolling in wealth, he may, through the second column of the *Times*, restore the value of the stolen property to its rightful owner, with interest added. Perhaps upon reading this he may return to the path of honesty; but I fear that, on the contrary, he will only laugh at how cleverly he robbed the friend who not only spared his life, but the lives of those suspected of his crime.

To our great joy the steamer returned from the sea on the 11th day of September. But our gladness was turned to sorrow, for two of the white men had died of fever during the passage down the river, and two others were carried ashore at Akassa invalided. We heard afterwards that they had been forwarded to Lagos, where they both died. The sad news had a very depressing effect upon everybody, as those who died were the youngest and strongest men on board, and, therefore, the more likely to live the longest. So much did it grieve and affect the living, that although in the enjoyment of rude, robust health, yet we began to lose interest in beautiful Lukoja, and heartily wished that the trading further up the Niger and also up the Binue was over for the season.

Massaba sent a long letter, written in Arabic, requesting us to send to him several hundred kegs of powder, a quantity of Birmingham trade muskets with suitable flints, and numerous other articles of which he stood in need. Massaba sent canoes about fifty feet long, five feet beam, and three feet deep, each canoe cut and formed out of a single tree. The goods were duly handed over to the chiefs, and were to be paid for in produce sent from Beda upon our arrival at Egga. Massaba's slaves, by order of their chieftains, took the powder to the river-bank and housed it over in a temporary manner by palm-thatch; but these slaves built huts close to the powder, and made fires, and when wind arose the sparks from the fires flew on to the thatch covering it, and we feared every moment a terrific explosion. This was too much; we did not like it at all, and decided that if

they would not shift quarters we should. They, at length,
paddled for about a mile up the river, and our hearts again
beat serenely. Two nights after the steamer's return,
about twenty Lukoja houses were destroyed by fire ; but, ·
as the powder was at a safe distance, it did not matter;
otherwise our gallant ship and her living freight might have
been blown skywards without giving us a chance to chant
" Nunc dimittis."

Although the average heat of the day during sunshine in
the mud huts is 98°, and from 108° to 120° in the sun (our
highest in the sun was 128°), yet in December, when the
Harmattan wind sets in, the thermometer registers before
sunrise as low as 65°. It is different, though, during the
day. The lowest that was experienced before sunrise during
the rainy season was 72°.

The calm, still nights now begin to be varied by the
occurrence of tornadoes, and they waken up everybody
properly. For ten minutes previously the wind, increasing
every moment in strength until it becomes a gale, and
briefly developes into a hurricane, blowing from S.E. to E.,
brings up a canopy of black clouds, with distant lightning
and thunder. Presently, it surrounds us like enchantment.
Rain falls in torrents, lightning plays all over the ship and
illuminates the electric conductors, and dances fantastically
over iron-work, causing blindness for a few minutes, whilst
the thunder deafens and rings in the ears long after the
fierce, but only temporary, disturbance of Nature lasts. The
thunder reverberates amongst the dark hills, and, passing
over them, is no · more heard. From half-an-hour to an
hour after the wind begins to blow, the inky clouds disappear to leeward. Meanwhile glimpses of distant scenery
on the mountain sides show vividly by the instantaneous
receding bright flashes, and these brilliant views are very

gratifying to the keen sense of sight, especially so when the crashing thunder ceases. Then all nature becomes calm, and

> " There's nought but stillness o' the night
> Where was sic din before."

The thermometer during a tornado falls from 25° to 35°. After the war of the elements is over, it rises again as fast as it fell, perceptibly changing from cold, yielding pleasant breathing, to close heat, and, as the moisture evaporates, it gives forth malaria, and then Europeans are most liable to take fever. The poor fellows who died could not be induced to sleep underneath the awning, but preferred to place their mats and pillows anywhere in the open air, exposed to the night dew. It is very pleasant at the time to do so; but it invariably brings on fever, and if the moon happens to shine, the human frame is liable to be shattered by moonstroke. Acting so unwisely on this river renders after-life miserably wretched.

One night a tornado proved so extra-violent that our anchor dragged, our mooring ropes broke, and the vessel drifted like a wreck upon a lee shore, which in this case was a soft bank overhung with trees; and, as the masts, spars, and rigging, by the wobbling to and fro of the vessel acting upon the keel and sides as fulcrum, broke off branches covered with noxious insects and reptiles, we felt horribly uncomfortable until daylight came, when all hands swept and garnished.

The Harmattan wind comes from the north-easterly direction, blowing over the great Sahara desert. In 1875 it did not commence until the first week in January, and before it began the arrangement of nature seemed to be changed to perfect calm and intensely suffocating heat. At sea, steamers running north of Sierra Leone during the Harmattan, with freshly-tarred rigging, or recently-painted bulwarks, find on the side next to Africa that the tarred rigging is powdered with fine sand, and that the newly-painted bulwarks assume the nature of sand-paper. It is imperceptible in its action, further than that towards the land the sky exhibits a dull, cloudy, but fiery appearance. On shore at Sierra Leone this peculiar wind is welcomed by recent European residents as affording cooler air to breathe and ability to walk about that exceedingly hot town regardless of the sunshine. But the older white residents and all the natives detest the Harmattan, for it brings to them colds and bronchitis, and deals death liberally amongst those of the natives who are weak in the chest, just as our horrible easterly winds do with people similarly affected. The Harmattan wind is so dry that nostrils become painful by the unseen but fine sand, inhaled as it is wafted from the desert; the backs of books bend outwards, and the veneer of furniture peels off in shreds.

Before leaving our conical mud huts for residence on the steamer, we were attacked in the middle of the night by ants. First a noise rose from one hut and then from another, but presently it was fully explained, for myriads of ants, probably prevented by some device from sacking the other huts, swarmed into mine and crept all over the bed. Apart from the disagreeable feeling of insects crawling over the person, many of them took biting samples to report to their commanding officers; so much so that I was obliged to rise from sweet repose and flee away, wiping and beating the hungry ants off with a Baden-Baden towel made of sackcloth. Somebody said, "Go to the ants, thou sluggard;" but he had evidently never been there himself, or he would not have given such injudicious advice. Perhaps it was meant as a very mild sanctimonious "sell." In this case the voice of the sluggard awoke and complained. That invaluable "cuss," the oldest inhabitant, told us that the visitation of

the ants was a merciful dispensation from Ju-Ju, and we
were quite willing to believe so, for in a very short time
they cleared out all other objectionable insects, including
wasps, centipedes, scorpions, beetles, and cockroaches; and
they carted the carcasses away, as the ancient Romans did
Egyptian obelisks, to their capital. Ants act exactly as
companies, regiments, battalions, brigades, and armies of
human beings do. You may kill thousands by one stroke of
a stick, and keep on smiting until the stick is worn out, or
you become tired and wait to go to bed, but they re-form
silently in martial order and continue their progress,
persevering in what they intend to perform, so that nor man
nor animal, unless speedy flight is available, stands any chance
against them. The only protection against ants is to take
ashes from the wood fire and make a line around your
dwelling. They cannot get over ashes.

The agent having appointed a competent young Englishman to take charge of the store and to conduct trading for
one year, assisted by an interpreter and a staff of servants
similar to the establishment at Onitsha, we are ready to
ascend the Upper Niger to the large town of Egga. We
leave the Bishop behind us, as he ascends no higher than
Lukoja, it being his most northerly station. Higher up, the
prevailing people are Mahometans; and wherever that is so
Christianity stands not the most remote chance of introduc-
tion. Before parting with him he told us, in the calm
unostentatious manner peculiar to him, and well known to all
who have the pleasure of intimate acquaintance with him, of
his being captured when a boy and sold as a slave for rum
and tobacco. In the simplest manner he relates having
been bought by the neighbouring chiefs and passed from hand
to hand, as good Mammy Peters was passed, as a medium of
coinage until arrival at Lagos, where now he rules as Bishop.

From that once infamous slave rendezvous—during the African experience of the author it was so—this poor, naked, forlorn boy was shipped by a Portuguese slave-dealer; but, fortunately for the furtherance of civilisation, the vessel was captured by an English man-of-war, and the living cargo landed at Sierra Leone. This boy was baptised Samuel Adjai Crowther; and at school his ability and aptness to learn, added to his gentle manners, gradually endeared him to all. After education, instead of taking to trading, he took to literature and the Church, and he has undoubtedly been the means of promulgating the benefits of civilisation amongst hitherto rampant savages. So highly was he esteemed, not only upon the West Coast of Africa, but also in England, that in 1864 he was consecrated the first coloured bishop of the Church of England, by the title "Bishop of the Niger Territory."

Life at Lukoja has got its advantages and the contrary. To Europeans, with their hearts where their home affections are, after a few weeks revelling in the strangely fascinating country, it becomes an abomination, despite the glorious scenery. But to those who, being jilted in love, feel inclined to wander "up the highest Andes, or down a horrible volcano;" or to those who are so formed by Nature to seek and enjoy seclusion, or to active and daring Nimrods—Lukoja presents all that can be desired to render life happy. We became indifferent to the big trees, the elephant, the tornadoes, and everything. Fortunately, we adapted ourselves to the food and drink of the natives, and for a little time the change was refreshing; but gradually we only partook of food sufficient to keep us up to our work. All that we required to render us supremely happy was some good English beef, also bread and cheese; but those gay and festive luxuries were a long way out of our reach.

CHAPTER VII.

LUKOJA speedily disappeared from our view as we steamed from it at six A.M. on the 14th day of September. We kept up full steam the whole day, making about ten knots an hour, and long after dark we anchored off the large town of Egga.

From Lukoja to Egga the Niger winds gracefully through a valley ranging from ten to thirty miles in width, abounding in rich soil and cultivated level districts, fringed in the distance on each side of the river by the flat-topped hills peculiar to this part of Africa. The river being now very high, in some parts it has overflowed the low-lying banks to the extent of five and six miles, and where that occurs the wide expanse of water presents the appearance of a great and continuous lake district.

There are numerous large villages, all formed of the singular-looking round mud huts; and where the current of the river has altered its course, it simply sweeps them away like water melting sugar. We passed close to half towns, and observed sections of hundreds of houses partially washed away, exposing to view the inmates in the act of leisurely removing. Their furniture did not appear very extensive; a few grass mats, country cloths, cooking pots, and perhaps a favourite house monkey, are quietly passed into canoes alongside the fast-disappearing houses; and families, as if it were quite a common affair, in the coolest manner migrate to more solid land, where we heard and observed them drumming and singing and building new villages of new mud huts, and thatching them with green palm-leaves. Mud is abundant and palm-trees are the same. It does not take five minutes to construct a temporary dwelling from palm-leaves, affording both shady and waterproof qualities, until the snug, cool, mud-walled, thickly-thatched hut, with pleasant-to-bare-feet asphalted floor, is ready to enter as the new home. This will last until the river again shows eccentricity, when the operations of flitting and fresh building have to be performed over again.

At Egga we commenced trading in earnest. One man was sent on shore to open shop in a hut; another was sent up to Beda, the capital of this Nupe country, for the same purpose; and we opened out our chief mart of commerce on board ship. For the English market, we bartered goods for tusks of ivory, weighing from 120 lbs. downwards. We also freely bought Shea butter, a valuable vegetable grease, hard in substance, and looking very much like white pomatum, and which will some day, when its qualities of hair-restoring are known, form a gigantic barber's advertisement. Somebody lacking a fortune ought to go violently into Shea butter. Example.—Two of our white men, wearing scanty hair, worn off their heads by frequent doses of African fever, get their polls shaven twice weekly by native barbers. It is really a most delicious operation. The barbers afterwards rub Shea butter well over those billiard-ball bald heads, and presently the unseen forest springs up, and heavy crops of capillature result.

Shea butter is collected from trees, the culture of which is carefully tended, and, when properly rendered into hard lard-looking material, is brought off in earthenware jars, each jar containing from one to fifteen gallons, and it is pleasant to see the jars tumbled on board and our bale goods diminish.

We also buy heaps of the teeth of hippopotami for the benefit of dentists at home, and wild boars' tusks, probably for the same purpose. For the markets on the West Coast we heap up the medicinal saltpetre called lubi, and also country-woven cloths of very thick durable material, cunningly and cleverly made in various pretty and quaint patterns, measuring from four to eight feet long and from one to five feet wide. The most prevalent colour is blue, on account of the abundance of the indigenous indigo. Many of these substantial cloths are interwoven with coarse red silk brought over Sahara from the Mediterranean seaboard; and, being highly valued in the West Coast towns, they yield considerable profit.

On the morning after anchoring off Egga, the chief of the town, a handsome young man, very tall, and endowed with regular and pleasing features, came off in a canoe, bringing with him, as a present for us, a slain buffalo, several live sheep and goats, pumpkins, calabashes of parched maize, large onions, and other truly welcome and much-needed provisions. We went wild over the onions, which are similar in size and quality to those imported into Britain from Spain. They imparted to us health, strength, and renewed vigour, especially when we found out, which we speedily did, what the natives ate in the shape and nature of lettuce and watercress. Then we went in steep for salad, and the engine-oil being purely vegetable—not that horrible petroleum stuff sometimes palmed off for Gallipoli, or olive—we used it freely. This, with a raw salt herring (the Krooboy's delight), after picking all the bones out and cutting it up fine and adding some fresh green pepper-pods, we found to be luxurious feeding.

Our generous benefactor, the young chief, was remarkably well-dressed in the long flowing tobe of the upper classes. He enclosed his lower extremities in the usual Turkish baggy trousers, and a broad-brimmed straw-hat, trimmed with red leather, covered his good head. Beneath the hat he wore a thin blue flannel cap. Suspended at his side was the customary straight sword with decorated brass handle, and also a highly-ornamented sharp dagger. He represented King Massaba, and worthily did he act his part. Other canoes filled with men, women, and children—well-dressed, ill-dressed, and rejoicing in no dress at all—came alongside, and the population crowded on board, so filling the deck that we could not move, and were compelled to ask the young swell chief for a few special constables to keep a clear space beneath the awning aft. He at once supplied the "bobbies;" but they layed on right and left, on men and women indis-criminately, with whips made of hippopotamus hide, causing painful-looking lumps to rise on the body, so that we gladly dispensed with their services, and tried how the law of kindness would act. We constructed a barrier of empty oil puncheons as a counter, behind which was our wholesale and retail shop. We broke off the iron hoops and cut open the well-packed bales of Manchester goods, and exposed Madras kerchiefs of glowing red and yellow colours, Turkey-red chintz and twills, red blankets, and a variety of eye-pleasing patterned cottons too numerous to mention. We also opened boxes of brass rods, likewise of brass pans called "neptunes," varying in size from a saucer to a sponge-bath. It is a remarkable feature in Central-African barter that the brightest articles command the best returns; hence it is that the tag-rag-and-bobtail adore all utensils made of brass, and they take great pride in keeping these showy jewels bright as gold. But the casks containing delicately-made boxes artistically illustrated on the outside, and inside filled with neatly-packed and ravishing soft silk-velvet robes for the aristocracy—beautiful green, brilliant magenta and scarlet, and all the colours of the rainbow—fairly overcome the most fastidious. Bright skies invariably cause humanity to love brilliant tints for apparel. Nature shows this by adorning birds with illuminated plumage and fish with sparkling jackets. Hence in our cold, cloudy climate ensues the natural use of corresponding sombre hues, black cloth, dark suicidal neckties, and funeral hats ; and even the melancholy sparrows and dull crows conform to Nature. We also exhibited cases of small German looking-glasses, matchets, and knives of various kinds, and all sorts of useful articles for common use in daily life, from the noisy fog-horn down to the entertaining penny whistle or the useful needle, and we were ready for any amount of trade, and only wanted customers—as Shakspeare might have remarked had he been up the Niger—to come on with the stuff, and cram us until the chief mate cries out " Avast ! The holds are full ! Enough ! "

As we opened each bale, case, cask, or ornamentally decorated card-built box, screams of frantic delight were uttered, like those arising upon a bright May morning from a school of laughing and happy boys or girls wandering through the Lowther Arcade, devouring the glorious toys exhibited with their festive eyes. The women turned up their optics in ecstatic rapture on merely feeling the nature of the rich silk velvets, which gave to them the same happy sensation as that experienced by rubbing a donkey's nose. Gentle reader, did you ever rub a donkey's nose ? If not, the next time you go to Cairo or New Brighton just try it, and you will add one more exquisite enjoyment to life. I was very sorry that the women could not afford to buy the velvet, and equally regretted that I was not millionaire enough to present each of them with what their sparkling eyes plainly showed that they loved and coveted.

We gradually found out that, for the purpose of fostering steady trade, we should not expose before the bewildered gaze of the community too many fine and superfine things at once. It was a mistake. The exhibition was, therefore, curtailed in the same way that we found prudent in smaller Lukoja; for showing their eyes "grieved their hearts," and they wanted too many good things for one tusk of ivory, or for a small jar of Shea butter, a lump of lubi, or even for a single country cloth.

Our trading agent was truthfully reputed as one of the most successful men on the West Coast or the interior for dealing with the natives. His long residence and prosperity at Lagos, of which colony he once acted as governor, and by the natives was christened "King of Lagos," out of their pure love for his manly qualities, entitled him so to be considered. Nothing disturbed his equanimity. He would buy a dozen tusks, wave his hand to the servants in attendance to produce the merchandise required for payment, in the midst of jabber and wrangle, and he would then turn to the next customer in regular order if even he, or she, only brought a single jar of Shea butter, exactly as a good physician accords interviews in regular turn to his patients, irrespective of their rank and worldly importance. But these Egga people vexed and annoyed us very much at first by very simple, and easily-seen-through, trade devices. For instance, the same tusk of ivory was offered over and over again, but by different people, and, although we marked the weight upon it in pencil and ink, they carefully obliterated the marks before submitting it for sale again. However, we soon discovered and remedied this simply display of cunning. It was proclaimed, through the interpreter, that after being at the trouble of placing pieces of cloth, counting brass rods, and

16

putting on the "top" of the lot needles, fishhooks, knives, looking-glasses, and other trifles before the owners of the ivory, and yet after all that the bargain was not completed, the rule would be to refuse tusks so frequently offered, which by talk-talk and useless palaver only wasted our precious time. To recognise the oft-returning tusks, and to ensure the rule being carried out correctly, we drilled a small hole, by means of a competent centrebit, near to the end over the hollow part of it, so as not to injure the valuable tusk ; and then, upon its next appearance, we either refused to purchase it or else bought it upon our own terms. Thus we drilled these innocents into earnestness, and gradually did a thriving and profitable business.

As we could not remain to trade after the river commenced to fall regularly, we told our constituents so, and they crowded the deck from early morn until we got tired out and shut up shop. Strange people came from afar and near in canoes, bringing our much-desired and profitable produce in large or small quantities ; the latter chiefly for amusement, to entitle them more to observe the strange white man and his doings than for trade. Some of our new friends, foreign even to Egga residents, came comfortably in their floating canoe-homes from far away up the Niger, even from beyond Timbuctoo. They were remarkably tall men, with most strikingly handsome and determined Jewish features, but still as glossy black in skin as the ace of spades. A temporary interpreter, called Dorego, a Houssaman, who had as a boy acted as servant to Dr. Barth during his long residence at Timbuctoo, understood partly what these strangers said, from which we gathered that they had come all the way from Morocco.

Dr. Barth, one of the most indefatigable of African travellers, took Dorego and another Houssa boy, called

Abiga, home with him, and had them well educated in
English and German.   They returned to Lukoja, where they
now reside, and they are of the greatest use, acting as interpreters to traders.   Their tales of European cities lighted at
night by artificial moons in the shape of gas, and the brilliant
shop windows filled with wondrous articles of value, have
spread widely amongst their neighbouring tribes.   The result
is that love and esteem for honest traders induce desire to
see more of them, and incline all to treat them with
kindness.

To facilitate commerce and give to our numerous customers
a fair chance to obtain what they wanted in equity (on our
side) for what we desired in exchange, it was found expedient
to open a second shop on board the steamer.   So the trading
agent stuck to the mart of commerce aft beneath the awning,
taking his seat at a table in front of the binnacle, for the
purpose of buying the large tusks of ivory ; and I opened a
friendly sort of opposition shop at the other end of the ship,
beneath the forward awning, so as to draw off idlers and the
bulk of crowding petty customers who were hardly worth a
"red cent."   I went in for trade with a will, and experienced
great delight in witnessing the manners and habits of people
so very much superior to the generally wretched beings on
the coast.   Constructing a counter of empty casks, I
exchanged all sorts of goods for various produce ; but, as
regards ivory, only for small tusks, called by the London
ivory-brokers " scrivelloes "—*i.e.*, those under twenty pounds
in weight.   All above that weight I sent aft with my love to
the trading agent ; for, through inexperience in purchasing
ivory, I might possibly be buying it recklessly at a loss,
which is certainly not the object of any trading expedition.
I had no interpreter in my shop, but managed by pantomimic
signs, absurd gesticulations, and "chaff," which the Egga

people seemed perfectly to understand; and I thoroughly enjoyed the fun and kindness displayed by my comical customers.

It is marvellous to witness the effect of our traders bringing to this region the manufactures of Europe, and carrying away in return the surplus produce of this strangely luxuriant country. Mutual intercourse invariably wears off those old-time prejudices which cause nations to dislike each other, whether civilised or savage, or mixed, or both. There is a common interest developed by the creation of new wants amongst the heathen, and habits of industry are thereby so engendered that they eagerly seek out whatever we require to enable them to get what they want. This becomes strikingly apparent, not only in their improved manner of living and dressing, but also in the establishment of better governing laws which naturally ensues.

The exported slaves, many of whom came from this part of Africa (the few re-captured were landed at Sierra Leone or Fernando Po, the rest were taken across the Atlantic to the West Indies, or to North and South America), wherever they were deposited, acquired wants unknown to them before, and wherever their descendants now exist, whether in communities of their own, or as subjects of colonies, or as citizens of the United States, no class contributes more to the development of commerce, for they are not given to hoarding wealth when they are inflicted with it.

Our primitive system of barter may, therefore, be taken as a sample of the means which will eventually civilize all Africa. Traders drive the small end of the wedge in first; it then follows for missionaries and philanthropists to do the rest.

Before commencing to barter goods for produce on this river, it is essential that the ruling powers be propitiated by presents of useful articles given from time to time as lawful tribute. Chiefs who are sensible will then afford every protection to foster and continue commerce, and it seldom happens after being started, and the mutual barter business is satisfactory, that traders are driven away.

Our floating shop is crowded with worthy and welcome applicants for British wares and merchandise. The women are far keener at trading than the men, and are much more pleasant to deal with. Male traders, exerting their superior strength, rudely hustled and shoved on one side numbers of the fair sex; but, as both brought equally good things to fill our vessel, we taught the gentlemen manners, and formed a row of ladies in the front, seated upon the chimes of our cask counter. Now, seated upon the sharp angular iron-and-oak combination forming the chime is not conducive to comfort, unless thick petticoats act similar to ships' fenders; but these ladies do not rejoice in, nor require, any under-clothing. However, they did not complain, and laughingly, covetingly, admiringly enjoyed the good view of our tiny exhibition and glorious array of brilliant things behind the counter. We had to threaten with a whip anybody disturbing the ladies until they had got what they wanted, when they were politely requested to clear out and let other produce-bringers come to the front.

To keep silence was impossible, nor would it have been at all agreeable or jolly. Every modulation of the human voice, from the yell to the attempted soft whisper, was uttered. A dozen arms were stretched out for several dozen articles, and ten dozen mouths shouted. For a short time, by attending to one customer, comparative order was obtained, and, by getting all that he or she had for sale, a certain barter-rate was established. For example, take jars of Shea butter averaging 60lbs. in weight. So many kerchiefs, looking-glasses, and fish-hooks were handed over for each jar, and a run of an hour would take place. When that article became scarce, more goods were demanded for it, which caused us to stop taking it, and appear as if we did not want it. Then we fixed a rate for lubi, and so on with antimony and country cloths. We packed the country cloths in the casks which had brought out civilised merchandise, and locked them up in the hold, so as to prevent the spread of kleptomania amongst our own Krooboys.

Some silly people brought us second-hand country cloths, but this evil practice I stopped by indignantly throwing one piece overboard into the river, and at the same moment, assuming an appropriate attitude, hissed out, "Kwara-Kwara!" The assembly roared heartily with laughter at the poor woman who had lost her cloth, and her downcast looks caused me to take her to the interpreter, and, giving her double the value of the cloth consigned to the river, I told her to tell everybody else that we would certainly throw overboard all cloths offered for sale that had been once worn. She did so; and, being thus encouraged and noticed daily, brought off canoe-loads of new cloths and lubi. I fancy that from that moment she was elected broker, and earned well-deserved commission.

To some of my customers, I presented, with great show of ceremony, odd trifles,—looking-glasses, metal spoons, fancy beads, and toy Pharaoh's serpents—which tickled them amazingly—mouth-organs, very inferior concertinas, and children's trumpets. It caused great merriment to cut from the piece of a dozen one bright red and yellow plaid kerchief, and, folding it neatly, with complimentary words—the tone of which indicated the tenor, and they understood it and pleasantly smiled—tie it around some fair lady's head, who gracefully bent forward convenient for adornment. Invariably the good lady returned on the following day with a handsome present of fresh eggs, nestling prettily in a basket lined with the prettiest ferns; or calabashes of freshly-parched maize (which proved as delightful to eat as delicate home biscuits), or fowls, or ducks, or gourds with large bodies and long necks (huge natural decanters) filled with palm-wine, or native beer, or delicious honey. Finding out that I was collecting curiosities, they brought fancifully-carved gourds, calabashes, boxes made of thin dry skins looking like parchment, opal beads, blue beads, brass snuff boxes, skin bottles, fans, and stout whips; also skins of animals, musical instruments, swords, spears, daggers, bows, and quivers of poisoned arrows, warning us to be careful and not to touch the barbs. These things did kind-hearted women bring daily, and, laying them upon the deck before us, gracefully bent one knee, and, with their expressive and bright eyes shining with true gladness and gratitude, at the same time placing their right hand over the heart, they expressed without language their deep respect for white men, and sometimes kissed the hem of a garment; but European garments are hard to kiss the hem of, especially as it was seldom that any of us entered into a coat. Each regretted not being able to return proper thanks. But bowing low, extending the open hands gently, bending the head, and smiling thanks was sufficient.

When the shopman went on shore and wandered wearily through the densely-populated town and the narrow streets, which soon caused faintness and languor, these good Samaritans would run out from their houses in every direction, take his hand and lead him into the midst of their families, and quench his thirst by exquisitely long drinks of new palm-wine, or equally refreshing draughts of cocoa-nut milk, and they would laugh and clap their hands with joy at witnessing our enjoyment. Presently, unasked for, from one or other of the neighbouring houses, they would bring calabashes of palm-oil-chop, fowls, or mutton-chops done up yellow like curry, with hot peppers added, and yielding a slightly pleasing flavour of palm-oil, reminding one of sleepily at midnight looking out of the train at Rugby or Peterborough, and becoming interested in the actions of the not very affluent but still practical philosopher whose duty it is to grease the axles, emitting from his dainty box the slight scent of palm-oil, which perfumes the carriage. But after the first taste and getting over the Rugby whiff, which is a mixed one and not pure, it is very good. Never mind what it is made of; as the Benin chief said, "What be good for white man be good for black man," and the converse holds good also, as the goose-and-gander axiom proves. No one will make a mistake in eating whatever the inhabitants of any country partake of, excepting professional cannibals; and then you yourself will most likely furnish the meal, especially if you be not addicted to smoking pipes until you are flavoured like an old meerschaum. Sierra Leone and Lagos people quaintly remark, "Them white men who sabby what be good, they like we country chop, and they be fit for live here and no die." To new comers the green peppers freely mixed with prepared food bring tears to the eyes and burning sensation to the swallow; but use begets liking, and dishes require to be highly seasoned for most tropical residents. Beef, mutton, goat, and fowl become tasteless, and dining on them is monotonous and unsavoury unless so flavoured.

The news of "white man's canoe" opened for trade soon spread, and numbers of *bona-fide* canoes came from Boussa, Raba, Beda, and other places, loaded with Shea butter and small quantities of ivory. Amongst these came a white man of a slightly yellow complexion, but apparently not so much sunburnt as we were. He was dressed in the flowing robes, and also wore the long straight sword, of the eminently aristocratic Houssas; and he had, in addition, a decent retinue of slaves attending upon him. A pipe-bearer being amongst them, as is customary in the East, added to his importance. He came to my shop first, and, glad to see a strange white face, I led him by the hand—it is the custom here in extending kindness—aft to the trading agent to give an account of his singular appearance. He explained in good French, which was familiar to the agent, that he was a native of Syria, and had just arrived across the desert with a loaded camel caravan from Tripoli. He appeared to be well known in the town, and frequently came on board during our stay, and, in return for presents, he gave us great cakes of sweetly refreshing dates, which added much to our comfort.

Cowries, as a medium of exchange, are current here. Silver coins are only prized to be worn as ornaments or hammered into rings. We brought £200 sterling in florins, fresh from the Mint, with that beautiful frosted appearance peculiar to new silver coins, and they were highly appreciated and speedily went for produce. Her Majesty's sovereigns and half-sovereigns find their way here from the coast in driblets, but the people have got no idea of their real value ; so they drill holes through the rim over the head of her Majesty, and the aristocratically-inclined ladies here wear them suspended around their necks as lockets. Sometimes they offer these coins for whatever strikes their fancy of trifling value, but the knowing old men of the village manage to get hold of stray gold, and when opportunity offers obtain its full value. Compared to the Delta savages, Egga people are partially civilised, and so long as Kings like Massaba are conquered by presents, so

long are white men perfectly safe in trading or going wherever they please; so that it is good policy to make suitable
presents to all Central-African potentates, and encourage
their despotic rule to keep their savage and half-savage
tribes from killing white explorers or traders. It will be a
very long time before Central Africans can be trusted with
mud-hut suffrage. Nothing short of iron-handed rule by
chiefs like Massaba can keep them in order. He forbids his
subjects, on pain of death, to purchase powder or guns, keeping deadly weapons and war material only for his regular
army at Beda; and we strictly complied with his orders not
to sell anything of the sort to his population. In fact he
had bought all the guns and powder left, and we were very
thankful upon seeking rest to think that no explosive substance existed beneath us.

It appeared very remarkable that the cry for rum ceased
at the Confluence—strangely coincident with the limit of the
missions, and the propagation of the religious and other
habits of white men. Rum is decidedly flat at Egga. We
could not sell a single gallon, and were obliged to take ninety
puncheons of it back to thirsty Onitsha. The people do not
like it, will not drink it, and are much better off without it;
but, in the order of events, they will take to the horrible
stuff, and, unfortunately, kindly too. We only parted with
a few hundred cases of Hollands gin, and that was more for
the sake of the attractive green boxes and pretty bottles than
for the liquor; but it would not be thrown away.

The first books, after learning to spell, which many boys
read with intense interest—before they attain to the age
when love-stories begin not to appear nonsense—are "Robinson Crusoe," "The Arabian Nights," and Mungo Park's
travels. In my case, Mungo Park became in after years the
favourite, as I had much to do with Africa and enjoyed the

friendship of several African explorers, so that naturally great interest followed in perusing books written about this great continent ; yet none ever effaced the well-remembered incidents in Mungo Park's simple narrative. Here, within a short distance of where his travels abruptly ended, I was most anxious to visit this spot as a pilgrim, to see where the most truthful, unassuming, determined, and one of the greatest of African travellers lost his life. I can understand his joy on beholding the Niger, after going up the River Gambia and undertaking that frightful land journey, during which his companions, stricken down by exposure, fatigue, and fever, died one-by-one, until only himself and another were left. His suffering from robbery, plunder, and ill-treatment by the various savage tribes through which he journeyed, oh ! so wearily, and then at last seeing the grand river and sailing upon its bosom. The object of his life attained. The great unknown river rolling onwards to the ocean, which he knew when he died as well as we know now, but which, from his death in 1805 until Lander descended it twenty-five years afterwards, was a sealed book. However, as fate would have it, trade was our object at Egga, and, as a trip to Mungo Park's rapids would not pay, we did not go there.

It is impossible to estimate the population of this town. Some travellers put it down at 18,000, and others at 50,000. It is built upon land slightly elevated over the river, is one mile and a-half long by half-a-mile wide, and now is surrounded by the river. Low-lying portions of the town are covered by the spreading water ; thus it is separated into islets. In these places canoe-ferry companies thrive by charging five cowries per head toll. The whole of the land forming the town is densely covered with the usual round mud huts, sensibly sheltered from rain and sun by thickly-thatched conical roofs. From four to a dozen huts form one residence, with ample room for walking about occasionally amongst flowers and pine-apples; the whole enclosed by high and thick mud walls. The streets are so narrow and tortuously crooked that there is only room for a man on horseback, at an easy walk, to navigate them; and they are horribly filthy with offal and other refuse, deposited for the hungry turkey-buzzards and lean dogs to clear away, as those useful birds and animals do in southern Egyptian towns and other warm regions. There are three mosques, the largest of which is 100 feet long by 40 feet wide. Beneath the wide verandah of it, and in the neighbourhood of the others, are sandal-makers busily engaged at work, also saddle and bridle makers. The saddles are like the high-pommelled Mexican saddles, originally, no doubt, introduced ages ago into Spain by the Moors, and from Spain to Mexico. Stirrups like overgrown shoes, and large, wicked spurs, are also met with. Weavers are also hard at work with their primitive but effective machines, and they rattle away for hours. Their labour is varied, however, by occasional snoozes over their looms. The web of the cloth is only from four to ten inches wide, but it is subsequently sewn together so finely that it takes clever eyesight to observe the joining. Thus are native cloths made. The patterns vary, and the good thick cotton is preferred on account of its thickness and durability by people upon the coast to the thinner English goods; but, strange to say, these interior natives infinitely prefer British bright cottons, and eagerly exchange, size for size, their much superior commodity. Red leather, like coarse morocco, is also worked up into the warlike shields, sword and dagger sheaths, quivers, slings, fetish charm-cases for home use and export, and a variety of other useful things. Instead of minarets, as in better-built Mahometan towns, the muezzin, or priest, ascends a row of mud steps on one side of the mosque—that next to Mecca—from the top of which he calls the faithful from labour to refreshing prayer at the appointed periods each day, according to the Koran. There is about the same difference between the mosque of St. Sophia at Constantinople and the principal mosque at Egga as that existing between St. Paul's Cathedral and one of the kirks on the Northern Orkneys; and just about the same difference, but reversed, between the hospitality of the respective peoples, as they each snooze in their "deevil-dodging" conventicles.

In early morning, or towards sunset, when favourable breezes blow, we sail our boat against the current for many miles; and when calm follows, as breezes soon die away, we descend rapidly by the current. Sometimes we depend altogether upon oars. The gig is manned by six of our strongest Kroomen, to work at the oars, and they make the graceful boat fairly fly. . We circumnavigate the town, rush across the smooth shallow water covering grass for miles and miles in every direction. In many spots great trees arise from the water covered with pelican, crown-birds, turkey-buzzards, and other large and strange birds, which have never heard the sound of a gun. They gaze unconcernedly at our beautiful boat, and no doubt look upon it as a large specimen of an aquatic centipede as the oars flash in the sunlight between each stroke. It is murder to shoot at these innocents, whose tameness, as Alexander Selkirk remarks, "is shocking" to tell. On occasional small islets are crocodile basking in the sun, with open mouths and slimy tongues attracting flies, which they enjoy as we do cardamoms. We shoot heavy rifle-balls, merely for target practice, at these ugly monsters, as upon our approach they wobble and roll into the water, but their carcasses are of no use, and their horrible smell causes us to avoid them. Occasionally we come across flocks of wild duck, and so numerous are they that, just after rising, a couple of barrels bring down a score of them, and they are capital eating. The pelican, when swimming, allow us to come close to them, as tame swans at home do; so it would be wrong to wring their confiding necks. Doves, of brilliant plumage, are difficult to shoot. They are as sharp on the wing as snipe, and rise as suddenly; but the flavour of pies made from them is sufficient to make us wary to capture as many as we can. On wild duck and dove we live like fighting cocks. We tried a crown-bird one day, weighing about a double-sized Christmas goose, but, although edible and filling, we preferred the duck and dove.

Some of the people here are wonderfully clever at mimicry. Occasionally, in the course of trading, white men utter exclamations which cannot be found in Holy Writ used in the same tone, neither in the Koran. Like mocking-birds we hear our customers repeating entire emphatic sentences of good but unparliamentary English. We noted that these were the smartest traders; so, as commerce progressed, we encouraged them, whether men or women, to act as brokers, and they quickly closed business transactions, and we gave them every assistance. It not only saved time, but was a mutual accommodation, especially to timid old people who had hoarded tusks of ivory for years as capital, concealed inside their huts in secret places, or perhaps buried underground to be better hidden in case of invasion, rapine, or robbery. The broker's commission is paid upon the spot after each act of barter, and in kind—kerchiefs, looking-glasses, fish-hooks, &c.; and a clever broker, coming on board with nothing but his ability, can fill a canoe by a good day's work.

A horrible fly, like a British horse-fly viewed through a magnifying glass, is the greatest torment in Central Africa. Its bite is intensely painful and draws blood; and if even you slay heaps of the "varmint," it does not appear to reduce the census. These interesting (when pinned as specimens) insects, buzz and worry about everybody all day long, and although an ox tail, with the part that makes soup extracted and a stick substituted, is constantly swished, yet they are artful dodgers, and alight on the back of the hand wielding the swisher. They actually draw blood through all clothing. Their nasty bites leave painful lumps upon the face and hands, as well as upon other tender parts of the suffering mortal frame, so much so that a photograph of any white man taken up the Niger, would not be recognised at home. We cannot make out whether these lumps develop into great and painful boils which afflict all our white men; however, we console ourselves that this disagreeable affliction indicates the absence of fever.

Our day's work commenced with early dawn, and before the sun became strong the best business of the day was transacted. But the terrific heat and dead calm caused our blood almost to burst bonds with suffocating anguish. The wide river, like molten white-heated glass, reflecting and re-reflecting from its surface to the white underside of awnings blinding heat, rendered breathing extremely difficult. We ought to have had a double awning, the underneath one of dark-green baize. I strongly recommend all awnings for the tropics to be so made, whether for a boat or for a ship's deck, with a space between each awning, which space acts as a non-conductor. As a relief during a change of rates before mentioned, my plan was to put a sentry over the opened bales of goods and retire to the inside of the paddle-boxes. In floating paddles one of them is always

horizontal. On this I stretched at full length. The ripple
of the downward stream through the lower part of the
blocked wheel caused a gentle current of air upwards over
the face and bare feet resting against the deliciously cold
iron, which iron is altogether in shade and partly in the water.
It was a dangerous thing to do, as, in one moment, inad-
vertently turning the wrong way, meant dropping into the
swift river, food for crocodile. However, half-an-hour's
sound sleep was very refreshing and health-restoring. But
one day my repose was disturbed, fortunately only a few
days before leaving. I was suddenly awakened by a cold,
clammy, slimy feeling across my bare feet, and instantly
starting wide awake, confronted a long snake. It had
floated from land on a detached little island of light grass,
which had stuck against the lower part of the paddle, and
Mr. Snake had wriggled himself upwards to escape from
death in the river. I speedily got through the manhole on
to the deck and closed the trap-door behind me, so as to
limit the progress of the snake. I then ran for a rifle, fixed
bayonet, and, upon return, pinned the obnoxious and intru-
sive reptile. It twisted round the bayonet and rifle barrel
and bit at the cold steel. The point of the bayonet went
through its middle and into one of the floats, so that its
days were numbered; but it caused considerable excitement
and trouble to get it on board, and the agent and I, over-
hauling a work on snakes, amicably argued and disagreed
about the species. It was a striped snake with distinct
yellow and black colours, and measured seven feet in length;
but it destroyed my mid-day siesta, for the peace of the
paddle had fled.

About four P.M. we cleared the ship of customers. Fancy
a Regent-street mart of commerce driving ladies and gentlemen out with whips at four P.M.! We then had a bath and

a change, and commenced fishing with rods and lines. We always caught quantities of good fish, and passed them to the galley to be cooked for our dinner at six o'clock. After dinner we were often so completely tired out and done up that, creeping underneath the mosquito-curtain, well tucked round a mat or mattress on deck to elude insects, and gradually with a soothing pipe falling asleep, was the only comfort, excepting the nightly tornadoes, during which we generally got pleasantly wet through and speedily dried again by the application of sackcloth without ashes. I adopted a dodge which was generally in use during fierce tornadoes, by taking an empty puncheon, clenching the nails projecting inwards, and throwing (when the rain began to fall) a mattress and pillow inside, I crept in afterwards, coiled up, and slept like a bow-wow. It was very jolly until the tornado was over. The puncheon was chocked on each side, which kept it from being blown by the strong wind of the tornado; but one night a practical joke was played upon me. The chocks were mischievously removed, and the puncheon commenced to roll before the wind, like the earth upon its axis, and I did not like the motion, but served the jokist out by sewing up his coat-lining, a trick common amongst mariners, and affording intense amusement to those in the secret, to see the unfortunate proprietor of the coat trying to get his arms wriggled through, and wondering what the "dickens" was the meaning of it. By means of somewhat similar eccentric conduct, good humour and laughter prevail over sadness where weary mortals have no other amusement. Shoes and socks form the only difference between night and day costume, which, when a man is fully clothed, weighs but little. Tropical outfit should consist of the thinnest woollen substance, well shrunk previously so that it will ·bear washing, for to yield comfort it has to be changed about

three times during the twenty-four hours.   But, after all,
life up the Niger, on board a hot ship, is not jolly.   Mark
Tapley would be suited to his heart's content, and come out
strong.

Our steamer was anchored fully two miles from the river-
bank fringing the town of Eggn, but we approached as close
to the population as the draft of water would permit, as bills
of lading say, "always afloat."   We were not only convenient
for trade, but handy to get paddled in a canoe to the town in
calm water, out of the swift downward current.   The wide
space of water is mixed up with low islands, on which flourish
groves of grass, appearing as healthy vegetation above the
surface.   This grass is very peculiar, for it more resembles
bamboo or thin sugar-cane than our notion of crops from
hayfields.   In the stem it is so long and strong that it not
only stoutly resists the action of the current, but at the
juncture of the leaves, branching right and left, it affords
accommodation for little birds to build nests.   These nests
are so quaintly and artistically constructed that looking at
them brings forth intense admiration of never-erring Nature
inspiring instinct into feathered songsters, teaching them the
necessity of forming a comfortable and dry home during
heavy rains.   The entrance to the nest is so skilfully formed
that the little landlord and landlady, the tiny representatives of our holy ideas of angels, can fold their wings and
simply slip underneath and over into the happy residence,
the roof of which the pretty builders have made waterproof
of fibre closely woven, and they somewhat resemble, on a
smaller scale, the nests of swallows.

Amongst these grass-built, light, and fairy palaces, which
we very much admired but did not touch—for birds forsake a
nest once desecrated by handling—on our arrival we stuck a
long pole firmly into the mud.   This pole was marked with

feet and inches, like those pertaining to railway-making or land surveyors, and we depended upon it to show the daily rise or fall of the river, which varied very much, operated upon by far-distant floods high up the country. Upon this index of rise and fall depended our time for terminating trade for the season and taking our departure. This pole it was absolutely necessary to watch carefully, for a vessel touching a bank upon a steadily-falling river remains there until the next year's accumulation of rainy flood enables it to float again. Several vessels have thus been unpleasantly detained. In some cases the natives plundered them. Captain, now Sir John, Glover, on a good steamer, got amongst rocks above Egga, and the vessel was wrecked. In my hut at Lukoja I wrote the subject of some of these letters upon greasy pieces of paper, by the light of a palm-oil spluttering illumination, on the table once belonging to Glover's plundered ship. He (Glover) walked across the country to Lagos, and it was a very tedious and difficult journey; but, as well as other Central African land travels somewhat similar, it enabled him to undertake the now historical march from the Volta to Coomassie subsequently with success. But before that he became Governor of Lagos, and no man alive knows Western and this portion of Central Africa better, nor how to deal more judiciously with the chiefs and kings, and usefully extend commerce by worthily representing the majesty of England; but this is wandering, so let us return to our "wethers" as Rabelais quaintly observes.

On the 30th day of October, 1871, Captain Stott, in the steamship "Victoria," stuck upon a bank between the towns of Egga and Lukoja on his way down the river, and there the ship was rendered a helpless machine until the river again rose and floated it off on the 6th day of August, 1872.

When he found his vessel aground he tried to get her afloat, but his seamanship could not remove a mountain. He was encumbered with a lot of passengers on board, who wanted to get to their homes on the sea-coast. These strangers, not wishing to abide with him, as the beautiful "Ancient and Modern" hymn suggests, travelled overland to Lagos. Thirty-five of them left the vessel on the 4th day of November, and, after enduring great suffering on the way, roughing it in a manner that is quite unknown to those residing in temperate zones, several of them pegged out life and were quietly interred in the bush. The rest arrived at Lagos on the 22nd of December.

Stott showed his thorough pluck as an Englishman. His crew numbered thirty, all being negroes excepting two other white men. He had fifty casks of Shea butter, and twenty-five tons of the same stuff in jars. He also had of his unsold outward cargo fifteen tons of salt, which is good, and better than fine gold here, for it yields the greatest happiness and luxury that can be imagined to all human beings in any hot climate. We lack a poet to express in suitable language the great value of salt all over the world, but especially in tropical regions. He had also seven tons of ivory, ready to be converted into artificial teeth for the benefit of shaky human civilised gums, or knife-handles, or stupid chessmen, or handles of tooth-brushes, or combs, hair-brush backs, billiard-balls, and a thousand other pleasing things to adorn daily life. He was crammed also with lubi and country cloths; and I have no doubt but that Stott swore heartily when he saw his ship high and dry on a bank in seven days after being stuck. But he remained faithfully by the vessel. All good sailors have true affection for their ships. One hundred feet length of her keel was not on a proper level with the formation of the bank; so, as the water fell and allowed him to do so, to save the ship from breaking up, he made everybody lively, and shored her up with blocks of wood, just as we see ships, standing upright in graving docks, steadied by artificial contrivances, bilge and keel blocks in their proper places, exactly as a well-regulated carpenter would approve. Fancy that ship on a sandbank in Central Africa and total wreck avoided by the inward impulse of duty to owners.

As the ship settled, Captain Stott discharged the cargo from the holds and stored it in a shed on shore. The three white men lived on board ship, and got to their home by an inclined-plane from the ground, as Noah very likely did with his family to and from his ark. The black crew erected a village on shore abreast the steamer, and got very "muchly" married and domesticated. To give an idea of the cheapness of food in this great and glorious country, abounding in everything that can render a hot climate endurable, from a beefsteak to an egg, or even to the sometimes despised onion, three and a-half tons of salt provided all the ship's company with food fit for princes, and, in addition, purchased a large quantity of rice to sell on the coast. When he got home the underwriters rewarded him, and he laughs and takes his glass of beer when the sun is over the fore-yard—eleven o'clock to the minute—like an old salt, and spins yarns of real Niger life which give delight to his audience.

Captain Stott had a favourite pig on board. Now, a pig is a homely animal, but wonderfully endowed with instinct, and as its virtues become known, before arriving at the bacon transformation, it is respected and admired. In addition, this pig boasted of English ancestry. It once belonged to the late Dr. Henry, a man well known about the Bights, and was in the habit of bathing daily, during the cool of the evening, in the river. It was, however, one day suddenly seized by a crocodile ; but, as the white men were enjoying themselves on the dry bank at the time, they shouted and threw missiles at the crocodile and frightened it away. The poor pig was then carefully doctored, duly recovered, and grunted many thanks. Its hams were, however, injured for life, and its "narrative," like Tam o' Shanter's grey mare's tail, was left behind.

At length the river began to fall, six inches, one foot, and two feet each day, measured by the pole. It rose again, and again fell. The fall had it and prevailed. So, on the 6th day of October, at ten A.M., we up anchor and steamed from Egga with our good, valuable produce on board, and everybody happy. Before dark on that same night, by means of full speed and the assistance of the swift current, we anchored of Lukoja, at the Confluence.

In addition to white men suffering from fever and dying, we buried four Kroomen, and many others of them are very ill of dysentery, caused by their gorging upon new yam, raw cassada, and unripe heads of corn. Kroomen eat all kinds of strange roots and vegetables, and they attend to each other during illness, until they learn by experience that white men know something of medicine and can generally afford relief. Having no medical man on board, we were obliged to study the book of directions supplied with each medicine-chest to each ship. Sometimes rash people innocently kill others by overdoses ignorantly administered. Krooboys gradually get to acquire such implicit faith in white men's supposed wisdom that they will swallow any medicine offered.

At Onitsha one of our Krooboys, after being ill all day, died. He was a fine young fellow, called Black Will, but [as soon as his strength was prostrated he succumbed, and we knew nothing of his illness until too late. His companions said not a word until they asked for a trade gun-case to act as a coffin. These gun-cases hold twenty long flint muskets, costing in Birmingham from seven to nine shillings each, and the cases are generally long, oblong, and bulky enough to bury people in, and are used for that purpose where the popular form of our inevitable last suit is not to be had conveniently. Black Will could not be got into the case on account of his length, so his fellow-country-men actually cut off his feet and placed one foot alongside each side of the head. It was an atrocious thing to do, but they did not think so, and even in the presence of death we could not help sorrowfully smiling.

Upon our return to Lukoja, our chief engineer, John Hunter, of Greenock, was taken ill of fever. I loved him and nursed him, and revelled with joy to see him come round. As an instance of unprofessional men serving out doses of medicine in dangerous quantities, our navigating skipper, who professed to know something of African fever, wanted to give John ninety drops of laudanum, over which the skipper and I had a row. Hunter was only a youth, and such a quantity of laudanum would have killed him straight off, and, as our worthy trading agent was also laid up with fever and deliri-ous, I could not appeal to him, so by sleight of hand managed to dodge the skipper, and administered to my patient twenty drops just as the turn of delirium occurred, which required artificial repose to assist youth to recover. I smoked many pipes and fanned mosquitoes away from my friend, and the next morning he awoke from calm slumber like a weak canary.

On the 8th of October, H.M.S. "Investigator," a tiny man-of-war, arrived, and we learnt with deep regret that her young commander, with whom I visited the King of Porto Novo, had died of fever, contracted at Porto Novo. This vessel, after taking in a supply of wood, proceeded up the river to Egga, with presents from the Queen to the King of Nupe, and we hope to fall in with her again after we return from the Binue river.

We went up the Binue. One day's steaming took us to the town of Yamana, off which we anchored, opened bales and fixed cask counters, expecting a numerous crowd of customers eager to trade; but, to our astonishment, very few people came off to the vessel, and they appeared to be police superintendents or Board of Trade surveyors. We politely showed these officials over the engine-room and vessel generally, stood them drinks, and told them through the interpreter what we had come for. They looked terribly frightened, shook their heads, and replied that they believed we wanted to get their King on board and take him prisoner to the reigning dignitary of Nupe. It is unnecessary to mention that we had not the remotest idea of doing anything of the sort, but they would not believe us.

Our agent charged them with peaceful messages, asking for audience, and stating that he would call upon the King and bring with him valuable presents. He showed them samples of goods, and made them presents of knives, looking-glasses, and other things, and did all in reason to induce them to think that all we wanted was to purchase ivory and Shea butter, giving them English goods in exchange. On the next day, no one coming off, we began to think that it was useless trying to do business with them; so, like unsuccessful pedlers, we packed up our wares. At length a man—their chief constable, no doubt selected for bravery—came in a canoe alongside, and told us that "we had better stand not upon the order of going, but go at once." He ordered us to shunt—mizzle—evaporate—disappear. The canoemen with him looked fierce and insolent. We observed large canoes ready to shove off from the bank, and, not being prepared for a fight, we retired upon instinct. The chief constable, in plain terms, told us if we would not immediately depart that, to quote after the Book of Proverbs, "the wrath of his King was as messengers of death"; that they would not only kill us all, but seize the ship. You can always tell when savages mean deadly mischief. They have a restless, nervous action in their legs and arms. Their eyes will not look you in the face, and suddenly become bloodshot. Then they stammer in their talk, and want to get behind you. When notably barbaric skunks act so, keep your hand upon your "pistuel" in your pocket, ready to blaze at the head or body the instant that they show fight. The body offers the surest target. Don't let them get behind you. Stick your back against something solid, and let them have it hot and straight. The man who draws a pistol and threatens hostile savages is lacking in sense. If you cannot by some device change their murderous intentions, as a last resort self-defence is justifiable. Do not draw your shooting-iron unless you mean to use it, and let it then speak for itself, or you yourself will, ten to one, as the marriage service says, "for ever after hold your peace."

After being ordered away, and taking the unaccountable conduct of the ruler of Yamana as a sample of the natives higher up the Binue, and also considering that if we proceeded further up upon a falling river we might, and in all likelihood would, get stuck for a year, and probably come to grief between the natives on one hand and the liability to fever on the other, we decided to abandon attempting to trade on the Binue. So we got up steam and anchor and returned to Lukoja, at the Confluence, for the purpose of taking on board the ivory and produce bought by the resident agent there, and then descend the Niger.

The Binue is wider at the Confluence than the Niger, but

it is doubtful which river brings from afar the largest quantity of water or drains the greater district. We know the source of the Niger, but not that of the Binue. The latter is entirely a matter of conjecture. Possibly it takes its rise in the same range of watershed which supplies the White Nile—the Nile flowing northward, and the Binue westward until its junction with the Niger at Lukoja. The waters of the Binue are very clear; those of the Niger, on the contrary, are extremely muddy; but, upon drawing a bucketful of the latter, the sediment soon falls to the bottom, and thereby yields clear drinking water. The same is the case with the Mississippi below its Confluence with the Missouri. This sediment, carried down stream during thousands of years, has formed the alluvial soil region called the Delta. The same occurs also with the Mississippi.

It is interesting to compare the rise and diverse direction of flow of the great rivers on the northern part of this continent with those in North America. In Northern Africa, on the western part of the continent, the Senegal, the Gambia, the Sherboro, and the Niger all take their rise in the same mountain district, situated south of the western portion of the Sahara Desert, and they run in different ways to the sea. The Senegal debouches into the Atlantic in $16\frac{1}{2}°$ N. and 16° W., the Gambia in $13\frac{1}{2}°$ N. and 16° W., the Sherboro just below Sierra Leone, and the Niger in $4\frac{1}{3}°$ N. and 6° E. Assuming the hypothesis that the Binue takes its rise in the vicinity of the White Nile on the eastern part of the continent, it issues into the Niger immediately below Lukoja, coming from due east; and the majestic Nile, overflowing from lakes, forming into cascades, continues its course through immense swampy districts, and, after being swollen by several tributaries, including the Blue Nile, it descends into lower levels over six cataracts, whence it streams like an eternal tide in the same direction, deep and silently, through the whole land of Egypt, rendering that exceedingly rich but narrow valley country, by the help of artificial irrigation, as fertile now as it was ages before the infant Moses was found cruising about in the frail craft in which the future lawgiver was as "captain, mate, and midshipmite," until Pharaoh's daughter captured the little derelict amongst the bulrushes. The great Nile, after lakes, cascades, swamps, rapids, cataracts, and confluences, having descended through 34 degrees of latitude, from $2\frac{1}{2}°$ S. to $31\frac{1}{2}°$ N., sweeps into the Mediterranean at 30° E. So that the Binue and Niger may be fairly compared with the Missouri and Mississipi, rushing in one direction; and the Columbia, receiving its source from the same region, rushes in an entirely opposite direction, exactly like the Nile. It is, therefore, extremely probable that the Nile and Binue in their infant state are close neighbours; but this remains to be proved. In North America, the Mississippi, the St. Lawrence, and the Columbia, all taking their rise in the centre of the continent, empty into both oceans; the Mississippi into the Gulf of Mexico at $28\frac{1}{4}°$ N. and 89° W., the St. Lawrence into the gulf of the same name at 49° N. and 62° W., and the Columbia into the Pacific at 46° N. and 124° W. This is in itself an argument in favour of the theory adduced.

The Niger, on a much smaller scale, somewhat resembles the mighty Mississippi from its mouth below New Orleans upwards. The rising land at Baton Rouge answers to Onitsha, and Vicksburg higher land to Iddah. But the delta of the Mississippi, in the Gulf of Mexico, exactly like the delta of the Nile between Alexandria and Port Said, is destitute of vegetation on its sea front; whereas the approaches to the Niger are densely crowded with mangrove-trees and impenetrable bush, which is accounted for by its tropical position.

Niger flat-topped hills and conical granite clusters, although great in their way, bear no comparison to the bold mountain scenery of the Columbia in Oregon. Nor, in a lesser degree, to the St. Lawrence, with its rugged Anticosti; and on each bank of that magnificent expanse of waters, its gracefully-cultivated slopes tapering upwards at right angles from the river, in long fenced-in plots of land, each enclosure forming a masterpiece of farming, and at the elevated end, fronting the highway, comfortable country mansions showing out amongst trees, each dwelling being a happy home in the New World.

It appeared strange to find in Lukoja that the consular agents were content to live in mud huts and sleep upon bamboo beds slightly elevated over the rudely-asphalted floor; and often even preferred a simple mat and hard leathern pillow placed upon the ground. Dr. Baikie so accustomed himself to the manners and customs of the natives—no doubt to enable him to learn their language thoroughly and compile his grammar—that his table-service consisted only of one silver table-spoon, which, in course of time, became half worn across the mouthful end by scraping the peculiar country pots clean of whatever had been cooked n them, scorning the intermediate use of dishes or plates, and literally taking " pot luck." His successors lived in better style, and also slightly improved upon the residence by coh-

ucting a mud shed between two of the circular dwellings, and they also raised the level of the floor to the extent of two feet, but no part of the roof is rainproof. I cannot help comparing this apparent disregard of comfort with the manner in which the first gold-diggers who migrated to California managed.

In that country, in those days, I arrived seeking gold like other needy fortune-hunters, and, working at some mines near to Placerville, El Dorado county, fell in with a few good Missourians and Kentuckians. They cut down pine-trees, and I assisted as well as any one not a backwoods-man could. In three days a comfortable log cabin, measuring thirty-six feet long, twenty-four feet wide, and nine feet high to the eaves of the roof, was created. The walls were made of straight pine-logs simply dove-tailed. The interstices were neatly filled with doughy clay. It had gable ends, and was roofed with split pine-boards, and tables, chairs, and bunks, acting as beds, were fashioned of the same material. A ten-feet-wide, lined with stone, fireplace yielded warmth during the rainy season. It was a very comfortable residence, and infinitely superior to Dr. Baikie's mud hut, measuring twenty-four feet in diameter, which daily, during heavy rains, required a wood fire in the centre to create dryness in the hot damp atmosphere. The smoke from this fire escaped unpleasantly down the throats of inmates: it also percolated through the leaky roof, and emitted volumes through the open doorway, presenting to outsiders the appearance of a dwelling on fire.

There are no men like Western Americans for ingenuity, especially displayed in fixing upon a spot convenient to good diggings, and creating from the abundance of the earth a snug home in the lonely forest. With salt pork, flour, molasses, pickles, vinegar, and Bourbon or Monongahela whisky, "toted" up from Sacramento city, added to the luxury of home-captured venison, bear's meat, and quail, flavoured with brine from the salt pork, we spent three of the jolliest years of early life in the glorious Sierra Nevada mountains—something pleasant to look back upon all through life and rejoice in when vanishing aloft like poor Tom Bowling. We held evening parties in winter, illuminated by pine-root torchlights and blazing oak-log fires. Our American cousins and staunch friends used to fill the house, and ask the only Britisher within thirty miles to read Shakspeare, Burns, or Byron, occasionally varied by relating anecdotes about the dear old country, which, notwithstanding trifling differences, all true Americans revere. They were born hunters and fighting men, most of them splendid fellows, and not afraid of encountering a "grisly bar," yet nursing their sick comrades with tenderness and manly affection. Each spring we separated into parties, " prospecting " for new diggings on the slopes of the Sierra Nevada range eastward and northward, sleeping all summer in the open air, with toes turned to a good fire, spinning yarns and making the grand old pine forest echo with our merriment. These men were the pioneers of California. They journeyed on foot with the assistance of packed mules at first, then with light four-wheeled wagons drawn by bullocks or mules over the rough country. Presently, they constructed roads, started comfortable stage-coaches, and gradually railroads, and on the rivers speedily ran steamboats, until now Pullman palace-cars traverse the continent, and steamboats traffic upon the rivers and seaboard, affording such luxury in travel not existing elsewhere in the World. But to return to Central Africa.

We felt very much vexed, as ill-fate would have it, that the natives of Yamana took it into their unwise noddles that we wished to do evil to them instead of good, and that they so churlishly refused to trade and drove us away. As we ascended the Binue from the Confluence, at about thirty miles distance on the north side, we observed a continuation of precipitous banks, averaging 100 feet in height, formed of strata of red sandstone above and white sandstone below. The banks of the other parts of the river, as far as we steamed up, are low, tapering upwards on each side to flat-topped hills, abundantly clothed with luxuriant vegetation, the same as that existing on the Upper Niger, until arriving off Yammaua, when again sandstone cliffs appeared.

Complete exploration of the Binue should be made without delay. Looking at it from a trading point of view, the opening-up of this portion of the sealed continent to extend commerce sufficiently justifies English merchants to subscribe money for the purpose. If they do not do so, and at once, enterprising explorers from other civilised countries will step in, and deservedly reap the benefit. Of course, the river is open to the world, the same as the sea. To whoever undertakes the adventure, I recommend a swift paddle steamer of light draft and extensive beam, after the manner of the Mississippi cargo-boats, furnished with double awnings fore and aft, well-armed, and loaded with suitable goods to trade with, and also to make presents to each petty king. Such a vessel need not allow the wretched rulers of tribes to dictate to them, but the reverse. It should have power enough to overcome moderate rapids, and when the conquering rapid appeared drop anchor, launch a couple of light boats fitted with small screw-engines and canoe-paddles, to use as oars are used, in case the engine came to grief. A score of Krooboys could carry each boat round the rapids on to smooth water above them, and away up river as high as possible. Returning down stream is easy work.

The creeks and banks of the Binue resemble those running into the Upper Niger. Overshadowing the latter, and also on higher ground, the wild grape-vine is abundant. The bunches are small, but the fruit is plump, light-green in colour, very tempting to the eye but delusive to the taste, being extremely sour. It very much resembles, both in colour and taste, the wild grape growing on the borders of creeks feeding the Sacramento river. California is now a wine-producing country. As these inhabitants become civilised, and experienced vineyard labourers are introduced amongst them, there is no doubt that this region will also produce wine enough to intoxicate succeeding generations pleasantly.

Fibres exist everywhere, not only in the shape of bark on huge trees, and in plantain and other forms, but also on long grassy vegetation, the outside shell of which peels off, and resists breaking with the strength of Irish flax. The natives collect it, and make serviceable twine and rope, fishing-lines, and woven hammocks, and various other articles of utility; but it is not yet collected in sufficient quantity to form an article of barter. At the foot of many trees quantities of a substance like gum exudes, which extends from two to three feet in thickness about the roots. The outside skin of this strange material is crusted over with a tough brown covering; forcing a ramrod through and withdrawing it brings forth a sample of pure bright-coloured gummy stuff, looking like the finer sort of molasses called golden syrup, but thicker in character. During a walk of three or four miles only, along the paths, many tons of this doubtless valuable gum can be collected. Besides cotton growing wild in many places, and other well-known products, there must be many valuable articles running to waste through sheer ignorance of those who at present ascend the rivers, which a man versed in natural science could at once point out and make public for the benefit of trade. It is, therefore, absolutely necessary that an experienced botanist and chemist should accompany the steamer proposed, or else, or in addition, that traders should be educated in natural science.

Apart from river navigation, it is impossible to open up the interior of a savage country unless by constructing a road.

The grand old Romans did this for the benefit of our tattooed and painted, wild-skin clothed and ragged, but sturdy ancestors. We ought to extend the same kindness to African savages, according to the improvement which we have made upon the old Roman road—namely, the railroad. Such philanthropy

"Is twice bless'd;
It blesseth him that gives, and him that takes."

Capital in Britain lies idle for want of employment. Here are simple paths which have existed since the descendants of Ham peopled this region. Nothing better is known as far as land travel is concerned. So let us put our heads together and construct a railway, similar to that between Douglas and Peel in the Isle of Man, between Lagos and Lukoja. The custom-house returns at Lagos show the increasing imports and exports. Taking the sample of the banks of the Niger and the accounts of people who have walked along the narrow paths from Lukoja to Lagos, there is no engineering difficulty, The chiefs owning the country will cheerfully accord permission and grant land for the railway, upon presents being made. Take the front of Government-house at Lagos as one terminus, and run the railway along the edge of the lagoon, handy to receive anything from or deliver anything to vessels at the wharves; then a bridge across the shallow sheltered lagoon, and, as mile by mile is constructed, the natives will yell with delight. Each mile laid down will pay by local traffic, and will certainly break down the petty jealousy existing amongst hostile tribes, who only require to know each other to throw away their bows and arrows and cease shooting trade guns at one another. Instead of fighting, they would collect produce to enable them to travel by railway, enlarge their ideas, and, instead of getting driblets of palm-kernels, palm-oil, and so on, as at present, they would take to

18

work in earnest. The increase of trade at Lagos, from published reports, will show what may be the future development if only fostered. It is distressing to meet poor women on the paths, staggering beneath heavy loads of produce on their heads, which they carry to the merchants, whilst their lazy husbands are fighting neighbours, dodging behind trees, killing one another now and then, and at the same time wasting their precious time and lives.

With regard to the traffic to be obtained from the Lukoja terminus. From the north-west canoes come from as high up the Niger as they can float. From the east, along the only partially explored Binue, canoes also arrive. Flat-bottomed river steamers can do the same as far as the rivers will allow them to float. Lukoja is a central point. I am confident that it would pay well as a speculation. But put that on one side. Think of the benefit that it would be to England in increasing markets for manufactured goods and receiving additional produce in return. And, lastly, reflect upon the fact that it would civilise the savage and prepare him for the missionary.

After delivering presents from the Queen to King Massaba, H.M.S. "Investigator" returned from her anchorage off Egga earlier than intended, owing to the unusually great subsidence of the waters. She steamed close to our vessel and anchored off Lukoja on the 18th October. We were ready to start down the river, but the "Investigator" required wood for fuel. Her commander selected a huge leafless tree which had been struck by lightning, and was convenient to the river-bank; so Krooboys were quickly set to work, who speedily cut it down and chopped it up into suitable billets to fit the furnaces. Meanwhile, before leaving the lonely representatives of the Crown and Trade of Great Britain, we clubbed our very limited and fast-disappearing

stores together, so as to enjoy a parting dinner in her
Majesty's mud huts. Admonishing our cook to "go to the
town and buy us flesh and wine," we were enabled to pass a
very merry evening—tinged, however, with grief at the
thought of those who had died, and regret at leaving good
fellows behind. Sadness is not good to dwell upon. We
became frolicsome and cheered up our hearts; for, verily, he
drinks good palm-wine in vain that feels not the pleasure of
it. We were separating never to meet again, so speeded the
parting moments pleasantly. None of the survivors of that
dinner will ever forget this verse :—

> " Then fill, fill your glasses with me, boys,
>   And pause just one moment to think, think, think,
>   That this may be the very last time, boys,
>   We ever again may drink, drink, drink."

Those who had never sung a song before did so, and were
encored. Had we been dining at the Mansion House, the
loyal toasts and the rest, even to the bishop of the diocese,
could not have been more properly given, nor more warmly
responded to. But every day must have an end; it was
early on the following morning though, and Krooboys, with
lanterns lighting our feet, so that we should not tread upon
puffed-adders or other night-wandering noxious reptiles,
guided our steps from the "royal mews" (as one of the
"Investigator's" fellows christened the stable-looking huts)
to the river-bank. The ship's gig took us on board. Steam
was up, and just before day broke we left enchanting Lukoja
for Igbegbe, where we anchored and remained that night,
and, receiving on board the good Bishop, two of his sons, and
their retinue, on the 20th October, at daylight, started down
the Niger with joyous hearts, admiring the wild mountain
scenery between Igbegbe and Iddah, and becoming interested
in a variety of new passengers. The deck is crowded with

them, bound for the coast; also with horses for Lagos.
Amongst the live stock are two very long-legged sheep,
return-presents from Massaba to the Queen. These brutes
kick up an awful row, especially at night, and cause much
breaking of the swearing commandment. If ever they arrive
at any royal palace, they will play "old gooseberry" amongst
the lords of the sheep-pens. It reminds one of the old times
in Palestine, when the anointed Kings of the period received
and gave presents; so we must tend the sheep carefully.

Descending the Niger is very different from going up
against the stream. We have in our favour a racing current
of from four to six knots an hour, and, as we steam at
least ten knots, our ship somewhat resembles an express
train skimming across a panorama, but to our gaze the
scenery unfolds itself. We anchored off Iddah and visited
the Attah. On this occasion the Bishop kindly acted as
interpreter, and many dry speeches were made, which the
Attah perceiving, he judiciously ordered in gourds and calabashes of palm-wine, and that rendered conversation more
fluent and agreeable. Presents were made. The Attah produced several ancient but bright brass utensils which needed
repairing. These were at once sent on board for that purpose,
and the engineer cleverly and speedily soldered the leaks,
made good the dinges, and polished them brightly, to the
great delight of the King.

It was deemed advisable to remain for that night at
anchor off Iddah. The rush of waters increased in volume
and strength so much that, afraid of drifting, we were
obliged to let go a second anchor and pay out more cable.
At midnight a tornado came on, with the usual accompaniment of thunder and lightning, but, being well inured to
them, the noise and flashes were unnoticed. However, as
the rain began to fall, a shriek startled all from sleep. One

of our Zouave Houssa soldiers, kindly lent to us by the
Governor of Lagos as a showy protection, was sleeping beside
a comrade on one of the paddle sponsons (those parts outside a steamer's rail fore and aft the paddle-wheel houses,
which are unprotected). This poor fellow, no doubt, felt the
rain patter upon his face, and sleepily turning to get on
board, forgetting which sponson he was lying upon, turned
the wrong way and fell overboard. The swift river carried
him away, but, by the continuous vivid flashes of lightning,
we could see him battling with the stream, vainly trying to
stem the current and make for the vessel, instead of striking
inshore for the bush. We heard his dreadful drowning cries,

> " And then, by toil subdued, he drank
> The stifling wave, and then he sank."

A lifebuoy was cut adrift and the gig lowered at once, but
the boat returned in a few hours with the lifebuoy, but
without the man.

At daybreak on the following morning we resumed our
journey, and during the same afternoon came to anchor off
Onitsha. Here we took stock, and ascertained that a very
good trade had been done in palm-oil, and moderately in
cotton ; so much so, that, after landing our produce at
Akassa, the steamer will have to return to Onitsha for
another load. Above two hundred kegs of gunpowder were
housed in a mud store, separated only by mud partition-walls
about eight feet in height from dwellings on either side,
beneath the one roof. Fires were burning in each residence,
the sparks from which were liable to, and did, fly over the
divisions and on to the tarpaulin covering the powder, and it
looked fearfully dangerous. The black clerks in charge and
their families did not seem to mind it. So accustomed do
these louts get to explosive articles, that they lose all sense
of fear, and recklessly play with danger. Occasionally they

get blown to pieces and scattered to the four winds. No doubt, after that interesting operation they would, if they could, like the rich man in Hades, send a few warning hints to survivors, but as yet they have not done so, for verily spiritual mediums confine their operations amongst wise-acres who are able to pay. It is their "forte" to do so.

The peculiar species of the palm-tree, from which the invigorating wine frequently alluded to is extracted, exists all over the west and south-west coast, and also in the interior along the banks of the rivers. These trees are looked upon as our farmers estimate cows yielding milk. A hole is drilled near to the top of each tree, beneath where the branches diverging form a graceful cluster, and a long-necked calabash is fastened underneath the orifice to admit the entrance of the juice running out therefrom. The wine is strained free from ants, swarming about all trees, and it must be used within twenty-four hours after oozing, during which time it is the most delicious and fragrant beverage known in Africa. On the second day it ferments and becomes an intoxicating liquor.

All surplus goods, including the rum which we were not able to dispose of up the rivers, were landed at Onitsha, for the purpose of trading for palm-oil and cotton. Large and unexpected quantities of palm-oil in jars had come in from adjacent villages; so much so that, after all the empty puncheons and casks had been filled, it became a puzzle what to do with the rest. The agent, however, readily solved this difficulty by starting Krooboys digging a pit, oblong in shape, five feet deep, and sufficiently long and wide for the purpose. This cavity he caused to be lined throughout with mud of almost the consistency of india-rubber, and the palm-oil was poured into it from the jars, there to remain until the steamer brought up fresh casks.

Since ascending the river the bank at Onitsha has become crowded with houses. A new village has sprung up, the natives of which each night, into the small hours, treat us with violently blowing horns, playing rude musical instruments, and dancing. During the day, close to the fishing-stakes and tall silk-cotton-tree, crowds of young and old ladies, and also gentlemen, from the city, quietly wade into the water and are scrubbed. The foam of country soap is considerable. They have not got the slightest idea of seclusion, for whole families troop into the water, and several generations rub, scrub, scrape, rasp, pare, and polish each other, materially assisted by native fibrous sponge and abundance of lather, like bucketsful of whipped cream, in the same way as practised in the Turkish baths in Turkey—not the miserably "cribbed, cabined, and confined" imitations of these excellent baths existing in many other places. As our steamer is anchored forward, and moored astern by a hawser round the cotton-tree, in a sort of bay counter-eddy of the stream, day and night we have a perpetual run of population, affording ample opportunity leisurely to observe their strange customs and amusements.

On the 25th October the little man-of-war arrived on her way down. The agent having that morning bagged a brace of wild guinea-fowl, we borrowed a piece of salt pork to flavour the birds, and invited the naval officers and the missionaries of Onitsha to a sumptuous temperance dinner. It was not exactly English without beer, but lively conversation which flagged not for one moment—the great secret of happiness during dinner—created a halo around decanters of water. On the next morning the "Investigator" started an hour before us, but during the day we passed her off Agberi, where she was taking in wood, plentifully piled there. We stopped the engine, and after a passing conversation, as our vessel drifted past her, we put on full steam and rattled away until it grew so dark that it was difficult to distinguish between the trees and the river, and long after night set in, we anchored below, and well clear of, the detestable village of Angiami, keeping steam up ready to start at daybreak.

The river is much more swollen than when we came up, for now hardly a vestige of land shows. Reaches of river flow through jungle and towns. In the latter—the houses of which are built upon stout limbs of trees, to resist floods—we observe inhabitants paddling along the streets and from house to house in canoes. Little children, partly in the water, rush to nursery doors, barred as ours are, and raise their infant voices with wondrous glee to see the steamer swiftly rush past like a roaring, screeching "Flying Dutchman." How these human beings manage to exist during their annual deluge is a mystery.

About noon the Atlantic was scented, and joyously we inhaled the welcome, health-restoring, fever-driving-away and bracing sea-breeze. Long before we came to a sight of the ocean, no Ju-Ju-man need tell us what was the matter. Each remarked to other, "How bright your eyes are! Hast been intoxicating?" Verily, we were doing so, by expanding lungs upon zephyrs from the vasty deep. After twisting through creeks, and suddenly opening out the broad Atlantic, the bonny blue line of our ocean home, we involuntarily gave a great "Hurrah!" and the steamer, bounding on as if she enjoyed the glorious sight also, was speedily anchored off Akassa.

The agent here, a youth of seventeen, during our absence had killed a python measuring fourteen feet in length. It was detected in the act of twisting itself fondly around a sheep, the numerous cries of which alarmed the sleeping natives, who in terrible fear awoke the young "massa," and, notwithstanding the dreadful fetish penalties (as snakes are held sacred here), and the running away in affright of the cowardly Akassa savages, the young fellow single-handed slew the python, and was preparing the skin to send home as a trophy.

On the 4th of November, at one A.M., in the midst of torrents of rain, taking charge of several missionaries' wives and their children, we started in an Akassa canoe to suit the meeting tides in the creeks to get to Brass River, there to meet the tender to the ocean steamers going up and down the coast from Bonny. In the first place, it was a matter of great difficulty to muster the Akassa canoemen, and, in addition to the stipulated goods for canoe hire, they demanded and got rum in advance, and also rum on the way. A dozen of these out-and-out savages paddled and shrieked songs, which, echoing from the thick mangrove bush in the solitary dark creeks, sounded, and our dim outline looked, in the early dawn, like a floating funeral conducted by demons. I became afraid of giving them too much rum lest they should get helplessly drunk, but the more they drank the faster they paddled. They stopped and struck for "another little drink all round" again and again, threatening unless it was supplied to run the canoe into the bush, or go back to Akassa. The poor women and children suffered greatly from the pitiless down-pour of rain, with no shelter to creep under, and they were frightened at the wildly excited savages, but they bore their troubles bravely and patiently, and a tin of biscuits served to cheer up the little ones.

It is no easy matter to preserve a smiling countenance amongst cannibals; however, after fourteen hours' of diplomatic distribution of rum, at length we entered and crossed over to the eastern side of Brass River, and landed at a trading store on the beach. On the following morning, the tender, like a pretty little welcome bird, arrived from the sea, and on the next afternoon it dropped anchor off Bonny-town, and that town, under ordinary circumstances, is not the liveliest of places; but listening to different voices in our own tongue offering welcome yielded intense happiness, for we were once more with our own countrymen.

CHAPTER VIII.

BONNY is the reverse of what its name implies. The houses forming the town are built, or rather thrown together, in a dismal swamp, overgrown, where dwellings are not, by the rankest kind of vegetation, and where the houses are, uncleanliness and nastiness reign supreme. Vultures stalk about perfectly at home amongst their favourite fetid food, and the insalubrious stench from both necessitates hard smoking of tobacco to counteract the evil effects of the poisoned air. If, after two or three hours' sojourn in Bonny and its marshy, jungly suburbs, a white man escapes fever, he may consider himself acclimatised. The voice of the bull-frog and cricket is heard night and day as staple music, varied by the plaintive "coo" of the dove and the weird shriek of the untutored grey parrot. From the moment of landing until getting afloat again, a sense of depression, caused by the exceedingly damp heat, affects the liveliest spirits. On the footpath from the beach to the village, past the Gree-Gree house, are many fine specimens of great trees with wide-spreading branches, and in every direction graceful clusters of vegetation and flowers attract the eye. Beautiful humming-birds, butterflies, dragon-flies, beetles, grasshoppers, and an infinite variety of insects, delightedly engross the attention ; but weariness soon sets in, and shelter from the sun is sought. Wherever chiefs or head-men reside, welcome shade, rest, and refreshment are cheerfully accorded ; but, as the lower orders of the populace are repulsive in appearance, and anything but cleanly in their habits, it is not advisable to study them too closely.

On leaving the vessel for the beach it is necessary to steer your boat carefully amongst a cemetery of wrecked hulks in every stage of decay. Once upon a time these vessels were proud English and Dutch East Indiamen, or huge wall-sided ships of war, which in their day of youth and strength were the pride of their country; but the worm undermined their constitutions and honeycombed their thick, solid timbers. Before that period, as that class of vessels became obsolete, owing to their slow-going, "bruise water" sailing qualities being eclipsed by modern clipper ships, and still more recent screw steamers, they were sold to African merchants and despatched to the rivers in the Bights. Their masts were cut down at the tops, and palm-thatched, lofty gable roofs housed in the whole deck fore and aft. The palm-thatch being prone to take fire, corrugated iron during late years has been substituted, and now prevails.

It is impossible for northern men to live in the town or upon the beach; so they reside on board the hulks. Let us inspect one of these floating homes of our countrymen, whose exile tends to contribute to our commerce and comfort. It is a huge vessel, very like an exaggerated toy Noah's-ark, anchored in the swift current, and it swings with the tide. A wide ladder-staircase reaches to the water's edge, protected by a substantial rail. Swift gigs bring visitors alongside this ladder, on to which we step, and, ascending the well-scrubbed and clean staircase, are ushered on to the sheltered, cool, and clean white upper deck, which is the living and entertaining hall, affording space enough in some vessels for a congregation of a thousand people. In addition to the roof over all, an under roof covers the whole of the spacious quarter-deck, forming a non-conducting space of air between,

which creates wonderful coolness and comfort. At the sides
and taffrail are curtains so constructed as to be lowered or
raised at pleasure. Madeira wicker-work chairs and sofas,
hammocks and couches, are handy everywhere, inviting repose, and the deck is so spotlessly white that, as the sailors
say, "you might eat your dinner off it." Comfortable bedrooms, offices, and bathrooms are constructed on this deck,
so that the favoured inmates may enjoy a greater amount
of fresh air than that finding its way through the old-
fashioned square ports into the old-fashioned grand cabins,
once the temporary homes of admirals, princes, and fair
ladies. These apartments are now occupied by white carpenters, coopers, and junior clerks. Beneath the quarter-
deck is the spacious old saloon, now converted into a trading
shop, with remnants of its gorgeous furniture still existing in
solid mahogany doors, tables, and sideboards, inlaid panel
paintings, and heavily gilt mouldings ; but the fine gold has
turned to dull yellow, so that the pride of bygone days is no
longer appreciated.

It is ten o'clock, and breakfast time. The gong, which
awoke echoes in many distant lands, sounds melancholy now,
as its deafening din peals forth expandingly from beneath the
roof, announcing the morning meal to the neighbouring
hulks, and also to those working on the beach. Everybody
has been busily employed since daybreak. Accra coopers,
either on the main-deck or in the store-houses on shore, have
been at work creating palm-oil casks from shooks and hoop-
iron ; whilst Krooboys have been engaged in melting or
rendering palm-oil to detect impurities, if any, and run it in
its fluid state into puncheons, ready for shipment by the
first steamer. Long canoes, laden with palm-oil, and paddled
by from twenty to thirty naked boys, lie close to the
ship on each side beneath the crane gangways. The traders

and chiefs owning the oil have been in the shop selecting goods of every variety in return for their produce. As the gong strikes, the mart of commerce is cleared of customers, and the iron open-work gate leading to it (the gate is meant for ventilation as well as security) is locked, and the chiefs invited up-stairs to breakfast on the quarter-deck. After the morning's work, and before breakfast, each white man revels in a bath, and that in many cases alone enables him to enjoy food.

If a stranger to the rivers, as you ascend the outer stair-case you are astonished by the ghost-like appearance of an over-grown white boy meeting you, ornamented with a bald head ; his once plump and ruddy features are shrunken and bleached yellowish-white. You feel very sorry for him, as, in reply to inquiry, he states that he has just got up from an attack of fever, during the delirium attendant upon which his hair was suddenly removed ; but, with brightening eyes, he adds cheerfully that his three years' term of servitude will soon terminate, and then he will gladly go home to his parents and friends. With every appliance at hand for comfort in the floating trading store, warehouse, and hotel combined, it appears a wonder that fever should overcome the pleasant sea-breeze ; but glance over the hulk's side and observe the colour of the water coming from nobody knows where—not from the Niger : it brings down malaria in solution. The same exists in its entirety in the swamps about the town, and on each side of the river ; consequently, as the sea-breeze ceases, the atmosphere becomes tainted, polluted, and unfit for white men to breathe.

During the rainy season, fog, and occasionally during the dry season, " smokes," generate haze, completely covering and concealing from view the low line of mangrove swamp on each side of the entrance to the New Calabar and Bonny rivers.

When this occurs during daytime, or should it happen to be night, the masters of steamers keep the lead going, so as to steer sufficiently clear of shoal water; and having run their distance, checked by previous observation, dead reckoning, and the patent log, they anchor and wait for daylight, or else for the fog to clear away, as the case may be; and generally, when the horizon becomes visible, they find themselves within a few miles of the dangerous bar outside Bonny River. The navigation from the sea into the river is tortuous, but the deep channel is defined by buoys. At first a break in the line of trees indicates one wide river, whereas there are two distinct streams. As you approach Rough Corner, the south-eastern point of Bonny River, Breaker Island opens out, and beyond it you see the New Calabar River, which comes from the Niger, and is the most easterly branch of its delta. Upon rounding Rough Corner smooth water is entered upon, and after six or seven miles' progress the mail steamer anchors convenient to her particular hulk, so as to haul alongside without much trouble and deliver or receive cargo.

As the steamer from England approaches, swift gigs, the pride of their owners, dart from every hulk. Each mercantile house trading at Bonny has its own hulk. One of the African steamship companies owns two—one for outward and the other for homeward cargo. The old company have an enormous floating warehouse and palatial dwelling, called the "Adriatic," formerly one of the huge wooden steamers of the Collins line; this vessel answers for cargo both ways. The gigs rushing for home news are each manned by six Kroomen, adorned with their favourite diamond RS (trade mark) cloths of wonderfully-brilliant hues. The Kroomen bend their agile and flexible bodies, developing Hercules-like muscular power, forcing the boats, bounding like marine flying eagles, alongside the steamer's ladder, and then a rush of white men on deck takes place. The president of the river association signs the G.P.O. receipt for the mail-bags, breaks the seals, and distributes the contents. Meanwhile the cork of the sodawater bottle is heard to pop, sounding like volunteer target practice. Residents welcome ships' officers and passengers, and invite all who can do so to go on board their cool hulks, so as to obtain some relief from the broiling-hot mail-boat. Two of the hulks rejoice in the possession of French ice-making and water-cooling machines. Ice is too cold to use with impunity. We made it up the Niger several times, but the change was too great for safety. Here decanters of water are placed beneath air-exhausters, a pump is worked, and the fumes from sulphuric acid, robbing the water in the decanters of its latent heat, in two or three minutes reduce it from fifty to sixty degrees below the temperature of the air. Each visitor waits for the frigid decanter of cooling liquid; and, before drinking, "Boo" is ejaculated all round—"Boo" being Bonny tongue for "good health."

"A short life and a merry one" may be said of many West African residents. In the past days most of the Bight traders were rude, uneducated men, who prided themselves upon coming in at the "hawse-hole, and going out at the cabin windows." Acts of wanton cruelty to white men, as well as to negroes, have been handed down by generations of the fraternity, combined with the time-worn name, "palm-oil ruffian." Of late years, however, "Courts of Equity" have been established in each river, which, in addition to the British Consul's occasional supervisional visits in a man-of-war, give law and order. The traders are not now addicted to midnight orgies; more opposition exists in trading matters, and money is harder to lay by than formerly; so, as banquets are expensive, and headaches result the next morning, they are not frequently held.

As all the hulks leak more or less, especially when the copper sheathing begins to give out, it is necessary to keep them pumped continually, for the accumulation of bilge-water is not only most offensive by its noxious exhalation, but also prejudicial to health. Iron hulks have been tried; but they soon corrode and leak also. One of the old Isle of Man boats, a venerable "Ben-my-Chree," lasted for many years, built over by a wooden terrace, verandahs, and offices, like a great Chinese junk; but she had to be beached at last, and now her tough, honest iron-work forms part of a wharf, and the tide ebbs and flows through the saloon where tens of thousands of Lancashire folk ate dinners and became "bilious." Still she rejoices in her pretty name.

The son and successor to the late King Peppel, George Peppel, is not of much account, although educated in England. He has not exactly ascended the throne of his ancestors, and does not consider it beneath his dignity to solicit for and superintend the washing of clothes for white men. Oko-Jumbo is one of the smartest traders and most influential chiefs. Apart from trading, he is most hospitable and affable with all white people; and he bears the same relation to Bonny that the chief Ja-Ja does to the neighbouring river eastward, called the Opobo, another new outlet of navigation and trade. Oko-Jumbo is about forty-five years of age, slightly above the middle stature, well built, inclined to portliness; and has bright sparkling eyes and an intelligent face. He looks clean, walks beneath an umbrella, and below that a light-coloured felt hat, and a variety of brilliantly-coloured thin cotton cloths extend loosely to his ankles. He wears a thin fashionable loose palctot over a thinner gauze singlet, rejoices in bare feet, has got rings on his fingers, and a gold-mounted cane in his hand. He always travels in a long yacht-like canoe, propelled with paddles by from twenty-four to thirty boys, arranged according to size, and a man standing aft steering with a longer-handled and larger paddle. This canoe goes along far faster than the Sultan's silver flying-dove caique skimming the Bosphorus, and the songs perpetually sung by his choral paddlers make the progress of Oko-Jumbo lively. He frequently sends his friends, from his own cookery, welcome dishes of food, consisting of fowl, shell-fish, yam, and in some cases luscious winkles in their shells, all mixed up and flavoured with herbs, peppers, and palm-oil, done up only as natives to the manner born can turn out this dainty food. Oko-Jumbo and several other important men, in addition to their own town residences, have farm plantations higher up the river, to which white men are invited and hospitably entertained.

The principal objects of interest to a stranger are the Gree-Gree, or Ju-Ju, house, the waste cannon, and the new Church Mission. The mud floor of the Gree-Gree house is literally paved with human skulls: the sides and door-posts are also lined and ornamented with the same grinning but jokeless, toothfull but fleshless, chops; and human bones are artistically arranged after the style adopted in the awfully-dull enclosed Campo Santo adjoining the convent of the Capuchins at Rome. In addition to skulls and bones, wicked-looking trophies of unrighteous warfare decorate the hideous interior.

Above Bonny-town, fronting the river and almost covered by vegetation, are great numbers of unmounted old cannon, pointed up and across the river. Nobody can give a correct account of how these guns were obtained. Probably they were sold to chiefs for slaves in the days that have fled; and this is not unlikely, as the natives are as fond of loud reports from heavy cannon as little boys at home rejoice in similar but smaller toys.

Bishop Crowther has built a small church on the beach, and established schools for boys and girls. Several of the chiefs' sons have been educated in England; and, as others follow the example set, combined with the mission, there is hope that the natives of Bonny will gradually improve from the savage state.

Breaker Island is a low, muddy, and sandy piece of land situated between the mouths of the two rivers, but inside the bar and fronting the ocean. The alluvial deposits brought down by both streams, added to the wash of sand by the tides, have formed it. It is tolerably well-wooded, yields a dry air, affords a pleasant change, and is a delightful place for picnic-parties. Some years ago a comfortable wooden house was erected upon it, in the midst of a grove, but now the place is going to wreck, and only a few iron bedsteads, drinking glasses, and a weather-beaten cork-screw remain. It is very strange that the white men neglect this comparatively healthy residence, which was formerly filled from Saturday until Monday with visitors from New Calabar on one hand and Bonny on the other. Each party brought food, drink, and Krooboys to build fires and cook. For patients in fever it is almost certain to effect a cure.

The white man's burial-ground is situated opposite to Breaker Island at Rough Corner, chosen because of its affording the only rise of land above the swamp district. There is no useless pomp displayed at funerals, nor external show of mourning; but, in all love and sincerity, kind-hearted fellow-countrymen form a sorrowful procession of boats, accompanying that containing the coffin of their departed brother, enfolded by the union-jack. Nothing can be more touching to the heart that the sight of the flag of our country fluttering in sunshine and sea-breeze, covering the bier carried from the boat across Afric's burning sand to the last home. The service is read by a friend amidst stifled sobs, and all is over.

Duke-town, off which trading hulks, similar to those at Bonny, are anchored, swinging with the tide as it ebbs and flows, is situated at a distance of fifty-five miles from the sea on the eastern bank of the Old Calabar River, above its confluence with the main stream, called the Cross River. The character of the intermediate country from the sea is dense mangrove forest, impenetrable jungle, and swamp, intersected with numerous creeks branching in various directions, forming islands, and affording short cuts between the rivers for navigation. Boats from vessels anchored at the mouth of the river, in trying to make Duke-town, frequently mistaking the proper course, get mixed up and lost in the lonely lagoon-like friths, because the appearance of each channel is so very much alike. The deepest channel is buoyed, and, when once known by practical experience, is so simple that on moonlight nights steamers proceed right up to their anchorage. It is a very hot place, for the sea-breeze does not last so long as upon the coast, and loses much of its purity by passing over mangrove.

Commencing with Duke-town, the flat country gracefully breaks into hilly districts, with, in many cases, cultivated valleys between. On the elevated land to the south of Duke-town, and upon another commanding spot above Creek-town. some eight miles higher up the river, on the north bank of a creek leading into the Calabar River, Presbyterian missions have been established for upwards of a quarter of a century.

The anchorage chosen for trading hulks extends from abreast the mission on the hill below Duke-town to three miles up the river, below Old-town. It is so shut in that the atmosphere becomes unpleasantly close and liable to generate fever, assisted by the filth on the river-bank fronting the town, which is a permanent abomination, air-polluter, and disease-diffuser. Europeans ought to reside on the high land, following the example set by the missionaries; but, with the exception of two traders, who have erected dwellings close to the level of the water, revelling in malaria, and frequently at night being visited by crocodile, the rest live on board hulks, as at Bonny.

Canoes flock down from distant villages each day, generally before and after daybreak, laden with palm-oil and palm-kernels to trade for goods. There are seven floating hulks in working order, and others in various stages of being broken up, as old age has rendered them useless.

As soon as the gun announces the mail steamer from England, boats shove off from the hulks, and also one belonging to the mission, a young missionary generally accompanying the latter. The president of the European traders' association opens the mail-bag on the steamer's deck, and, reading aloud the addresses, each nominee grasps his own. The missionary has got two black boys standing behind him, each boy provided with a basket. He holds out his hands imploringly, as if seeking for benediction, and eagerly clutches the letters, newspapers, and book-packets destined for the missions, passing them behind his back to the boys; but his own personal communications he consigns to his own bosom, and when his boat flies away, like a welcome Mercury he may be observed, with his head bent down, absorbed in wonder, reading " book " from far-away home.

Those who recollect Prince Albert's visit to Liverpool in 1846, when he laid the foundation-stone of the Sailors' Home, will doubtless remember, just before that time, a strange-looking iron house temporarily put together on that

site.   It rejoiced in two stories, was surrounded by a wide
verandah, and attracted curiosity from its differing so much
from our street houses.   It was taken to pieces, shipped out
to Old Calabar, and erected, for the then ruling dignitary, in
the centre of Duke-town, forming a prominent feature
amongst the native houses.   Upon the death of the ancestor
to the present King Archibald, it was gutted, partially destroyed, and abandoned, as is customary; and the then usual
human sacrifices were made about it; but still its iron walls
exist.

Through the influence of missionaries and traders, the
wholesale destruction of human life formerly attendant upon
the death of a chief is not now openly practised.   In several
instances it has been altogether abolished; but still the natives
adhere to their accustomed and harmless fetish ceremonies.
When a man of note dies, his family place small sheds on the
paths leading upwards from the valley where the wretched
town exists.   They furnish the sheds with a couch and pillow,
an umbrella, bottle of rum, pipe and tobacco, and whatever
else the dear departed was partial to, but notably the rum;
so that, on leaving the Duke-town vale of tears, the ethereal
should not lack tangible comforts to render, in a poetical
manner, parting associations pleasant.   If by a certain time
the rum is still found intact (and few heathen are found
irreligious enough to drink it and substitute water or air), the
bottle is broken and the contents spilled, so that the defunct
may scent it aloft amongst other spirits.   When people are
suspected of witchcraft, murder, robbery, or any crime
coming within the code of offences defined by the chiefs, the
accused is compelled to eat the celebrated Calabar poisonous
bean.   If the bean is cast forth, the prisoner is declared
innocent; but should death result, guilt is considered
sufficiently apparent to justify the verdict of "palaver set."

Natives who are detected in the act of committing serious crime, or perhaps stealing, especially if the thief happens to be a slave, are executed at once in the most brutal, cold-blooded, merciless manner. The mouth of the victim being gagged, he is laid across a turned-over canoe, his back broken by clubs, and the body thrown into the river, or placed in the bush, as they call it " land chop " for crocodile. Should the tide be at low ebb, the doomed one, in addition to being gagged, is trussed like a fowl, placed in the water, fastened by stakes into the mud, and left to perish as the waters rise overwhelm him. " But there ; enough of gruesome deeds." Let us inspect the peaceful missions.

Duke-town Mission is presided over by the Rev. Mr. Anderson—one or two young missionaries, Mrs. Anderson, and several other white ladies assisting, principally in the education of children. Service is conducted each Lord's Day, morning and afternoon, and also each Tuesday, in the native tongue, the Efik. In the English language service is held every Sabbath at 5 P.M., so that during the cool of the day Europeans may arrive in boats at the foot of the Mission hill. Worship is over before dark, after which Mr. and Mrs. Anderson kindly invite the white men, who certainly are overcome by fatigue at climbing the steep hill, to partake of a refreshing cup of tea, reminding many forcibly of quiet Sunday evenings at home. Their kindness to their fellow-countrymen, as well as to the natives, does not cease here ; for, when traders become ill, they are invited to try change of air at the Mission, and frequently lives are prolonged in consequence. The gardens surrounding the Mission are in a high state of cultivation, well adorned with luxurious exotics, principally obtained from the West Indies, and the buildings, with lofty rooms and cool verandah, are clean and sweet, showing plainly that delicate hands contribute materially to comfort. At any time of the day visitors are heartily welcomed, and fruits of the most tempting nature and delicate flavour offered and partaken of, varied by useful and pleasant conversation.

The late Rev. J. Bailie, once missionary here, showed a party of us a wonderful collection of curiosities which he had gathered with great care. Amongst them was a tub containing lively samples of the electric eel. Upon touching the fish with your finger a smart series of shocks resulted. These eels are used for particular diseases in children, the child in its bath being rolled about amongst them. There were also boa-constrictors' and crocodiles' eggs undergoing the process of incubation. At the proper time, when breaking the shell to introduce the latter into the world, it instantly opens its jaws and shows fight. Mr. Baillie informed us that upon one occasion, having obtained a boa-constrictor's nest with the eggs glued together, the skin of the mother snake was rolled round the nest, and skin and eggs boxed up and sent to Edinburgh. When the box was opened, twenty-eight living snakes sneaked out, like the unexpected reappearance of the " four-and-twenty blackbirds baked in a pie." The household lifted up their voices and fled, leaving the establishment in possession of the African visitors until zoological assistance arrived.

It is very amusing before service to note the eagerness with which the youth of the vicinity wait for their turn to ring the church-bell, at the sound of which well-dressed men, women, boys, and girls—but recently the worst of savages—flock along the shaded lanes leading to the temple of the curious new religion, carrying their Bibles and hymn-books, and good-humouredly greeting neighbours. The building rapidly fills. All the windows and doors are open, and when the wind blows through it is very pleasant. Inside the main entrance is a box to hold the copper, and also brass rods, bent like croquet stakes, which form the current coin contributions of Old Calabar. A plate is also at hand convenient for subscriptions from white men. The finance is looked after by one of the ladies. The precentor is a young negro, rejoicing, as all converted negroes do, in exaggerated white shirt, collar, and extensive wristbands, contrasting well with his glossy black skin, black broadcloth Sunday suit, and patent-leather boots. His voice is pitched so high and shrill that none but natives, especially women and children, can follow the tune, but all join in the singing, and excellent time is observed. Coming out of church, young and old people group together on their way to their villages, and thus a new style of spending Sunday becomes gradually adopted by many natives.

During a stay of three weeks on board the hulk "Dawstone," belonging to my travelling companion, we enjoyed ample means of transit on the waters ; and, when tired of walking on the land, occasionally mounted an attendant donkey, which duly brayed discontent upon being laden. The resident trade manager, Captain J. B. Walker, F.R.G.S., who has stayed for many years at Old Calabar, took us occasionally some two miles over a hill through the bush to his own model farm and schoolhouse. For a lay missionary, trader, and country resident combined, he has done wonders towards civilising his *protegées*, and he has thereby earned not only the warm esteem of the missionaries, but also the approbation of their society at home. One morning very early we went in the hulk's six-oared gig eight miles up the river to Creek-town. This boat, provided with a canvas awning lined with green baize, afforded grateful shelter from the heat of the sun, and, regulating the side curtains, moderated the unpleasant dazzling glare reflected from the sunlit dancing waters. Upon landing at Creek-town, the first object that met our view was a big slave chained by one leg to a tree, allowing him space to get into the water from one extremity of the iron tether, and stretching in the opposite direction to creep beneath a low palm-thatched shelter from the sun, like a watch-dog. Upon inquiring "Why this bondage?" we were informed that the man was a "tief." His conscience, however, did not appear to smite him much, for he laughed heartily and ate plantains, sitting crosslegged on the ground nursing his manacled ancle, and anon appeared splashing in the water. The chain composed his full suit.

A wide grass-grown space leads direct to the boats' landing, gradually uphill for the distance of one mile to the mission, which by walking certainly appears twain. On our right is the double palace of King Eyo Honesty the Seventh. A large but cracked bell, erected midway in the thoroughfare, announces his name and title in raised letters cast when the bell was. We knew his predecessors; so pay a visit. This Eyo is a portly, good-humoured young man, and lives in his comfortably cool ground-floor mud palace huts, opening inwards, and hidden from vulgar gaze by a blank wall which encloses the quadrangular space. But his show palace literally astonishes all by its being fantastically painted Prussian-blue and flake-white. It is situated on the hilly side of the mud palace, is two stories high, built of wood, has got a wide verandah surrounding the upper floor, displays a variety of tinted glass-door window-panes, which Eyo tells you to look through at the landscape and observe the really fine views extending in every direction. Under the influence of blue, yellow, red, and green, the kaleidoscopic diversity of his kingdom is pleasing, and so is the King. He exhibits his crown, but does not place it upon his head. We would not like him to do so; it would be too much for our nerves all at once. It is a great big exaggerated affair, made in Holland, and therefore Dutch, like the gold of which it is composed. It is studded with enormous precious stones, bright jewels made of glass, and looks fine, or, as the natives admiringly remark, "proper." In his principal audience room is a likeness of the Queen, cut from the *Graphic*, and gummed against the wall in a good light, and it is the best "old master" in Eyo's gallery. He shows with pride a photographic album, and then kindly invites us down-stairs to the other palace, where in the courtyard a band of rude music plays, whilst a very ugly old man sings comic songs, which tickle those amazingly who can appreciate the jokes. Even the armed retainers acting as a guard of honour cannot help bursting out with laughter right in the eyes of Eyo the Seventh.

We visit several chiefs in their lairs, and my friend is introduced as the merchant to whom they owe so much palm-oil. One old man was ill in bed, but keen love for trade shone through his sparkling eyes. The entrance to his bedroom was crooked and roundabout, but from the foot of his sleeping couch he let us escape from his dark room into sunshine by a private entrance. This venerable chief slept amongst bale goods and produce, as if he wanted to dabble with them until his eyes closed for ever. We were glad to get away, dodging amongst lean pigs, skeleton poultry, and unhealthy cur-dogs, and ascend to the Mission, from whence we had the best view of the luxuriant surrounding country. In the distance was the Duke-town Mission. Between both flag-signal messages are arranged. The Rev. H. Goldie is the principal of this Mission, and he kindly placed his bath-room at our disposal—the greatest act of kindness which one white man can extend to another in the tropics.

My companion was so fatigued by walking in the sun,

and became so exhausted, that we abandoned the idea of undertaking a week's journey and sojourn higher up stream to visit the interior Mission. We passed a delightful day, principally in the shade, occasionally visiting Mr. Goldie in his well-stocked library, and observing the destruction caused by book-devouring insects, Mrs. Goldie superintending the culinary part of comfort, and, with Mr. Campbell, a very young missionary, and two young ladies inspecting the education of youth, the day soon showed signs of closing. In the school-house was a boy albino, a white negro, with red wool, but weak eyes. This child read a chapter of the New Testament in Efik. Adjoining the school buildings are the graves of missionaries, one of whom (the late Mr. Edgerly) was well known to our party. As the sun declined towards its wonted west, the principal of the Mission took us over his hill and valley plantation, which has taken twenty-five years to bring to its present state of perfection. He grows cinnamon, coffee, orange, citron, castor-oil, tamarind, African, East and West Indian trees, and enjoys the benefit of acres upon acres growing wild pine-apples, but he has been unsuccessful with cotton, as a description of fly destroys that useful plant. In the back verandah of the Mission were eight or ten black infants sleeping upon pieces of carpet mats. These little things, having been unfortunately born twins, were doomed to death by the fetish objectors to fecundity, but the good missionaries saved their little lives and will try to bring them up.

It is well known in the river that the home society allows the missionaries about here barely enough to live upon, and that although boasting of what has been done towards civilisation, and the extension of Christian teaching by the people sent out, yet it is said to be extremely niggardly in its conduct to its devoted servants.

The model palm-oil trader's voice is heard long before daybreak resounding beneath the dark, dismal roof of the hulk, summoning coopers, carpenters, white men, Accra men, and Krooboys from slumber to labour. After coffee and biscuits to the white men, he goes in a boat to the beach, tumbles out the sleepers there, and sets each gang to their particular work. In a house on the beach he enjoys a bath with cold water obtained from a handy spring; after which he goes wandering round until the sun, silently creeping over the hill, darts its fierce hot rays over all, showing out, painfully to the eyes, the startling difference betwixt light and shade. Everything is still, save the noise made by the men at work. Not a zephyr breathes through the trees. Heavy drops of dew shine out on all vegetation, sparkling like diamonds. The stench from the river-bank is—perceptible. All is dull, listless, and melancholy in the extreme, until the sea-breeze sets in. He then returns on board, presides at the barter business half an hour before breakfast, when he enjoys another bath, and, whilst completing his toilet, prays aloud in his thinly-partitioned cabin, and is heard all over the quarter-deck. It is rather uncomfortable for his clerks to hear their names mixed up in soliloquy; but thus he warns them of shortcomings, not only in earthly, but hulkly and other affairs. The Krooboys well know the measured accents of the final Lord's Prayer, for then they pass the signal to the galley, and the hot rolls, hot plates, hot yam, hot coffee, and hot fowls come forth, and so does the man. A long grace precedes and winds up the meal. Meantime, if a canoe announces its advent by distant singing and drum-beating as it approaches, the trader keeps one eye upon it, recognises it, rubs his hands, and, mentioning the canoe-owner's name, states—" Ah, that fellow is coming at last with the palm-oil

which he owes ;" but, lo ! the oil passes on the other side of
the way, like the Levite.   Upon this the trader drops his chops
and knife and fork, and loudly orders "Tobin" to jump
into a skiff canoe and follow.   The man alluded to,
who happens to be the biggest and cleverest nigger
on board, does so, and, returning, reports—"Tree
puncheon live for Harry Hartz, saa," meaning that three
puncheons of oil have gone to Harrison's hulk, of which Mr.
Hartz is agent.   This is trial number one, and the day is
full of them, mixed up with pleasant *bona fide* purchases.
Meals follow in succession, sleeping and getting up again.
On Saturdays at one o'clock all trading ceases until Monday.
All hands wash and scrub the ship inside and out.   On
Sunday morning a banner with the strange device "BETHEL"
flutters from the tall flagstaff.   At half-past ten the ship's
bell tolls for church.   Boats bring visitors from other hulks ;
white men and Accra mechanics, with their Bibles and prayer-
books, assemble around a large table, at the head of which
officiates the model.   Krooboys, with arms twined round
each other's neck, packed and sticking together as closely as
soles at Billingsgate, quietly go to sleep.   One Sabbath an
irreverent dog, wandering about looking for something to
bite at, at last laid hold of a sleeping Krooboy's leg, the
owner of which awoke and "went for that dog."   The model,
reading with the emphasis of the real, and proud of the
appearance of Michael Angelo's Moses, was in full swing,
but the disturbance caused an addition to the text—" Unto
whom I sware in my wrath,——Jim, turn that con—— dog
out."   The model keeps no liquor in his hulk, nor ever says
"Here goes it" ; and thus his weeks, months, and years
pass pleasantly away.

   In this river, as in others, a medical man resides, who is
paid so much per head for attendance upon each hulk.   Two

men, taking turns of six months out and six home, generally work amicably together; and although the natives have their own professors, yet, as they get to know more of the habits of Europeans, they eagerly seek the advice and prefer the physic of the white doctor.

Wherever white men are gathered together for trade, natural and healthy competition exists; but when fierce opposition, furthered by the injudicious practice of giving credit, instead of sticking to simple barter, prevails, it tells its own tale in the long run. Here, more than elsewhere on this coast, is this evil exemplified. It seems reasonable that natives whose private house, and, say for the absurdity of the thing, hotel and travelling expenses, are not extravagant, should be better able to pay produce for goods than receive goods for probable, speculative, uncertain, and, in very many cases, never-forthcoming produce. A clever native goes up river, brings down a few puncheons of palm-oil, sells them to one of the hulks, obtains goods, sometimes to double their value, goes away, brings down more produce, obtains more credit, deals with rival hulks, and goes on as long as it suits him to do so. Suddenly the clever native dies or disappears for ever; and what security then has the trader got for his debt? Of a truth, the credit system with savages is bad in principle. They undersell each other, and therefore accumulated debts figure in home merchants' books as value to come forth at some future time. When will African merchants instruct their agents to use common sense by entirely abolishing the credit system?

Upon leaving the Old Calabar River, steering southwards towards the River Cameroons, or, as mariners say, " hugging " the eastern extremity of the Bight of Biafra, the dreary swamps, with their monotonous line of mangrove-trees springing from universal mud, and therefore appearing about the same height, fringing the entire seaboard of the Bights, and yielding anything but pleasure to the eye from the painful uniformity, vanish at once. Suddenly the scenery and country totally change in character to a grand mountain region, and the remarkable change is most welcome.

The Cameroons Mountain gradually rises on its north side from mangrove swamp; but on the south it is separated by the river of the same name from a moderately hilly district. Viewed from a distance, it resembles in outline a gigantic pyramid. Its sea base extends for thirty miles. Steaming close to the land opens out small bays, dotted with pretty islands wooded from the water's edge, and far upwards on the highland sides are valleys, cañons, and deep shady chasms abundantly clothed with infinite variety of great trees, growing according to the temperature, influenced by the altitude, until, at the elevation of 13,700 feet, the solitary peak towers in azure. Its aspect continually varies according to the position of the sun. Every tint, from the faintest neutral barely distinguishable from sky to the golden colours of sunrise and sunset, charms the senses, and causes a feeling of wonder that all this healthy district should remain unused and running to waste ; for its slopes afford sites for residences where patients from along the whole coast can readily get to and rapidly recover.

Here it is well to record what has been done tending towards utilising the healthy mountain slopes. On the shores of Ambas Bay, situated twenty miles westward of the entrance to the Cameroons River stands the new settlement of Victoria, whose existence dates from the time when, by Spanish intolerance, the Baptist Mission in Fernando Po was compelled to abandon that island in 1858. Twelve years before that date, a Spanish Commissioner sent by his Government to Fernando Po to claim possession of the island, had ordered the Baptist Missionaries to depart, but it was not until 1858 that they left. A few of the oldest and most respectable negro families, the heads of whom (originally slaves, re-captured and liberated by British men-of-war) accompanied the missionaries. The site of Victoria was purchased by the Mission from the natives. The settlers soon cleared it and erected homes, where they reside with enough of the comforts of life to induce contentment. They live at peace, and are governed and kept in order by their oldest men. They have their school and meeting house. They trade a little in palm-oil. The sale of spirits being prohibited, they are kept sober, and are certainly better-behaved citizens than their brethren remaining on the island of Fernando Po. A few years ago they were fortunate in having Mr. George Thompson, of Glasgow, to reside amongst them. A man of talent and large-heartedness, he left his home, where he was a prosperous architect, to establish a sanatorium on the slopes of the magnificent mountain for the use of all the white men obliged to reside up and down the coast. He is engaged upon that good work now. Meantime he has become as a father to the Victorians, being patient to a degree with them, instructing them in all acts of kindness and charity, and, both by his purse and good example, aiding and forwarding their moral and material prosperity.

Rounding the southern extremity of this lofty mountain, we enter the Cameroons river, and steaming thirty miles upwards brings us to Aqua-town, off which hulks are anchored for the purpose of trading with the natives, as in the rivers already described. Aqua-town is built upon elevated land on the southern bank of the river; it is laid out at right angles, and the gardens surrounding many of the residences, together with shady trees in the streets, show that the people are endowed with some taste; in fact, they are much more intelligent than those of Benin, Brass, Akassa, Bonny, or even Old Calabar. The women are decidedly better-looking than those in the other rivers, and pay more attention to personal adornment, especially shown by trimming their hair in a variety of lumpy designs, of which the sugar-loaf pattern is the prettiest, as it towers aloft ornamented with bright glass beads and cowrie-shells.

The Rev. A. Saker, Baptist missionary, has been established here, and at Fernando Po till he was driven out, for nearly thirty years. In the first place, he taught the natives to make bricks—with his own hands mixing the clay, moulding, and turning out the useful article. He set the example of building by constructing his solid mission-church, school-house, and residence, on an appropriate site commanding a magnificent view of the Cameroons Mountain, the river winding through distant valleys, bounded by far-away blue mountains inland, and seawards, dimly apparent, the island of Fernando Po. He also taught them boat-building, handling the axe and the adze with dexterity, and, with equal application of general knowledge, instructed them how to dress huge blocks of stone brought from the foot of the great mountain. His premises are well drained, and every part is clean and kept in good order. As usual at all missions on this coast, not only resident traders but casual visitors are heartily welcomed, and the best of everything grown on the mission grounds is produced for their gratification and comfort, even to pudding made from the bread-fruit. Generations of children have been, and are, educated at his schools; and, take Mr. Saker altogether, he is undoubtedly one of the best missionaries in Africa, simply because he has persevered in inculcating into barbarian minds useful lessons pertaining towards civilisation.

It may not be out of place, whilst alluding to practical missionaries, to note what Mr. Burton, the head of the American mission at Sherboro, has done. Apart from churches and schools in full operation for many years past, he selected a well-timbered spot convenient to ample water power yielded by a creek running into the Sherboro river. This he has utilised in such an enterprising manner, by getting suitable machinery out, and erecting a saw-mill, that he now supplies the whole of the colony of Sierra Leone with durable hard wood in the shape of planks, beams, and boards, in great demand for building purposes. The profits of this lumber trade are applied to defray the expenses of the mission; and the happy result is, that instead of being a burden upon the Parent Society of the United States, from its own earnings it pays its own way and gradually extends its usefulness. Such men as Burton and Saker are invaluable, and they are the true type of what missionaries should be amongst savages.

Fifty miles' sea-journey west of the mouth of the Cameroons river, and then the anchor, belonging to the tiny speck on the ocean containing atoms of humanity, is dropped in the waters of Clarence Cove, on the north-eastern end of the beautiful island of Fernando Po, which rises from the sea like a twin brother of the Cameroons Mountain. Its bays develop into valleys fringed by mountain ridges, and luxuriant vegetation, similar to that on Cameroons, crowns all, towering aloft into indistinctness, capped by the peak, 11,000 feet high. The northern side of the island fronts the neighbourhood of the Old Calabar river, coming from which at early dawn, as you leave Tom Shott's Point for only a sixty-mile run across, the twin giants rise with the sun, changing from sky-blue to gold and purple, looking like colossal Gog and Magog saluting each other as great guardian gods of earth, waking from sleep to overlook equatorial Africa.

Clarence Cove affords good anchorage for vessels of any size, by keeping well clear of a rock below water, which is buoyed and situated not far from King Will's Point, the eastern promontory sheltering the cove. A Spanish guard-ship keeps time and order. The beach is lined with palm-oil stores, coal stores, and various huts connected with traders. An inclined plane of a road leads up a steep hill to the town of St. Ysabel. The barracks, governor's house, English consulate, the hospital, and a few other buildings, together with a sprinkling of mounted and unmounted cannon, over-look the bay. Behind the promenade, on which these buildings are erected, dwell the descendants of liberated slaves landed when the island was under the protection of England, with the addition of similar people who have come from Sierra Leone and Lagos. These blacks, under Spanish rule, have been rendered docile and obliging, for they have had the bumptious notions, fostered by English misrule in English West-African colonies, driven out of them, and at the same time they are so kindly treated that they do not desire change. It is well-known that wherever French, Spaniards, or Portuguese rule in Africa, niggers are com-pelled to be civil.

To the left of Clarence Cove is Alburkah Bay, where, overgrown with vegetation, lies all that is left of the first Niger exploring steamer, after which the bay is named. To the right is another and very romantic-looking indent of the sea, studded with pretty islands. At the foot of tall trees the English Government possess a coal depôt for the use of the African fleet: in front of it lies the worn-out "Vindictive," once an English man-of-war.

Fernando Po belongs to Spain, and is used as a place of

banishment for political offenders ; hence a Spanish governor and white soldiers hold possession, but make very little use of it other than to pass away their lives as lazily as possible. The few white women who have been induced to leave Europe soon turn to the complexion of saffron, and, although adorned in finery, much given to the use of scent, and surrounded by every luxury and comfort that the climate affords, or that the kindest attention can bestow, yet they dwindle, peak, and pine, and look as unhappy, and as much out of place, as the almost unknown gorgeously-attired wax effigies in Westminster Abbey.

The trading here, for palm-oil only, is in the hands of English merchants and the descendants of liberated slaves, some of whom migrated from Sierra Leone and established business before the Spaniards assumed their right to govern the island. Previously Spain allowed the English consul to act also as Spanish governor, and "old coasters" well remember Captain John Beecroft, of Birkenhead, and his genial rule and wise administration of justice. He is buried where he wished to be, on King Will's Point, in front of and overshadowed by a great silk-cotton-tree, beneath which he daily passed many hours looking across the waters at his beloved Africa. This inscription speaks truth :—

Beneath this Monument
Are deposited the remains of
JOHN BEECROFT,
Spanish Governor
Of the Island of Fernando Po,
And Her Britannic Majesty's Consul
For the Bight of Biafra,
Who died June 10th, 1854,
Aged 64 years.

This Memorial was erected by the inhabitants of the Colony of Clarence as a testimonial of their gratitude for his many years' fatherly attention to their comforts and interests, and for his unwearying exertion to promote the happiness and welfare of the whole African race.

Further along King Will's point is a monument erected to the memory of those who died on the Niger Expedition of 1841. Beecroft's memorial was sent out in pieces, but for ten years they remained lying beneath the big cotton-tree until Captain Graham, of H.M.S. "Danac," in 1869, had what was left of it erected. This shows the neglect of the townspeople to the memory of their best benefactor, a man who, with his whole energy, entered into nearly all the treaties still existing between the British Government and the native chiefs for the suppression of the export slave trade and the encouragement of lawful commerce. In 1853 I frequently walked with Governor Beecroft over his favourite promenade on King Will's Point. It happened that Mrs. Matthews, who had kindly nursed me during the fever, spoke to Governor Beecroft, when he visited me on my recovery, about Richard Lander's grave. She pointed out where it was, and said that a stone sent out from England covered it. The spot was concealed by thick jungle and trees. Governor Beecroft employed Kroomen to clear away the rank vegetation, and the tombstone, hidden for twenty years, again saw light. It will be remembered that Richard Lander was the first white man who descended the River Niger.

The successor to Governor Beecroft, who officiated until the Spaniards took charge, was called sometimes Governor James Lynslager, but oftener "Daddy Jim." He was a native of Holland, was wrecked when a boy and cast forth from the sea with a broken leg, and therefore became addicted to a wooden one. He waxed wealthy, married a black wife, in accordance with the rites of the Church of England, of which he was a strict member, and, as a mark of welcome and friendship to his numerous acquaintances, was wont to suddenly unship his timber limb and throw it at their heads. He was a most hospitable but very eccentric host. If a dinner prepared for guests did not suit his idea of correctness, he did not hesitate to destroy it, which spoliation invariably caused at first surprise, followed by merriment. After this he naturally insisted upon "pot luck," which was thoroughly enjoyed. It did not matter whether those whom he entertained were admirals or skippers; if anything went wrong "Daddy Jim" drew the cloth, and nobody could prevent subsequent assault and battery upon somebody blameable, unless, by stealing his loose leg, he was reduced to hopping about like a lame rooster. I met him shortly before his death at the '62 Exhibition, and waited to càtch the leg, as, upon observing African features, he at once, full of joy, reclined upon a sofa and placed his hands convenient to loosen his missile, but, suddenly recalling to mind that he had mounted a cork substitute, curiously fastened and concealed by a broadcloth cover corresponding with the genuine article, his display of feeling found vent and satisfaction in the nearest refreshment-room. When the Spaniards came, "Daddy Jim" retired into private life, after which Hutchinson, Burton, Charles Livingstone, brother to the great African explorer, and Hopkins, succeeded as British consuls, and now Hartley reigns.

The aborigines of the island, called "Bubis" (rendered by Sierra Leone people appropriately into "Boobies"), are extremely shy in their manners, and live entirely by themselves in bush villages. They are repulsive in appearance, and their principal dress is a wide-brimmed straw hat, fastened behind through straw and wool by means of a long wooden skewer, leaving both ends of the skewer exposed to view. A grass string, with fetish cowrie-shells hiding the string, or the vertebra of a snake, ornaments the abdomen; and either, or both, constitutes an inexpensive outfit. But the women who come to market with palm-oil, yams, or the usual run of produce of their village plantations, are gradually adopting the habit of adorning their waists with cloths. They are a quiet, inoffensive race, and take great pleasure in painting themselves with red earth. In early youth ornamental scars are incised upon various parts of the body, similar to the practice in Niger countries, and when the rainy season comes on they carefully rub their entire persons with palm-oil, thus enjoying a cheap waterproof suit. In cases of marital infidelity, the "Booby" divorce-court judges chop off at the wrist the right hands of the faithless wives; and, from the number of one-handed females wandering around loose, the court seems to pay, and such forlorn ladies are obliged to utilise the left hand.

This island is about the size of the Isle of Man. If you can fancy Mona rising from the waves into a peak four or five times the height of Snaefell, and imagine it abounding with primeval forest peculiar to the tropical and temperate zones, until human sight cannot distinguish vegetation from bare outline, the resemblance will be complete. A road has been cleared of jungle to a distance of five miles up-hill, where a few houses have been erected, and the purity of the atmosphere at only the height of 1,500 feet above the sea-level is apparent in the speedy recovery of the few invalids who avail themselves of its benefit. What, then, must be 'the advantage of constructing a road still higher into temperate regions, even to occasional snow, approaching the Clarence or Cameroons peaks? In other countries advantage would be taken of ascent to pure breathing, but here apathy and indifference prevail over common-sense and energy. Nothing can be more simple than to start a comfortable hotel 10,000 feet above the sea-level, which would yield the climate of Madeira close to the

Equator, and give to all Europeans who are obliged to dwell on the West Coast of Africa a chance to prolong life.

This leads to the subject of white men bringing out their wives to this coast before healthy hilly residences are prepared for them. Such conduct is not only unwise, but criminal. Nothing can justify it. It is more especially cruel, unmanly, and inhuman in the case of children. Here is but one instance of common occurence. " Oh, mamma dear ! Oh, papa dear ! Look ! Look at a boat full of Kissy Minsels !" two little children exclaimed with frantic joy on approaching that hotbed of all that is bad—Sierra Leone, whilst observing a boat full of negroes coming towards the vessel. Their white faces were flushed with heat as they rushed about the deck beneath the awning, prettily dressed in airy white clothing, gaily trimmed with broad blue ribbons, all ready to go on shore. The careful captain, after leaving England, as soon as the little ones got their sea-legs on—and children soon manage that—had the poop railing netted, so that they could not fall into the sea. They scampered over the ship, yielding delight to every one on board, from the forecastle, where kind-hearted brawny fellows nursed them and told them queer tales, to the galley, and also chock aft. The cook had always something for them. They knew every officer's cabin, and where he kept his sunshine pictures of home. Chumming with the butcher, they visited the sheep in their pens, the pigs in their houses, and the poultry in the hencoops, and as the rolling of the vessel occasionally jerked sea-water up the scuppers on to the main-deck, which was their safest playground, they laughed with glee, and then looked down the scuppers at the bright blue ocean streaked with foam as the ship bounded along, silently pondering for a little while—(who knows what strange thoughts these innocents pictured of the

wonders of the deep in their fairyland fancies?)—until
presently another roll of the ship, perhaps, gave them a
startling shower-bath, and then they ran off to mamma as if
they had encountered a dragon, to seek for sympathy and
dry clothing. That passage out passed like a happy dream.
Everybody thought at night of devices to amuse the children on the next day. But, and it is extremely painful to
think of it, six weeks after landing at Sierra Leone they were
both quietly at rest in the cemetery. Had they remained in
England, they would only have been young people in the
twentieth century.

CHAPTER IX.

TO show an increase of trade to and from the West Coast of Africa since December, 1852, when the first of the African Steamship Company's vessels left England and called at the various ports enumerated, terminating with Fernando Po, it is necessary to state that they sailed monthly from each end until 1868, when the British and African Steam Navigation Company commenced running their ships also once monthly, and both companies extended their places of call beyond Fernando Po. They occasionally visit the Portuguese islands of Prince's and St. Thomas; thence to Gaboon, situated just north of the Equator, on to Black Point, Landana; and then up the river Congo to Banana Creek, in latitude 6° 25' S., longitude 12° E.; next, to Kinsembo, Ambrizette, Ambriz, and St. Paul de Loanda, in latitude 9° 10' S., longitude 13° E., which is at present their southern limit. Now, instead of only monthly communication as far as Fernando Po, steamers about five times the size of the "Forerunner"—the pretty and appropriate name of the pioneer vessel for December, 1852—leave Liverpool at one terminus and Bonny at the other every Saturday. Each company also despatches a steamer monthly, alternately, as far as St. Paul de Loanda; and each, in addition, possesses a large tender, constructed of light draught, so as to enable it to cross the bar of Lagos lagoon harbour, and also the bars of the minor rivers in the Bights of Benin and

Biafra.　These tenders bring cargoes, consisting of huge casks of palm-oil and other produce, to transfer to the receiving hulks and ocean steamers at Bonny.

The Dutch traders at Banana Creek, river Congo, have also a regular set of steamers plying to Holland.　The Portuguese Government has subsidised a line between St. Paul de Loanda and Lisbon, calling at their continental and island possessions, and the French Messageries Maritimes have an organised service, amongst other places calling at Goree and Senegal.　Furthermore, private firms build or charter and run ocean steamers to and fro, as well as smaller ones for every available place up rivers, as feeders both to ocean steamers and sailing vessels; so that, in fact, steam launches are gradually taking the places of canoes; river steamers of light draft are becoming common in lieu of lumbering sailing cutters; and everywhere, wherever trade justifies it, traders run steamers of their own to and from Europe ; and thus King Steam has extended his benefit-yielding comfort and speed even to benighted Africa.

We left Fernando Po just before sunset, and after twenty-three hours' steaming southerly, inclining towards the east, on the next afternoon entered the Gaboon river.　The French town is situated on the north side of the river, at a little distance from its mouth; and anchored off it, in smooth water, is the guardship, a French man-of-war, and several French trading vessels.　We stop the steamer until a boat from the guardship approaches, receives her mails, and grants us permission to proceed about three miles higher up, where we come to anchor abreast a cluster of English trading factories, called Glasstown, to deliver mails and cargo.

On the following morning, at early dawn, all the passengers who feel inclined for a ramble on shore land in the captain's gig instead of a surf-boat, as the water is not rough

like that upon the open seashore. The first thing that
strikes one is the abundance of ironstone rock, similar to
that at Sierra Leone, lining the bank. At low water these
rocks show out covered with clusters of good eating oysters,
and then it is well to employ Kroomen collecting them for
use on board, to be partaken of with bread-and-butter and
bottled stout. The English traders heartily welcome stray
visitors, and oblige us with one pony and one donkey. I
believe that to be the entire census of the equine race of
Glass-town. We start towards the French town along the
beach. The animals soon get tired, and so do the outsiders.
Repose for the former about half-way is a happy thought,
and equally so for the latter, and a drink for both ; also for
those who, walking, speedily overtake the cavalcade ; for do
we not see a store before us! Those mounted look very
like Don Quixote and Sancho Panza, and they are properly
ridiculed, for it is a moot point, as Æsop indicates, whether
the men should not carry the animals ; for the poor things
can hardly drag themselves along beneath a tropical sun.
Entering the castle courtyard—a cluster of sheds stuck in
soft sand—the steeds are looked to. Nobody is about, which
certainly appears strange, but sounds of revelry come from
the upper floor of the two-storied store ; music and clapping
of hands and women's and children's voices peal forth.
There is no fear of Rosinante and the donkey bolting; for the
weight of the riders, the heavy sand, and the hot sun have
told upon all four, as well as upon the pedestrians. Forming
a procession, we ascend the outer staircase to the verandah
and knock at the door ; but the revellers do not hear the
knocking ; so we make bold to lift the latch and enter, and
there we see a man playing the melodious concertina, drawing it in and out as a sort of ferocious accompaniment to
stringed instruments played by others, while comely dark

damsels twirl about to the great delight of their children squatted on the floor; and, strange to say, the children are much lighter in colour than their mothers; but this peculiarity is not confined to Gaboon. Evidently the good man of the house (undoubtedly European) is abroad. The music and dancing cease, and the babes begin to howl. We request the performers to "go ahead mit de moosic;" but, like a mad bull or a mob charging an organ grinder playing "Madame Angot," the harmony ceased; however, gradually fear merges into confidence, for the little ones crowd around the strangers, and a few trifling presents restore peace. Bottled beer quenches thirst, and then we proceed onwards to a change of nationality, and enter a French village, prettily situated on rising ground overlooking a wharf, on which produce is piled for shipment to France. There is actually a paved street here, and an air of comfort very pleasing in Africa. A boat comes from a French vessel, and we are kindly invited by the people landed to partake of their fruit and delicious salad in a verandah, beneath the shade of trees, which completely shuts out the hot sun. This is so enjoyable that we linger until a gun is fired from our steamer—"Hoop-la!" "Allez!"—compels tearing ourselves away from our newly-made but warm-hearted friends.

Leaving Gaboon at five P.M., forty-one hour's steaming along the coast brought us, on the second forenoon, abreast Black Point, which is a fine open bay. Three hours' anchoring sufficed to discharge cargo; three more hours' steaming, and then Landana, one of the most picturesque places on the south-west coast of Africa, and one of the richest in produce. In addition to delivering goods brought by the vessel from England, we gladly commenced to take on board cargo in return, consisting chiefly of palm-oil, palm-kernels, and ground-nuts. A stay of two days enables us to ramble over the hills and valleys in the vicinity. One man goes out shooting pretty birds to preserve as specimens ; another takes photographic views; others prefer the shade. There are Dutch, Portuguese, and English factories, and all cheerfully entertain strangers. As the ship is anchored three miles from the land, we prefer to spend the nights on shore, enjoying large prawns, rock-oysters, fresh fish, radishes, capsicums, and pleasant company.

There are so many stations to call at upon this coast, and as there are no lights exhibited to indicate headlands or harbours, it is necessary to leave any anchorage to time arrival about daybreak at the next place. Thus we steamed from Landana at ten P.M., and daylight on the following morning showed us off Shark's Point, the southern side of the entrance to the great river Congo. We encountered a strong current of mighty water forcing itself out to sea. Steaming near to the southern bank for a few miles, the vessel's head was pointed to the north side, and she steamed into a branch of the Congo called Banana Creek, where we anchored in perfectly smooth water, close to wharves belonging to Dutch, French, Portuguese, and English merchants. This is the most convenient place upon the whole coast for vessels discharging or receiving cargo, and will become a gigantic depôt of transit for produce from, and manufactures to, the vast interior drained by the mighty rivers. Undoubtedly, the river Congo is the ocean outlet for Livingstone's Lualaba.

Banana Creek curves round into the Congo, forming a promontory of low land, and upon this the trading factories are built. The water is sufficiently deep to load vessels lying alongside the wharves. The stores erected towards the neck of the tongue of land are compelled to keep Kroomen on watch each night to warn the sleepers if foes invade. These timid sentinels sit around large bonfires and call to each other at intervals, as well as to know that all are wide awake as to keep mutual courage up. We spent two nights in one of these places, but could not sleep for the yelling of the Krooboys. They were extra watchful, for, shortly before, a band of natives from the mainland crept quietly toward the stores to steal whatever they could lay hands upon. Our host was warned in time, and from the strong verandah a six-pounder, charged with slugs and nails, was fired at the moving mass, and all hands fired Sniders. The foe retreated, leaving two of their party, who couldn't do so any more.

The Congo remains yet to be properly explored. It is the biggest stream in Africa. The produce of the vast regions which it drains must come to its mouth. Traders are only peddling at present, for they are sorely beset by the worst of savage savages. It is time that some civilised government established a fort on the first high land up the river, manned by black soldiers and officered by white men, assisted by a few armed steam launches to punish river pirates, to destroy refractory villages, and thereby protect the peaceful trading community.

From Gaboon to St. Paul de Loanda the line of coast rises into pleasant-looking country, which in many places strongly resembles the park-lands of home. In the far distance glimpses are obtained of blue hills, and nearer are occasional granite rocks peeping out of forest, looking like comfortable country houses. The valleys are clothed with long grass, through which creeks and rivers, fringed with graceful vegetation, roll into the Atlantic. Near to the mouths of the streams navigable for canoes, or else at the termination of old and well-worn paths, trading factories are established, so as to be convenient to barter goods for produce as it arrives from the far interior.

The French possess Gaboon, the Portuguese Ambriz, St. Paul de Loanda, and the district about the river Coanza. All other places north of Ambriz belong to the natives; but each is in reality ruled by the most sensible trader, who judiciously manages the savage tribes so as to keep them from plundering his own and also his fellow-traders' stores. At these places it is absolutely necessary to be prepared at all times for wily attack. Each white man carries his life in his firearms. The natives must be cajoled, or else coerced and frightened into subjection; but they are arrant cowards, for when an outbreak takes place much shouting is heard, a few shots are fired, and probably nobody hurt; so trade is soon resumed, as the blockade of rum, consequent upon the cessation of traffic, does not yield a state of bliss to savages who have once tasted.

The barter trade south is very similar to that north of the Equator, varied, however, according to the peculiar fancy of the different inhabitants for certain goods in return for produce natural to the different districts. The principal products are palm-oil, palm-kernels, india-rubber, coffee, ivory, gum, bees-wax, ground-nuts, fibres, castor-oil beans, and a little cotton; which are bartered for chiefly by guns, powder, prints, cloths, earthenware, brass rods, red and blue beads, knives, matches, rum, and gin.

It takes nine and a-half hours to steam from the river Congo to Ambrizette, where the natives are especially ferocious in their conduct. They are so given to lawless habits and stealing, and so prone to deeds of violence, that the traders are obliged to arm their faithful people, and keep constantly on the watch for assault, plunder, and ill-usage. Take one of their trading-stores—that part where goods are kept. It is like an ordinary shop, without windows, but with counters and shelves containing a selection of articles of every sort suitable to the wants of savages; but the thieving customers are not admitted. A strong door, shut and bolted, debars their entrance. This door is five feet high, and just over it, from a space of about two feet, the grinning heads of the negociators peep and yell. The trader or his clerk attends to them. These truly "rum" customers— for they adore the fiery fluid as much as Niger Delta savages— have taken their valuable articles of barter, whether palm-oil, palm-kernels, ground-nuts, india-rubber, fibre, or anything else saleable in England, to other sheds forming a portion of the factory, the man attending to which has given them a small piece of paper "book;" in fact, a receipt form filled up with the weight and quantity of whatever has been delivered. These vouchers are held aloft over the five-feet door, and the owners fight for being first served, just as paupers in Italy do at gratuitous soup distributions, flourishing their basins and spoons. Each native trader is attended to in turn. Our friend Mr. Carr presided, and his quiet, but sarcastic play of the native language to his eager constituents, who wanted to get the bright prints, knives, guns, and orders on the magazine keeper for gunpowder, as quickly as possible, and be off, amused us very much. Mr. Carr told his servants what goods to hand over for the tickets, and away the happy recipients went, usually a demijohn of rum accompanying them; and then, like a lucky boy at school receiving a basket of apples, friends attended, and, the demijohn being frequently sampled, songs naturally arose.

One party, beneath the graceful shade of a baobab-tree situated a little way back from the main thoroughfare of a footpath, got so overwhelmed with pleasure by passing the liquor around freely, poured from the demijohn into a second-hand sardine-box, that if a ladder had been placed before them they would only have looked upon it as a smooth deal board. Under the serene sky, surrounded by agreeable society, they gradually were overcome, and then lovely woman stepped in to the rescue and corked the demijohn.

One of our passengers, wandering two miles from the trading stores towards the native village, fixed his camera to take a dry-plate view of the collection of huts, when a crowd of women came forth, and, seeing a bright eye below a piece of black velvet, as he was focussing the view, shrieked wildly that an evil eye was fixed upon the town. They speedily collected a mob, and commencing to stone the amateur photographer, smote his head and smashed his mahogany case; but the lens escaped injury. It was useless to try to explain matters, for suitable language was wanting. But the sudden appearance of a trader, who, with a stick, struck out right-and-left, and the production of a coloured vignette, the wonder of inspecting which, like a ray of civilisation illuminating obtuse intellect, changed the current of their thoughts, caused them to cease stoning and smile, and the man still lives.

At Ambrizette there is a large flat space of ground which at certain times is lower than the Atlantic. Into this sea-water is run; it is allowed to evaporate, and a quantity of salt is then collected. A somewhat similar process for the production of salt is practised near Ostia, at the mouth of the Tiber, where the extensive salt marshes, which Livy mentions as having existed in the time of Ancus Martius, in the seventh century B.C., are utilised for the same purpose at the present day.

We leave Ambrizette without regret, and, forty miles further on, anchor off Kinsembo for two hours to deliver cargo and mails, and ten miles more bring us to Ambriz, where a headland on the south side protects an iron wharf boasting actually of a set of steps, so that a ship's boat, instead of a surf-boat or canoe, can land people from the ship, anchored three or four miles distant. At the shore end of the iron wharf is the Portuguese custom-house, and also in the immediate neighbourhood a cluster of general stores; from behind them—the stores—an excellent road has been made (by convict labour) sloping gently uphill to an extensive and healthy plateau, where the traders reside in comfortable dwellings, built for security from fire in a straggling manner widely apart. The Dutch house appears to be the best, for beneath the shade of trees the inmates can enjoy their leisure hours, fanned by the welcome fresh air from the south, from whence comes the coolest breeze in this southern hemisphere.

The scene on the steamer's deck is now something unusually interesting and exciting. She commenced at Landana to take homeward cargo, although still bound further south with English cargo. At each place canoes come off, peddling grey parrots, blue-nosed monkeys, pretty little monkeys, if any monkey can be called pretty, and big ugly ones; also snakes, young crocodile, and a great variety of birds; likewise excellent mats, made of grass woven into fancy patterns, curious spears, bows and arrows, fancy gourds, porous earthenware water-coolers, and an infinite variety of pleasing curiosities.

Sixty miles south of Ambriz we anchor off St. Paul de Loanda. This harbour ranks next to Banana as regards shelter and calm water—wonderful aids to working ship's holds. The harbour is formed by a long narrow island, dotted with marine villas peeping out from groves of cocoa-nut palms; but the bay is so shallow about the landing-places that vessels of any ordinary size are compelled to bring up as far away as three or four miles from the wharves fronting the town ; however, this inconvenience is partly obviated by the use of steam launches employed to tow cargo-barges alongside.

There are steamers on the American river plan, and English-built steamers plying to factories up the Coanza river, the mouth of which is situated fifty miles south of Loanda, and from the Coanza comes most of the produce shipped from Loanda.

In the city, fronting the bay, there is a tolerably good plaza, with a statue in the centre to a general who did bravely by the colony, as the inscription records. A promenade garden also exists in the vicinity of the Governor's residence, situated on a hill overlooking the town. At each of these places the military band plays twice weekly, on which occasions the youth and beauty of Loanda assemble to listen to the music and bill and coo before dinner. It is interesting to walk through the market streets, where open-stall stores are managed by the natives, exposing to view a variety of goods, peddled as at Sierra Leone. Each morning there is abundance of delicious fruit for sale, and fresh fish, which the bay abundantly yields; but toiling through the sand enervates the strongest. Ascending the surrounding hills, to obtain a view of the country and houses scattered around, necessitates the use of the machilla, a sort of cot-hammock with side curtains, carried by two men, each at one end of a round stout pole resting on their shoulders, with their easy-going fare slung between and pleasantly jerked along. But, during the heat of the day, either walking or being carried in the machilla soon creates unpleasant warmth and weariness; so that shelter is naturally sought in the billiard-room on the plaza, or else in the English consul's, or some other friendly house. Here I must remark that the English consul always heartily welcomes his countrymen if they are at all worthy of recognition.

The bells ringing from the old churches sound pleasant, but it is melancholy to observe that many of them, and also the solid residences, built from two to three hundred years ago, are hopelessly going to decay; but still Loanda is the metropolis of the Portuguese possessions on this coast: yet, as they make it the place of banishment for their convicts, who present by no means a lively, well-fed, or healthy appearance (convicts rarely do), it is apparent that Portugal reckons Loanda not good for anything better. It has had a bad time of it since the export slave trade was abolished; but enterprising merchants—English, American, and some from the island of St. Helena—have of late years made legitimate trade lively; for, in addition to starting local steam traffic, they have erected modern stores and houses; and, from its commanding position, its sheltered harbour, and its aptability to become the terminus of a future railway into the interior, Loanda will, phœnix-like, rise from its ashes and become a great outlet for valuable produce from the rich inland region; and, on the other hand, equally an extensive field for civilised manufactures with which to buy the produce.

The hired labourers employed by the merchants come from the Cabenda district, situated between the Congo and Landana. These Cabenda-boys somewhat resemble Krooboys not only in willingness to work for pay, but the inveterate habit of stealing anything that they can carry away is common to both tribes, and both are equally addicted to telling lies. The black population of Loanda furnish domestic and local labour for the Portuguese community, and, as the water obtained from wells about the town is brackish, many of them are engaged bringing, by bullock-carts and canoes, drinking water from the River Bengo, situated about sixteen miles north of Loanda. Rain-water, collected in tanks, is freely used, but during the dry season fresh-water is scarce and dear.

The want of a proper system of drainage and removal of collections of offal and garbage makes Loanda unhealthy. Upon landing, a horrible stench is at once apparent; worse than that in front of Duke-town, Old Calabar, because there is more of it. Like most tropical places built upon sloping hills, with whitewashed houses showing out of occasional clumps of luxuriant vegetation, surmounted by the clear sky and brilliant sunshine, Loanda looks too good to be true; and, similar to Constantinople, but on a very much reduced scale, its beauty fades as you step from the boat on to the wharf. Coming from the pure sea-breeze surrounding the ship, you inhale foul air, and keep on doing so until getting accustomed to it, and you express no surprise on being informed that death frequently plays havoc amongst the population.

The European cemetery is pleasantly situated about a mile outside the town; it is carefully attended to, well adorned with flowers, and is one of the prettiest spots about Loanda. Blacks are deposited in another burial-ground. As they are carried to their long home, the corpse is laid down at about every hundred yards to rest the bearers, when the procession of mourners, crowding around it, shout their grief with emphasis, clap their hands, and dance wildly. Upon returning to the late residence, it is considered a point of honour on the part of surviving relations, in justice to the memory of the departed, to supply refreshments, and sorrow is so much drowned by rum and gin flowing freely from bottles and demijohns, that alternate weeping, laughing, and dancing, peculiar to the different tribes to which the mourners originally belonged, result. They form a common "platform" of joy over strong drink.

It is painful to talk to white men here who speak the purest English, and, after casually conversing upon anything coming uppermost, to be told by those who have noticed you that you have been yarning with a convict out upon surveillance, and that he cannot go beyond certain bounds. It rather staggers one, but the Portuguese Government appears to be very lenient towards offenders who possess the ability to earn their own living apart from goal discipline, and yet, at the same time, serve out their term of exile. Heaven knows that existence at Loanda upon the most favourable terms is banishment and punishment enough on this earth.

Let us turn to a gay and festive scene. We have been here for one week, and have made many friends, including several good fellows who are to leave for England on the following morning by our steamer. A parting banquet in their honour is announced to take place on the island opposite to the city. We sail across the bay, and, landing at about two P.M., wander along the shore, picking up pretty shells and tying the collection in handkerchiefs to take home, where, placed behind a door, they are duly forgotten. Our temple of entertainment is a long, one-storied, substantially-built house, with a promenade on the flat roof, after the manner of those at Jerusalem. It is the seaside residence of the principal of the firm giving the *fête*. We are ushered into a scene rarely to be found excepting in extravaganza on the stage or in the Arabian Nights' Entertainments. The long undulating Atlantic waves break on the west of this narrow isle of Loanda, yielding the sad monotonous sound which we know so well; for is it not echoed at home, and sea memories revived, by listening to the murmur of the shell? On the eastward the placid bay unfolds itself, rippled only by a gentle breeze, wafting numerous sailing-boats across from the city. In the wide verandah, surrounded by soft sand, amidst a grove of waving palms, a table is spread, and all but the roof open to the air. It is laid out as perfectly as at the "Star and Garter." But what do the boats bring? One is loaded with cases of champagne and Rhine wine; another with cases of cognac and barrels filled with soda-water bottled in Britain; another has a huge machine to make soda-water, and there are cooks, waiters, fruit, and provisions in profuse abundance. Presently two boats crowded with men attired in military uniform approach. Are we to be shot or taken prisoners, or is war about instead of sherry and bitters? These boats contain the military band, twenty-eight in number—counted before dinner. Then come boats with ladies, three English and six Portuguese; then follow in other boats the young fellows, the middle-aged fellows, and the old fellows, and gradually the old fellows call the young fellows "old fellows"; but such is life. A junior member of the firm judiciously orders everything and plays host to perfection. We commence at half-past three P.M., and the festivities last for twelve hours.

Before dinner was over the band began to play an air from "The Grand Duchess"; and if that will not loosen people's tongues and make their legs quiver with a sort of riotous joy beneath the table, nothing will. In the room, with open windows, dancing was started and kept up; social parties formed, chatting pleasantly; and, during intervals of music, strolls by moonlight through the grove cooled the dancers. In addition to the band, whilst its members were enjoying their food and liquor leisurely and quietly, our host, who had imported native merry-makers, caused them to exhibit their antics, which were so true to nature that everybody laughed until they could laugh no more, and some, so much overcome with joy, simply rolled over or lay back and howled with delight. It might be properly designated a sort of Italian opera and savage pantomime, flavoured with ball-room costume, mixed up with Portuguese and

English songs. Meantime the moon shone brightly, giving deep shade to the palms, and the sea on one side, and the bay on the other, assumed brilliant silvery hues, so that perfect peace and happiness prevailed; and thus

> "The minutes wing'd their way wi' pleasure."

With regret everybody bade others adieu, and then the city people returned to their homes and the wanderers to their temporary club on board the ship bound for England.

With the exception of exploring the river Binue to its source, and also wandering up the river Congo, and actually proving that it is the outlet of the great stream and system of lakes discovered by Livingstone, and known as the Lualaba—very little remains to substitute definite positions upon the map of Africa for the hitherto unpleasantly vague term "unknown regions."

It is now universally agreed by geographers that the Congo, and not the Nile, drains the vast district of Western Central Africa situated between the third and twelfth parallels of southern latitude. This view is strengthened, and all but made perfectly clear (only lacking personal survey to complete Livingstone's and Cameron's travels), by comparing the rainy seasons north and south of the Equator, and collecting from natural facts their effect upon the Nile, the Niger and Binue, and the Congo respectively.

North of the Equator the rainy season commences in May and June. The further north the earlier clouds begin to discharge their volumes of water. For instance, at the Gambia, in 13° north latitude, it begins in May, whereas in the Bights of Benin and Biafra, in from 4° to 5° N., rains are not looked for until June, but they last until November. Further north they cease earlier.

South of the Equator the rainy season commences in September and October, and ends in March. The further south, the earlier it begins and terminates; so that about the Equator, all across the Continent, rain prevails during the greater part of the year. Hence the existence of highland spongy receptacles of water and great lakes, from whence rivers derive their sources and run in various ways to the sea, according to the direction of the decreasing altitude.

The Nile on one hand, and the Niger and Binue on the other, rise at the same time, and the average increase in the depth of water, from the lowest about April until the highest at the end of September or beginning of October, is the same in both rivers, the one taken at Cairo, and the other at the Confluence of the Niger and Binue at Lukoja—namely, thirty-five feet. It is evident, therefore, that they are both subject to the influence of the rainy season peculiar to the African portion of the tropic of Cancer, although, in the case of the Nile, partly fed from south of the Equator; and not unlikely the same is also the case with the Binue; yet, notwithstanding southern position, which is overcome by the altitude of their sources and the habit of water to roll downhill, both are subject, as already remarked, to Northern African seasons.

The river Congo, the mouth of which is in 6° 25′ south latitude, is at its highest in January or February; hence it is fair to assume that its waters are collected from the region well south of the Equator, as its rise and fall are in accordance with the rainy season peculiar to the tropic of Capricorn on this continent.

The width of the Congo at its mouth is from six to seven miles. It runs into the Atlantic at the rate of six miles an hour, in one united body of water, without a delta. There is no accumulation of sand at its debouchure, as is the case with nearly all African rivers, because the strong deep stream forces the alluvial deposit—which with smaller rivers settles, the action of tide on one side, and river on the other, forming shallow water called bars—straight into the ocean, and the muddy colour is apparent far out at sea, tainting the deep blue water, similar to the outflow of the Amazon and the Mississippi.

And now, in bringing my African travel to a conclusion, although I should be sorry to think that I may never revisit Africa, let us consider why this part of Africa—say, from the Gambia to Loanda—has not long before become as well known as the most remote countries, and been made to yield a corresponding increase of trade. In the first place, the climate is against the residence of Europeans, so that they only stay for a while to obtain what they require and leave it. In the next place, the natives on the seaboard have not yet appeared sufficiently intelligent or honest enough to be trusted to any extent with goods to trade with in the interior. Again, the strong power of England, in suppressing the export slave traffic, has been successful too recently to show any very marked improvement resulting in straightforward honest trade. The savage luxury obtained by the sale of slaves is not yet forgotten by inland chiefs. War upon them is costly both in life and treasure, and the result of repeated lessons has not been altogether satisfactory. Years must elapse before a decided and steady change for the better takes place. The negro youth educated at the various mission schools, and at the public cost in English colonies, must gradually imbibe honest habits and become trustworthy. Then educated black men will take the place of Europeans, for the ordinary run of white men cannot, for even half the allotted span of life announced by David, exist in tropical Africa.

Missionaries, acting as schoolmasters, combining general knowledge with the inculcation of habits yielding personal comfort, instructing the apt youth of their particular districts in the arts of brick-making, boat-building, house-building, draining villages, and anything that affords happiness, are benefactors to the African race ; and, by leading a pure and blameless life, they not only gain the respect of the natives by their quiet, unostentatious manner, but gradually pave the way for the trader. But this sort of progress between missionaries and traders is too slow for the last quarter of the nineteenth century. We must go ahead ; and, by starting railways where rivers are not, as well as from the heads of navigation into the interior (all of which will pay dividends if honestly managed), not only increase the number of missionaries, but develop trade; and that is the main point, apart from sentiment.

As native chiefs cannot now sell slaves for export, it slowly dawns upon their minds that better use may be made of slave-labour at home in cultivating the land. They are doing so. They can grow anything tropical, and thus produce increases, and goods in return follow; and, by the adoption of modern means of transit, the vast interior will be opened out and become so well known that invalids obliged to winter south will be able, about A.D. 1900, to take a through-ticket, land at the Congo, proceed by a river steamer up to a railway, run across to the Nyanzas, staying at good hotels all the time, and then go on to Gondokoro and down the Nile to Cairo. Happy will be the people of the next century !

At present, the male African takes no thought for the morrow ; time is not of the slightest value to him, want of food does not trouble him. It comes naturally, for women everywhere perform the greater part of the hard work, even to tilling the soil, leaving the men either to fight for ideas, tribe with tribe, or to pass their time away in luxurious but inglorious indolence.

The palm supplies material for building houses, the thick stems of leaves form uprights, the thinner ones walls, and the leaves yield water-proof thatch. The stems are also easily made into beds, sofas, chairs, and tables; the fibre forms thick rope or thin cord, and the latter is used for fishing lines and nets, or woven into mats, or mixed with cotton into durable cloth. The palm-tree also supplies oil, and fruit to eat and wine to drink. Cotton is indigenous and capable of cultivation in vast regions. Of huge trees canoes are made; and gourds, varying in size and shape from a drinking cup to the largest size of wash-basin, answer for many domestic uses. The art of pottery, fashioned after the manner of ancient Egyptian models, is prevalent everywhere. The rude manufacture of iron from ore has been practised since man existed. Wild animals, domestic animals, and birds abound. Fruits of the earth grow spontaneously, or with little cultivation ; so that wherever rivers run, the land may be truly said to overflow with milk and honey.

Thus Nature has been kind in abundantly furnishing this land with valuable but uselessly-excessive produce, unless commerce steps in to take the surplus away, and, in return, supply the people with goods, which they ardently covet when they see them. It may seem wicked to tear these innocents away from their savage but happy habits ; but it is to our and their advantage to offer them civilised manufactures of all sorts ; and it is considered proper to introduce the Christian religion, so as to compete with the Mahometan in gaining converts from Paganism. To do so effectively a modern system of travel and transit must be adopted. It is well to recollect that, before the Romans introduced road-making and religion, England enjoyed no better bush-paths for traffic than those of savage Africa now.

Bleak northern countries, overflowing with genius and

skilled labour, able to fashion rough material from anywhere into useful commodities, giving comfort and enjoyment to the whole world, lack that which Africa is able to yield. Africa requires unlimited supplies from our industrial districts. She opens out her arms for everything that we can manufacture, and will return kind for kind ; and she is beginning to play her part in the history of the world, which will not only enrich, but astound succeeding generations.

THE END.